For Exams Scheduled After December 31, 2017

FINAL REVIEW
FINANCIAL

UPDATES AND ACADEMIC HELP
Click on Customer and Academic Support under CPA Resources at
http://www.becker.com/cpa-review.html

CUSTOMER SERVICE AND TECHNICAL SUPPORT
Call 1-877-CPA-EXAM (outside the U.S. +1-630-472-2213)
or click Customer and Academic Support under CPA Resources at
http://www.becker.com/cpa-review.html

This textbook contains information that was current at the time of printing.
Your course software will be updated on a regular basis as the content
that is tested on the CPA Exam evolves and as we improve our materials.
Note the version reference below and click on Customer and Academic
Support under CPA Resources at http://www.becker.com/cpa-review.html
for a list-of available updates or to learn if a newer version of this book is
available to be ordered.

V 3.1

BECKER
PROFESSIONAL EDUCATION®

COURSE DEVELOPMENT TEAM

Timothy F. Gearty, CPA, MBA, JD . . . . Editor in Chief, Financial/Regulation (Tax) National Editor

Angeline S. Brown, CPA, MAC . . . . Director, Product Management and Curriculum, U.S. Accounting

Valerie Funk Anderson, CPA . . . . Manager, Accounting Curriculum

Stephen Bergens, CPA . . . . Manager, Accounting Curriculum

Patrice W. Johnson, CPA . . . . Manager, Accounting Curriculum

Tom Cox, CPA, CMA . . . . Financial (GASB & NFP) National Editor

Steven J. Levin, JD . . . . Regulation (Law) National Editor

John B. Pillatsch, MAS, CPA . . . . Sr. Director, Product Management

Pete Console . . . . Director, Educational Technologies

Brian Cave . . . . Manager, Software Development

Dan Corrales . . . . Manager, Curriculum Quality Assurance

James McKimson . . . . Manager, Software Quality Assurance

Danita De Jane . . . . Director, Course Development

Anson Miyashiro . . . . Manager, Course Development

John Ott . . . . Manager, Visual Design

Tim Munson . . . . Team Lead, Course Development

Linda Finestone . . . . Sr. Course Editor

Naomi Oseida . . . . Course Development

Eric Vasquez . . . . Course Development

CONTRIBUTING EDITORS

Teresa C. Anderson, CPA, CMA, MPA

Katie Barnette, CPA

Jim DeSimpelare, CPA, MBA

Melisa F. Galasso, CPA

Holly Hawk, CPA, CGMA

Julie D. McGinty, CPA

Sandra McGuire, CPA, MBA

Stephanie Morris, CPA, MAcc

Michelle Moshe, CPA, DipIFR

Peter Olinto, JD, CPA

Sandra Owen, CPA, MBA, JD

Michelle M. Pace, CPA

Jennifer J. Rivers, CPA

Josh Rosenberg, MBA, CPA, CFA, CFP

Jonathan R. Rubin, CPA, MBA

Michael Rybak, CPA, CFA

Denise M. Stefano, CPA, CGMA, MBA

Elizabeth Lester Walsh, CPA, CITP

Permissions

Material from *Uniform CPA Examination Selected Questions and Unofficial Answers*, 1989–2017, copyright © by American Institute of Certified Public Accountants, Inc., is reprinted and/or adapted with permission.

Any knowing solicitation or disclosure of any questions or answers included on any CPA Examination is prohibited.

LICENSE AGREEMENT—TERMS & CONDITIONS

DO NOT DOWNLOAD, ACCESS, AND/OR USE ANY OF THESE MATERIALS (AS THAT TERM IS DEFINED BELOW) UNTIL YOU HAVE READ THIS LICENSE AGREEMENT CAREFULLY. IF YOU DOWNLOAD, ACCESS, AND/OR USE ANY OF THESE MATERIALS, YOU ARE AGREEING AND CONSENTING TO BE BOUND BY AND ARE BECOMING A PARTY TO THIS LICENSE AGREEMENT ("AGREEMENT").

The printed Materials provided to you and/or the Materials provided for download to your computer and/or provided via a web application to which you are granted access are NOT for sale and are not being sold to you. You may NOT transfer these Materials to any other person or permit any other person to use these Materials. You may <u>only</u> acquire a license to use these Materials and <u>only</u> upon the terms and conditions set forth in this Agreement. Read this Agreement carefully <u>before</u> downloading, and/or accessing, and/or using these Materials. <u>Do not</u> download and/or access, and/or use these Materials <u>unless</u> you agree with all terms of this Agreement.

NOTE: You may already be a party to this Agreement if you registered for a Becker Professional Education CPA Final Review program (the "Program") or placed an order for these Materials online or using a printed form that included this License Agreement. Please review the termination section regarding your rights to terminate this License Agreement and receive a refund of your payment.

Grant: Upon your acceptance of the terms of this Agreement, in a manner set forth above, Becker Professional Development Corporation ("Becker") hereby grants to you a non-exclusive, revocable, non-transferable, non-sublicensable, limited license to use (as defined below) the Materials by downloading them onto a computer and/or by accessing them via a web application using a user ID and password (as defined below), and any Materials to which you are granted access as a result of your license to use these Materials and/or in connection with the Program on the following terms:

During the Term (as defined below) of this Agreement, you may:

• use the Materials for preparation for one or more parts of the CPA exam (the "Exam"), and/or for your studies relating to the subject matter covered by the Program and/or the Exam), and/or for your studies relating to the subject matter covered by the Materials and/or the Exam, including taking electronic and/or handwritten notes during the Program, provided that all notes taken that relate to the subject matter of the Materials are and shall remain Materials subject to the terms of this Agreement;

• download the Materials onto any single device;

• download the Materials onto a second device so long as the first device and the second device are not used simultaneously;

• download the Materials onto a third device so long as the first, second, and third device are not used simultaneously; and

• download the Materials onto a fourth device so long as the first, second, third, and fourth device are not used simultaneously.

The number of installations may vary outside of the U.S. Please review your local office policies and procedures to confirm the number of installations granted—your local office's policies and procedures regarding the number of allowable activations of downloads supersedes the limitations contained herein and is controlling.

You may not:

• use the Materials for any purpose other than as expressly permitted above;

• use the downloaded Materials on more than one device, computer terminal, or workstation at the same time;

• make copies of the Materials;

• rent, lease, license, lend, or otherwise transfer or provide (by gift, sale, or otherwise) all or any part of the Materials to anyone;

• permit the use of all or any part of the Materials by anyone other than you; or

• reverse engineer, decompile, disassemble, or create derivate works of the Materials.

Materials: As used in this Agreement, the term "Materials" means and includes any printed materials provided to you by Becker, and/or to which you are granted access by Becker (directly or indirectly) in connection with your license of the Materials and/or the Program, and shall include notes you take (by hand, electronically, digitally, or otherwise) while using the Materials relating to the subject matter of the Materials; any and all electronically-stored/accessed/delivered, and/or digitally-stored/accessed/delivered materials included under this License via download to a computer or via access to a web application, and/or otherwise provided to you and/or to which you are otherwise granted access by Becker (directly or indirectly), including, but not limited to, applications downloadable from a third party, for example Google® or Amazon®, in connection with your license of the Materials.

Title: Becker is and will remain the owner of all title, ownership rights, intellectual property, and all other rights and interests in and to the Materials that are subject to the terms of this Agreement. The Materials are protected by the copyright laws of the United States and international copyright laws and treaties.

Use of Navigator 2.0: If your employer or college/university has instructed Becker to use its Navigator 2.0 to track your studies, the following will occur: a) once you have activated your software (course log-in), you will be asked to set up your study planner. In order to do this, you may be required to provide information about yourself as part of the Program registration process, or as part of your continued use of the Materials. You agree that any registration information you give to Becker will be shared by Becker with your employer or college/university ; and b) once that is done, Navigator 2.0 will automatically track if you are behind in your studies based on your study planner, your office location, your service line within the firm, your college/university course, which course parts were purchased (Audit and Attestation, Financial Accounting and Reporting, Business Environment and Concepts, and Regulation), what format are you using (online, live, self-study), your course progress, study time details (hours/min in course, # of log-ins, last log in), exam progress details including: whether you applied to take the exam, and if so, the state to which you applied; whether you received your NTS (notice to schedule), and if so, its expiration date; whether you scheduled your exam, and if so, the date; whether you received any scores and what they were; and the number of attempts to pass each of the four parts.

Navigator 2.0 Liability Provisions: You hereby waive any claims, causes of action, and damages, and agree to hold harmless and indemnify Becker and its affiliates, officers, agents, and employees from any claim, suit or action arising from or related to your use of the Materials, the sharing of any of your information by Becker with your employer or violation of these terms, including any liability or expense arising from claims, losses, damages, suits, judgments, litigation costs and attorneys' fees.

SUBJECT TO THE OVERALL PROVISION ABOVE, YOU EXPRESSLY UNDERSTAND AND AGREE THAT BECKER, ITS PARENT CORPORATION, SUBSIDIARIES AND AFFILIATES, AND THE OFFICERS, AGENTS AND EMPLOYEES OF THOSE ENTITIES, SHALL NOT BE LIABLE TO YOU FOR ANY LOSS OR DAMAGE THAT MAY BE INCURRED BY YOU, INCLUDING BUT NOT LIMITED TO LOSS OR DAMAGE AS A RESULT BECKER SHARING YOUR INFORMATION WITH YOUR EMPLOYER OR COLLEGE/UNIVERSITY.

THE LIMITATIONS ON BECKER'S LIABILITY TO YOU IN THE PARAGRAPHS ABOVE SHALL APPLY WHETHER OR NOT BECKER HAS BEEN ADVISED OF OR SHOULD HAVE BEEN AWARE OF THE POSSIBILITY OF ANY SUCH LOSSES ARISING.

Termination: The license granted under this Agreement commences upon your receipt of these Materials. This license shall terminate the earlier of: (i) ten (10) business days after notice to you of non-payment of or default on any payment due Becker which has not been cured within such 10-day period; or (ii) immediately if you fail to comply with any of the limitations described above; or (iii) upon expiration of the period ending eighteen (18) months after you log-in to access the Materials, that is, the first time you visit the Becker Program homepage at https://online.becker.com and log-in using your user identification and password; or upon expiration of the twenty-four (24) month period beginning upon your purchase of the Material, whichever of these periods first transpires (the "Term"). In addition, upon termination of this license for any reason, you must delete or otherwise remove from your computer and other device any Materials you downloaded, including, but not limited to, any archival copies you may have made. The Title, Exclusion of Warranties, Exclusion of Damages, Indemnification and Remedies, Severability of Terms and Governing Law provisions, and any amounts due, shall survive termination of the license.

Your Limited Right to Terminate this License and Receive a Refund: You may terminate this license for the in-class, online, and self-study Programs in accordance with Becker's refund policy as provided at http://www.becker.com/cpa-review/resources/cpa-exam-review-policy and as listed below.

Cancellations and Refunds: To cancel your enrollment and receive a refund, contact Becker Professional Education at 800-868-3900.

Textbooks should be returned within 10 days of notification of withdrawal. Students should contact Becker for a "Return Materials Authorization" number prior to shipping returns. Students should ship materials by certified mail or an alternative traceable method. Flashcards and the material license fees for the Becker Promise are non-refundable. The cost to return materials is the responsibility of the student. Refunds will be made within 30 days from the date of cancellation. Non-receipt of shipment disputes must be made with 90 days of original purchase date.

All returns must be sent to: Becker Professional Education.
Attn: Becker Returns, 200 Finn Ct., Farmingdale NY, 11735

For **Online CPA Exam Review Course and CPA Final Review course students***, a full tuition refund (less any applicable savings and fees) will be issued within 10 days of initial purchase or first login, whichever comes first.

For **Live Format and Cohort Program CPA Review students***, a full tuition refund (minus all applicable savings) will be issued to students who withdraw on or before the 5th business day or if students do not attend any part of the course (no-shows) after the start date of the scheduled section and provided that electronic course materials are not accessed. Thereafter, no refund will be issued as full access to course content has been granted.

Under certain circumstances, a live class may be cancelled up to 5 days in advance of the scheduled start date. Students will be provided with rescheduling options which could include access to self-study materials when live courses are not available. If rescheduling efforts are not successful, a refund for the cancelled course section may be issued and access suspended provided that the section content has not been accessed.

No Shows are students who never attend a live/live online class and do not access any portion of the course software/electronic materials.

For **Atlanta Intensive and Final Review students***, a full tuition refund (minus all applicable savings) will be issued to students who withdraw on or before the 2nd class of the first scheduled part. Thereafter, no refund will be issued as full access to course content has been granted.

For **SkillMaster Workshops**: A full refund will be issued to students who withdraw at least 10 business days before the scheduled workshop. Thereafter, no refund will be issued.

(*Applicable in all states except those noted below.)

The following cancellation policy is applicable for students in Alabama, Arkansas, District of Columbia, Kansas, Kentucky, Louisiana, Nebraska, Nevada, New Hampshire, New Mexico, Oklahoma, West Virginia:

If cancellation occurs within 3 business days of registration, all monies paid by the student will be refunded even if classes have already started.

A full tuition refund (minus all applicable savings and fees) will be issued to students who withdraw on or before the 5th business day after the start date of the first scheduled section; thereafter, students are entitled to a prorated refund (minus all applicable savings and fees) for the unused portion through 60% of the part taken (75% in Arkansas and DC).

For example, the refund for a candidate who withdraws after completing 12 hours (3 sessions) of Audit classes will be calculated as follows:

- Amount Paid $1131.00
- Amount to be Prorated $1131.00
- 8 Hours Cancelled / 20 Hours Scheduled × $1131.00 = $452.00 (Amount Refunded)
- Residents are not required to submit written notification of withdrawal.

New Hampshire Students: Any buyer may cancel this transaction any time prior to midnight of the third business day after the date of this transaction.

Oklahoma Students: Becker Professional Education is licensed by Oklahoma Board of Private Vocational Schools, 700 N. Classen Blvd. #250, Oklahoma City, OK, 73118.

Classroom Locations: University of Oklahoma, 307 West Brooks, Room 200, Norman, OK 73019, Oklahoma Christian University, 2501 E Memorial Rd., Edmond, OK 73136, and Oklahoma State University, 108 Gunderson Hall, Stillwater, OK 74078.

Tennessee Students: At a minimum, refunds are calculated as follows:

Date of Withdrawal During:	Percent Refund of Tuition (Less Administrative Fee)
First day of scheduled classes	100%
Balance of week 1	90%
Week 2	75%
Weeks 3 and 4	25%
Weeks 5–8	0%

Refunds are to be prorated as of last day of actual attendance, notification is not required. All monies paid by an applicant will be refunded if requested within three days after signing an enrollment agreement and making an initial payment.

Holder in Due Course Rule: Any holder of this consumer credit contract is subject to all claims and defenses which the debtor could assert against the seller of goods and services obtained pursuant hereto or with the proceeds hereof. Recovery hereunder by the debtor shall not exceed that paid by the debtor. (This Federal TradeCom Regulation became in effect 5/14/75.)

Becker Professional Education is licensed by Oklahoma Board of Private Vocational Schools, 700 N. Classen Blvd. #250, Oklahoma City, OK, 73118.

NON-REFUNDABLE ITEMS: Charges for Flashcards, Supplemental Multiple-Choice Questions, 0% APR* Financing Processing Fee and the Becker Promise material license fee are non-refundable.

*Annual Percentage Rating

Attendance: To review Becker's attendance policy, please visit http://www.becker.com/cpa-review/resources/cpa-exam-review-policy

Exclusion of Warranties: YOU EXPRESSLY ASSUME ALL RISK FOR USE OF THE MATERIALS. YOU AGREE THAT THE MATERIALS ARE PROVIDED TO YOU "AS IS" AND "AS AVAILABLE" AND THAT BECKER MAKES NO WARRANTIES, EXPRESS OR IMPLIED, WITH RESPECT TO THE MATERIALS, THEIR MERCHANTABILITY OR FITNESS FOR A PARTICULAR PURPOSE AND NO WARRANTY OF NONINFRINGEMENT OF THIRD PARTIES' RIGHTS. NO DEALER, AGENT OR EMPLOYEE OF BECKER IS AUTHORIZED TO PROVIDE ANY SUCH WARRANTY TO YOU. BECAUSE SOME JURISDICTIONS DO NOT ALLOW THE EXCLUSION OF IMPLIED WARRANTIES, THE ABOVE EXCLUSION OF IMPLIED WARRANTIES MAY NOT APPLY TO YOU. BECKER DOES NOT WARRANT OR GUARANTEE THAT YOU WILL PASS ANY EXAMINATION.

Exclusion of Damages: UNDER NO CIRCUMSTANCES AND UNDER NO LEGAL THEORY, TORT, CONTRACT, OR OTHERWISE, SHALL BECKER OR ITS DIRECTORS, OFFICERS, EMPLOYEES, OR AGENTS BE LIABLE TO YOU OR ANY OTHER PERSON FOR ANY CONSEQUENTIAL, INCIDENTAL, INDIRECT, PUNITIVE, EXEMPLARY OR SPECIAL DAMAGES OF ANY CHARACTER, INCLUDING, WITHOUT LIMITATION, DAMAGES FOR LOSS OF GOODWILL, WORK STOPPAGE, COMPUTER FAILURE OR MALFUNCTION OR ANY AND ALL OTHER DAMAGES OR LOSSES, OR FOR ANY DAMAGES IN EXCESS OF BECKER'S LIST PRICE FOR A LICENSE TO THE MATERIALS, EVEN IF BECKER SHALL HAVE BEEN INFORMED OF THE POSSIBILITY OF SUCH DAMAGES, OR FOR ANY CLAIM BY ANY OTHER PARTY. Some jurisdictions do not allow the limitation or exclusion of liability for incidental or consequential damages, so the above limitation or exclusion may not apply to you.

Indemnification and Remedies: You agree to indemnify and hold Becker and its employees, representatives, agents, attorneys, affiliates, directors, officers, members, managers, and shareholders harmless from and against any and all claims, demands, losses, damages, penalties, costs or expenses (including reasonable attorneys' and expert witnesses' fees and costs) of any kind or nature, arising from or relating to any violation, breach, or nonfulfillment by you of any provision of this license. If you are obligated to provide indemnification pursuant to this provision, Becker may, in its sole and absolute discretion, control the disposition of any indemnified action at your sole cost and expense. Without limiting the foregoing, you may not settle, compromise, or in any other manner dispose of any indemnified action without the consent of Becker. If you breach any material term of this license, Becker shall be entitled to equitable relief by way of temporary and permanent injunction without the need for a bond and such other and further relief as any court with jurisdiction may deem just and proper.

Confidentiality: The Materials are considered confidential and proprietary to Becker. You shall keep the Materials confidential and you shall not publish or disclose the Materials to any third party without the prior written consent of Becker.

Use of Your Data: You understand that you will be providing personal information if you register for the Program and that the following will occur: (a) once you have registered, logged in, and activated your account, you will be asked to provide information about yourself as part of the registration process, or as part of your continued use of the Materials. You agree that any registration information you give to Becker will be used and stored by Becker. By using the Materials, you hereby consent to Becker retaining your personal information for purposes of the Program and for future purposes in marketing to you regarding other Becker Products.

Waiver of Liability: You hereby waive any claims, causes of action, and damages, and agree to hold harmless and indemnify Becker and its affiliates, officers, agents, and employees from any claim, suit, or action arising from or related to your use of the Materials, the use and storing of any of your information by Becker, or violation of these terms, including any liability or expense arising from claims, losses, damages, suits, judgments, litigation costs, and attorneys' fees.

SUBJECT TO THE OVERALL PROVISION ABOVE, YOU EXPRESSLY UNDERSTAND AND AGREE THAT BECKER, ITS PARENT CORPORATION, SUBSIDIARIES AND AFFILIATES, AND THE OFFICERS, AGENTS, AND EMPLOYEES OF THOSE ENTITIES, SHALL NOT BE LIABLE TO YOU FOR ANY LOSS OR DAMAGE THAT MAY BE INCURRED BY YOU, INCLUDING BUT NOT LIMITED TO LOSS OR DAMAGE AS A RESULT OF BECKER USING OR STORING YOUR INFORMATION WITH YOUR PROFESSOR OR COLLEGE/UNIVERSITY.

THE LIMITATIONS ON BECKER'S LIABILITY TO YOU IN THE PARAGRAPHS ABOVE SHALL APPLY WHETHER OR NOT BECKER HAS BEEN ADVISED OF, OR SHOULD HAVE BEEN AWARE OF, THE POSSIBILITY OF ANY SUCH LOSSES ARISING.

Severability of Terms: If any term or provision of this license is held invalid or unenforceable by a court of competent jurisdiction, such invalidity shall not affect the validity or operation of any other term or provision and such invalid term or provision shall be deemed to be severed from the license. This Agreement may only be modified by written agreement signed by both parties.

Governing Law: This Agreement shall be governed and construed according to the laws of the State of Illinois, United States of America, excepting that State's conflicts of laws rules. The parties agree that the jurisdiction and venue of any dispute subject to litigation is proper in any state or federal court in Chicago, Illinois, USA. The parties hereby agree to waive application of the UN Convention on the Sale of Goods. If the State of Illinois adopts the current proposed Uniform Computer Information Transactions Act (UCITA, formerly proposed Article 2B to the Uniform Commercial Code), or a version of the proposed UCITA, that part of the laws shall not apply to any transaction under this Agreement.

NOTICE TO STUDENTS: ACCET COMPLAINT PROCEDURE

This institution is recognized by the Accrediting Council for Continuing Education & Training (ACCET) as meeting and maintaining certain standards of quality. It is the mutual goal of ACCET and the institution to ensure that educational training programs of quality are provided. When problems arise, students should make every attempt to find a fair and reasonable solution through the institution's internal complaint procedure, which is required of ACCET accredited institutions and frequently requires the submission of a written complaint. Refer to the institution's written complaint procedure which is published in the institution's catalog or otherwise available from the institution, upon request. Note that ACCET will process complaints which involve ACCET standards and policies and, therefore, are within the scope of the accrediting agency.

In the event that a student has exercised the institution's formal student complaint procedure, and the problem(s) have not been resolved, the student has the right and is encouraged to take the following steps:

1. Complaints should be submitted in writing and mailed, or emailed to the ACCET office. Complaints received by phone will be documented, but the complainant will be requested to submit the complaint in writing.

2. The letter of complaint must contain the following:

   a. Name and location of the ACCET institution;

   b. A detailed description of the alleged problem(s);

   c. The approximate date(s) that the problem(s) occurred;

   d. The names and titles/positions of all individual(s) involved in the problem(s), including faculty, staff, and/or other students;

   e. What was previously done to resolve the complaint, along with evidence demonstrating that the institution's complaint procedure was followed prior to contacting ACCET;

   f. The name, email address, telephone number, and mailing address of the complainant. If the complainant specifically requests that anonymity be maintained, ACCET will not reveal his or her name to the institution involved; and

   g. The status of the complainant with the institution (e.g., current student, former student, etc.).

3. In addition to the letter of complaint, copies of any relevant supporting documentation should be forwarded to ACCET (e.g., student's enrollment agreement, syllabus or course outline, correspondence between the student and the institution).

4. **SEND TO:**

   ACCET
   CHAIR, COMPLAINT REVIEW COMMITTEE
   1722 N Street, NW
   Washington, DC 20036
   Telephone: (202) 955-1113
   Fax: (202) 955-1118 or (202) 955-5306
   Email: complaints@accet.org
   Website: www.accet.org

Note: Complainants will receive an acknowledgement of receipt within 15 days.

Financial

Final Review Sections

Financial Section I | *Conceptual Framework, Standard-Setting, and Financial Reporting*

A   General Purpose Financial Statements
B   Cash Flows
C   Public Company Reporting: SEC
D   Public Company Reporting: Earnings per Share
E   Public Company Reporting: Segment Reporting

Financial Section II | *Selected Financial Statement Accounts*

A   Trade Receivables
B   Inventory
C   Property, Plant, and Equipment (PP&E)
D   PP&E: Nonmonetary Exchanges
E   Investments
F   Intangible Assets
G   Impairment of Intangible Assets and PP&E
H   Payables and Accrued Liabilities
I   Long-Term Debt
J   Equity
K   Revenue Recognition
L   Compensation and Benefits
M   Income Taxes

Financial Section III | *Select Transactions*

A   Accounting Changes and Error Corrections
B   Business Combinations
C   Contingencies
D   Derivatives and Hedge Accounting
E   Foreign Currency Transactions and Translation
F   Leases
G   Research and Development
H   Software Costs
I   Subsequent Events
J   Fair Value Measurements

(continued on next page)

(continued)

Financial Section IV | *State and Local Governments*

A   State and Local Government Concepts

B   Form and Content of CAFR

C   Financial Reporting Entity

D   Typical Items and Specific Types of Transactions

Financial Section V | *Not-for-Profit Accounting and Reporting*

A   General Purpose Financial Statements

B   Revenue Recognition

Introduction

Final Review is a condensed review that reinforces your understanding of the most heavily tested concepts on the CPA Exam. It is designed to help focus your study time during those final days between your Becker CPA Exam Review course and your exam date.

This Book

Becker's Final Review is arranged based on the AICPA's blueprints. The blueprints outline the technical content to be tested on each of the four parts of the CPA Exam. The blueprints can be found in the back sections of Becker's main CPA textbooks.

The Software

The Final Review software uses an interactive eBook (IEB) format. Watch the introduction video in the Final Review software for a tour of the IEB features.

We recommend progressing through this course in the following order:

- Review the IEB content, including the video introduction to each topic and the lecture audio associated with each page of the IEB.
- Work the embedded multiple-choice questions for each topic as you progress through the content.
- Work the related multiple-choice questions in the question bank for each topic. There are links from the IEB to the question bank.
- Once you have completed all of the IEB sections, topics, and multiple-choice questions, do the practice Simulations in the software.

Becker Customer and Academic Support

The Becker Customer and Academic Support area is your source for course updates, supplemental materials, and academic support. Just click on Customer and Academic Support under CPA Resources at:

http://www.becker.com/cpa-review.html

You can access customer service and technical support from Customer and Academic Support or by calling 1-877-CPA-EXAM (outside the U.S. +1-630-472-2213).

I

Conceptual Framework, Standard-Setting, and Financial Reporting

1 Income Statement and Statement of Retained Earnings

1.1 Reported on Income Statement

1.1.1 Income (or Loss) From Continuing Operations (Gross and Net of Tax)

Income from continuing operations includes operating activities (i.e., revenues, costs of goods sold, selling expenses, and administrative expenses), nonoperating activities (e.g., other revenues and gains and other expenses and losses), and income taxes.

1.1.2 Income (or Loss) From Discontinued Operations (Net of Tax)

The (normal) loss from discontinued operations can consist of three elements: (1) an impairment loss; (2) income/loss from actual operations; and (3) a gain/loss on disposal. All of these amounts are included in discontinued operations in the period in which they occur.

1.2 Reported on Statement of Retained Earnings

1.2.1 Change in Accounting Principle (Net of Tax)

The cumulative effect of a change in accounting principle is presented net of tax. It is the cumulative effect (calculated as of the beginning of the first period presented) of a change from one acceptable method of accounting to another ("GAAP to GAAP" or "IFRS to IFRS") because the new method presents the financial information more fairly than the old method.

Question 1-1

Allison Corporation's current year income from continuing operations before taxes was $1,000,000 before taking the following items into consideration:

- Depreciation was understated by $100,000.

- A strike by the employees of a supplier resulted in a loss of $200,000. This strike was the first such strike that Allison had encountered.

- The inventory at December 31 of the prior year was overstated by $300,000. The inventory at December 31 of the current year was correct.

- A flood in Allison's Houston facility destroyed equipment worth $500,000. The facility had just been rebuilt from damages that occurred in a flood in the prior year.

What was Allison's adjusted income from continuing operations before taxes?

    1. $1,000,000

    2. $900,000

    3. $700,000

    4. $500,000

? Related Questions

For related questions, go to the online question bank:

➤ FR-00305

➤ FR-00320

➤ FR-00350

➤ FR-00451

2 Comprehensive Income

Comprehensive income includes all changes in equity during a period, except those resulting from investments by owners and distributions to owners. Comprehensive income is net income plus other comprehensive income.

Other comprehensive income includes:

- Pension adjustments
- Unrealized gains and losses on available-for-sale debt securities
- Foreign currency items
- Effective portion of cash flow hedges
- Revaluation surplus (IFRS only)

Question 2-1   FR-00335

Szuba Corporation reported the following transactions for the current year:

Sales	$500,000
Cost of goods sold	300,000
Operating expenses	100,000
Cash dividend	50,000
Unrealized gain on available-for-sale debt security	10,000
Unrealized gain on trading debt security	20,000

Ignoring income taxes, Szuba should report other comprehensive income of:

1. $80,000
2. $10,000
3. $60,000
4. $30,000

Related Questions

For related questions, go to the online question bank:

➤ FR-00439

3 Notes to Financial Statements

Notes are an integral part of the financial statements. The first note is the summary of significant accounting policies, which includes methods, policies, and criteria (e.g., methods: LIFO, FIFO, straight-line). The other notes provide the details of the financial statements.

IFRS requires an explicit and unreserved statement of compliance with IFRS in the notes to the financial statements.

Question 3-1   FR-00850

A major research university receives over half of its grant funding from a single federal government agency. The university's rationale for disclosing this in the notes to the financial statements is most likely to:

1. Show the vulnerability if that particular funding source were to disappear.
2. Show the need for additional funding sources to augment current grant inflows.
3. Highlight the strength of the relationship between the government and the university.
4. Quantify what would happen to future grant revenues if that funding source went away.

? Related Questions

For related questions, go to the online question bank:

➤ FR-00851

Task-Based Simulations

Task-Based Simulation 1: Calculations

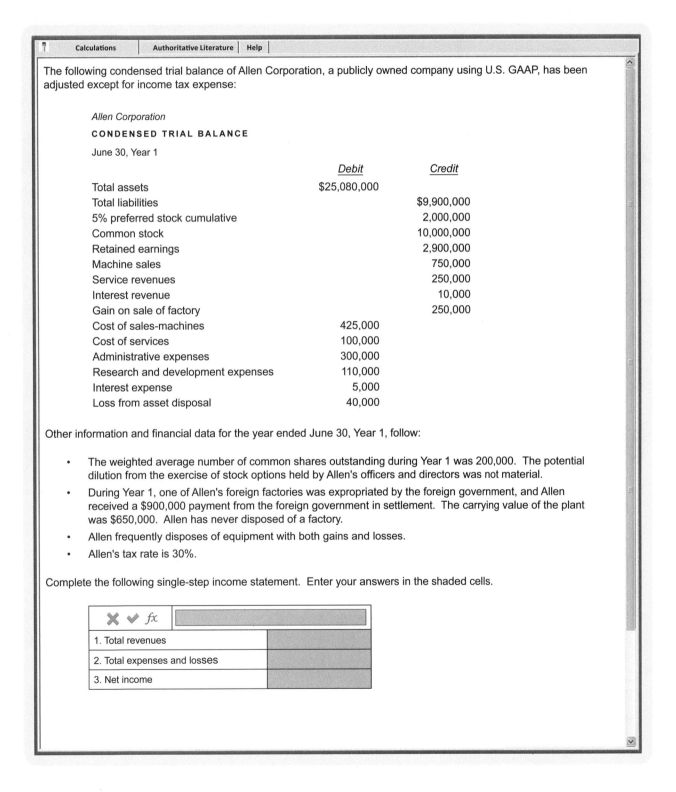

| Calculations | Authoritative Literature | Help |

The following condensed trial balance of Allen Corporation, a publicly owned company using U.S. GAAP, has been adjusted except for income tax expense:

Allen Corporation

CONDENSED TRIAL BALANCE

June 30, Year 1

	Debit	Credit
Total assets	$25,080,000	
Total liabilities		$9,900,000
5% preferred stock cumulative		2,000,000
Common stock		10,000,000
Retained earnings		2,900,000
Machine sales		750,000
Service revenues		250,000
Interest revenue		10,000
Gain on sale of factory		250,000
Cost of sales-machines	425,000	
Cost of services	100,000	
Administrative expenses	300,000	
Research and development expenses	110,000	
Interest expense	5,000	
Loss from asset disposal	40,000	

Other information and financial data for the year ended June 30, Year 1, follow:

- The weighted average number of common shares outstanding during Year 1 was 200,000. The potential dilution from the exercise of stock options held by Allen's officers and directors was not material.
- During Year 1, one of Allen's foreign factories was expropriated by the foreign government, and Allen received a $900,000 payment from the foreign government in settlement. The carrying value of the plant was $650,000. Allen has never disposed of a factory.
- Allen frequently disposes of equipment with both gains and losses.
- Allen's tax rate is 30%.

Complete the following single-step income statement. Enter your answers in the shaded cells.

✖ ✔ fx	
1. Total revenues	
2. Total expenses and losses	
3. Net income	

A   General Purpose Financial Statements

1.   Total Revenues

Revenues:	
Machine sales	$750,000
Service revenues	250,000
Interest revenues	10,000
Gain on sale of factory	250,000
Total revenues	$1,260,000

2.   Total expenses and losses

Expenses:	
Cost of sales machines	$425,000
Cost of services	100,000
Administrative expenses	300,000
Research and development expenses	110,000
Interest expense	5,000
Loss from asset disposal	40,000
Income tax expense	84,000[1]
Total expenses and losses	1,064,000

3.   Net income

Net income	196,000

[1] Income tax expense = Total revenues = $1,260,000
Total expenses other than taxes = $980,000
Difference (pretax income) = $280,000
$84,000 = 30% x $280,000

Task-Based Simulation 2: Comprehensive Income

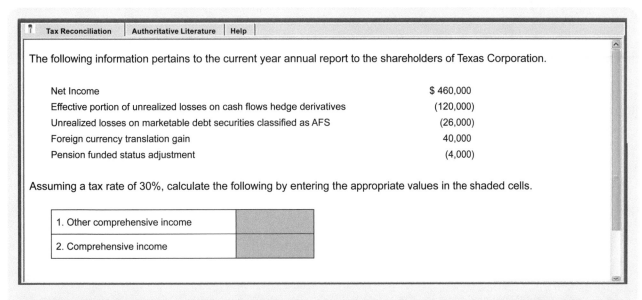

| Tax Reconciliation | Authoritative Literature | Help |

The following information pertains to the current year annual report to the shareholders of Texas Corporation.

Net Income	$ 460,000
Effective portion of unrealized losses on cash flows hedge derivatives	(120,000)
Unrealized losses on marketable debt securities classified as AFS	(26,000)
Foreign currency translation gain	40,000
Pension funded status adjustment	(4,000)

Assuming a tax rate of 30%, calculate the following by entering the appropriate values in the shaded cells.

1. Other comprehensive income	
2. Comprehensive income	

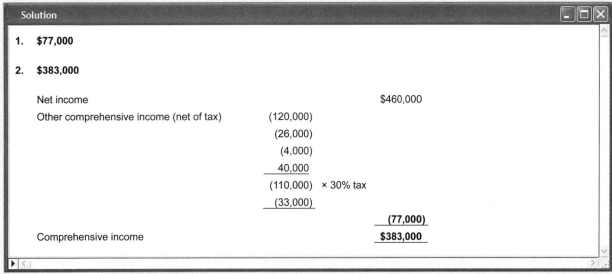

Solution

1. **$77,000**

2. **$383,000**

Net income		$460,000
Other comprehensive income (net of tax)	(120,000)	
	(26,000)	
	(4,000)	
	40,000	
	(110,000)	× 30% tax
	(33,000)	
		(77,000)
Comprehensive income		$383,000

1 Methods of Presentation

The direct method and the indirect method are the two methods of presentation for the statement of cash flows. The two methods are identical except for the cash flows from operating activities and for some disclosures. A presentation of cash flow per share is prohibited. Both U.S. GAAP and IFRS encourage the use of the direct method. Regardless of the method of presentation, the sections of the statement of cash flows are:

- Operating activities (CFO)
- Investing activities (CFI)
- Financing activities (CFF)
- Supplemental disclosures

Investing and financing activities are the same presentation for the direct and indirect methods. There are two approaches to presenting the operating activities but the results are the same. Under U.S. GAAP, operating activities require a reconciliation of "net income to net cash" for both methods. In addition, the direct method requires a cash basis income statement.

2 Operating Activities (Indirect Method)

The indirect method (reconciliation of net income to net cash) begins with accrual net income and reconciles it to cash flow from operating activities by adding noncash amounts, such as depreciation, amortization and losses on dispositions of assets and subtracting gains on dispositions of assets. Other adjustments to next income include changes in current assets and current liabilities, such as A/R, A/P, inventory, etc.

Indirect Method

Letterman Inc.
Statement of Cash Flows
For the Year Ended 12/31/Year X

Cash flows from operating activities:		
Net income		$ 50,000
Adjustments		
Decrease in accounts receivable	$ 25,000	
Increase in inventory	(10,000)	
Increase in accounts payable	20,000	
Increase in income taxes payable	6,000	
Total adjustments		41,000
Net cash provided by operating activities		91,000
Cash flows from investing activities:		
Cash paid to purchase equity securities	(3,000)	
Net cash used in investing activities		(3,000)
Cash flows from financing activities:		
Cash dividends paid	(2,000)	
Net cash used in financing activities		(2,000)
Net increase in cash and cash equivalents		86,000
Cash and cash equivalents at the beginning of the year		99,000
Cash and cash equivalents at the end of the year		$185,000

Question 2-1   FR-00323

Sykes Corporation's comparative balance sheets at December 31, Year 2 and Year 1, reported accumulated depreciation balances of $800,000 and $600,000 respectively. Property with a cost of $50,000 and a carrying amount of $40,000 was the only property sold in Year 2. Depreciation charged to operations in Year 2 was:

1. $190,000
2. $200,000
3. $210,000
4. $220,000

? Related Questions

For related questions, go to the online question bank:

➤ FR-00413

3 Operating Activities (Direct Method)

The direct method is a cash basis income statement. The statement is prepared by adjusting the accrual amounts reported in the income statement to the cash basis. A "reconciliation of net income to net cash" is required under U.S. GAAP. The totals for the "reconciliation" and "cash basis income statement" are the same. Operating activities include:

- Cash received from customers
- Cash paid to suppliers and employees
- Operating expenses paid in cash
- Interest received and paid
- DIvidends received (but not dividends paid)
- Taxes paid
- Purchase and sale of trading securities classified as current assets

Question 3-1   FR-00368

In its year-end income statement, Black Knights Company reported cost of goods sold of $450,000. Changes occurred in several balance sheet accounts during the year as follows:

Inventory	$160,000	decrease
Accounts payable-suppliers	40,000	decrease

What amount should the Black Knights Company report as cash paid to suppliers in its cash flow statement, prepared under the direct method?

1. $250,000
2. $330,000
3. $570,000
4. $650,000

Related Questions

For related questions, go to the online question bank:

➤ FR-00428
➤ FR-00453

Direct Method
(preferred presentation)

Letterman Inc.
Statement of Cash Flows
For the Year Ended 12/31/Year X

Cash flows from operating activities:

Cash received from customers	$125,000	
Cash paid to suppliers and employees	(30,000)	
Income taxes paid	(4,000)	
Net cash provided by operating activities		$ 91,000

Cash flows from investing activities:

Cash paid to purchase equity securities	(3,000)	
Net cash used in investing activities		(3,000)

Cash flows from financing activities:

Cash dividends paid		(2,000)
Net cash used in financing activities		(2,000)
Net increase in cash and cash equivalents		86,000
Cash and cash equivalents at the beginning of the year		99,000
Cash and cash equivalents at the end of the year		$185,000

Same

Reconciliation of net income to net cash provided by operating activities:

Net income		$ 50,000

Adjustments to reconcile net income to net cash provided:

Decrease in accounts receivable	$ 25,000	
Increase in inventory	(10,000)	
Increase in accounts payable	20,000	
Increase in income taxes payable	6,000	
Total adjustments		41,000
Net cash provided by operations		$ 91,000

See Indirect Method

4 Investing Activities

Investing activities generally involve changes in non-current assets, inclusive of the purchase or sale of property, plant, investments, equipment and marketable securities (excluding trading securities classified as current assets). Depreciation expense and/or the accumulated depreciation on assets disposed of, and gains/losses on assets disposed of, are a few key accounts that must be considered in determining the balance of the cash used or provided by the investing activities.

Question 4-1   FR-00441

The Year 11 balance sheet of Cool Tools Inc. reported the following fixed asset balances:

	Year 11	Year 10
Fixed assets	$160,000	$128,000
Accumulated depreciation	(53,000)	(41,000)
Fixed assets, net	$107,000	$ 87,000

On January 1, Year 11, Cool Tools purchased fixed assets for $50,000 and sold fixed assets with an original cost of $18,000 and a book value of $6,000 for $10,000. Cool Tools made no other long-term asset purchases or sales during Year 11. What is Cool Tools' net cash used in investing activities and the amount of the depreciation adjustment to the operating section of Cool Tools' statement of cash flows prepared using the indirect method?

	Net Cash Used in Investing Activities	Depreciation Adjustment in Operating Section
1.	$32,000	$12,000
2.	$32,000	$24,000
3.	$40,000	$12,000
4.	$40,000	$24,000

5 Financing Activities

Financing activities generally involve changes in non-current liabilities and stockholders' equity, including payment or retirement of long-term notes, long-term bonds, the issuance or re-acquisition of company stock, and dividends paid.

Question 5-1 FR-00308

During Year 1, Brianna Company had the following transactions related to its financial operations:

Payment for the retirement of long-term bonds payable (carrying value $740,000)	$750,000
Distribution in Year 1 of cash dividend declared in Year 0 to preferred shareholders	62,000
Carrying value of convertible preferred stock of Brianna converted into common shares	120,000
Proceeds from sale of treasury stock (carrying value at cost $86,000)	95,000

On its Year 1 statement of cash flows, net cash used in financing activities should be:

1. $717,000
2. $716,000
3. $597,000
4. $535,000

? Related Questions

For related questions, go to the online question bank:

➤ FR-00398

---

6 Noncash Investing and Financing Activities

Certain transactions do not affect cash: purchasing assets with a note, entering into a capital lease, or exchanging bonds for stock. Look for a transaction that is, in effect, a barter transaction. These transactions are not included on the body of the statement of cash flows but are included in supplemental disclosures.

7 Cash Equivalents

Cash equivalents are short-term, highly liquid investments (maturing 90 days or less from the date of purchase) that are readily convertible into cash or so near their maturity that the risk of a change in value is insignificant. Cash equivalents are included with cash in the statement of cash flows.

Question 7-1   FR-00383

Kong Co. purchased a three-month U.S. Treasury bill. Kong's policy is to treat as cash equivalents all highly liquid investments with an original maturity of three months or less when purchased. How should this purchase be reported in Kong's statement of cash flows?

1. As an outflow from operating activities.

2. As an inflow from investing activities.

3. As an outflow from financing activities.

4. Not reported.

? Related Questions

For related questions, go to the online question bank:

➤ FR-00338

➤ FR-00353

8 IFRS vs. U.S. GAAP

IFRS allows more flexibility than U.S. GAAP in classifying cash flows related to interest, dividends, and income taxes. The following table summarizes the classification differences between U.S. GAAP and IFRS:

Transaction	U.S. GAAP	IFRS
Interest received	CFO	CFO or CFI
Interest paid	CFO	CFO or CFF
Dividends received	CFO	CFO or CFI
Dividends paid	CFF	CFO or CFF
Taxes paid	CFO	CFO, CFI, CFF

IFRS classifies taxes paid as CFO, but allows allocation to CFI or CFF for portions specifically identified with investing and financing activities.

9 Additional Supplemental Disclosures

Interest paid and income taxes paid must be disclosed.

Question 9-1   FR-00463

Which of the following supplemental disclosures to the statement of cash flows is not required when the indirect method is used?

1. Income taxes paid.
2. Reconciliation of net income to net cash provided by operating activities.
3. Interest paid.
4. Noncash investing and financing activities.

Task-Based Simulations

Task-Based Simulation 1: Cash Flows

| Cash Flows | Authoritative Literature | Help |

Below are the consolidated workpaper balances of Marigold Inc. and its subsidiary, Rose Corporation, as of December 31, Year 1 and Year 2:

Assets	Year 2	Year 1	Net change increase (decrease)
Cash	$313,000	$195,000	$118,000
Marketable debt securities for trading, at cost	175,000	175,000	- 0 -
Allowance to reduce marketable debt securities to market	(13,000)	(24,000)	11,000
Accounts receivable (net)	418,000	440,000	(22,000)
Inventories	595,000	525,000	70,000
Land	385,000	170,000	215,000
Plant and equipment	755,000	690,000	65,000
Accumulated depreciation	(199,000)	(145,000)	(54,000)
Goodwill	57,000	60,000	(3,000)
Total assets	$2,486,000	$2,086,000	
Liabilities and Stockholders' Equity			
Current portion of long-term note	$150,000	$150,000	$ - 0 -
Accounts payable and accrued liabilities	595,000	474,000	121,000
Note payable, long term	300,000	450,000	(150,000)
Deferred income taxes	44,000	32,000	12,000
Minority interest in net assets of subsidiary	179,000	161,000	18,000
Common stock par $10	580,000	480,000	100,000
Additional paid-in capital	303,000	180,000	123,000
Retained earnings	335,000	195,000	140,000
Treasury stock at cost		(36,000)	36,000
Total liabilities and stockholders' equity	$2,486,000	$2,086,000	

Additional information:

1. On January 20, Year 2, Marigold Inc. issued 10,000 shares of its common stock for land having a fair value of $215,000.
2. On February 5, Year 2, Marigold Inc. reissued all of its Treasury stock for $44,000.
3. On May 15, Year 2, Marigold Inc. paid a cash dividend of $58,000 on its common stock.
4. On August 8, Year 2, equipment was purchased for $127,000.
5. On September 30, Year 2, equipment was sold for $40,000. The equipment cost $62,000 and had a carrying amount of $34,000 on the date of sale.
6. On December 15, Year 2, Rose Corporation paid a cash dividend of $50,000 on its common stock.
7. Deferred income taxes represent temporary differences relating to the use of methods for income tax reporting and the allowance for financial reporting on accounts receivable.
8. Net income for Year 2 was as follows:
   Consolidated net income: $198,000
   Rose Corporation: $110,000
9. Marigold Inc. owns 70% of its subsidiary, Rose Corporation. There was no change in the ownership interest in Rose Corporation during Year 1 and Year 2. There were no intercompany transactions other than the dividend paid to Marigold, Inc. by its subsidiary.
10. Sales were $2,200,000.
11. Purchases were $1,500,000.
12. Goodwill was determined to be impaired by $3,000.

(continued)

(continued)

For each account below, reconcile the beginning and ending balances to assist in determining the effect on cash flows for the year ended December 31, Year 2. Double-click on the shaded cells of Column B and select from the list provided. Enter the corresponding amounts in the shaded cells of Column C.

	Marigold Inc. and Subsidiary **Consolidated Statement of Cash Flows** for the Year Ended December 31, Year 2		
Cash Flows From Operating Activities:			
	Total adjustments		$0
	Net cash provided by operating activities		$0
Cash Flows From Investing Activities:			
	Net cash used in investing activities		$0
Cash Flows From Financing Activities:			
	Net cash used in financing activities		
	Net increase in cash and cash equivalents		
	Cash and cash equivalents at beginning of year		
	Cash and cash equivalents at end of year		$0
Supplemental Disclosure of Noncash Investing and Financing Activities:			

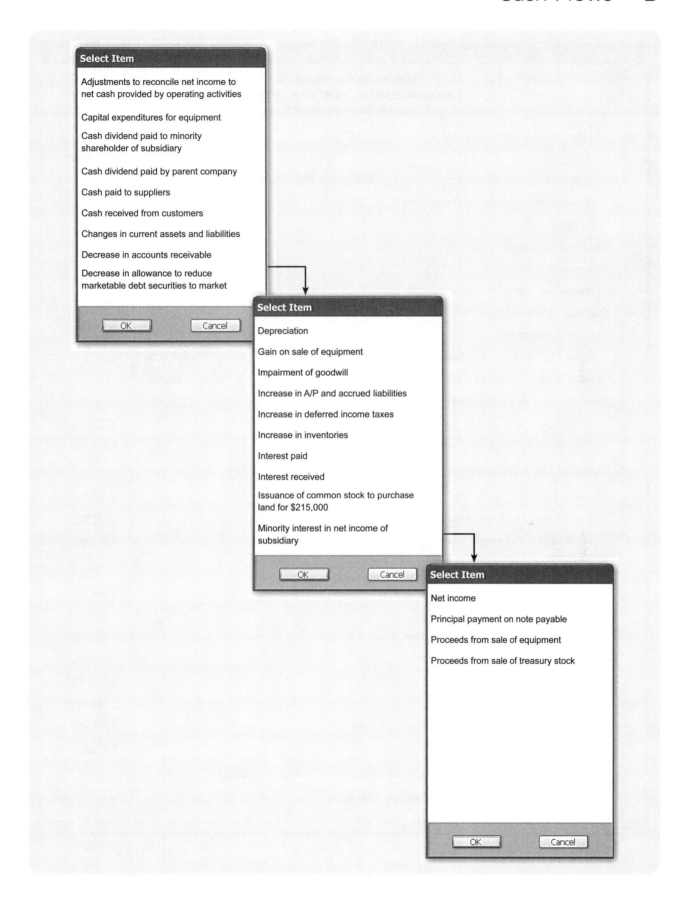

Select Item

Adjustments to reconcile net income to net cash provided by operating activities

Capital expenditures for equipment

Cash dividend paid to minority shareholder of subsidiary

Cash dividend paid by parent company

Cash paid to suppliers

Cash received from customers

Changes in current assets and liabilities

Decrease in accounts receivable

Decrease in allowance to reduce marketable debt securities to market

OK   Cancel

Select Item

Depreciation

Gain on sale of equipment

Impairment of goodwill

Increase in A/P and accrued liabilities

Increase in deferred income taxes

Increase in inventories

Interest paid

Interest received

Issuance of common stock to purchase land for $215,000

Minority interest in net income of subsidiary

OK   Cancel

Select Item

Net income

Principal payment on note payable

Proceeds from sale of equipment

Proceeds from sale of treasury stock

OK   Cancel

B   Cash Flows

Marigold Inc. and Subsidiary
CONSOLIDATED STATEMENT OF CASH FLOWS
for the Year Ended December 31, Year 2

CASH FLOWS FROM OPERATING ACTIVITIES:

Net income		$ 198,000
Adjustments to reconcile net income to net cash provided by operating activities:		
Minority interest in net income of subsidiary	$ 33,000	
Depreciation	82,000	
Impairment of goodwill	3,000	
Gain on sale of equipment	(6,000)	
Changes in current assets and liabilities:		
Decrease in accounts receivable	22,000	
Increase in inventories	(70,000)	
Increase in A/P and accrued liabilities	121,000	
Increase in deferred income taxes	12,000	
Decrease in allowance to reduce marketable debt securities to market	(11,000)	
Total adjustments		$ 186,000
Net cash provided by operating activities		$ 384,000

CASH FLOWS FROM INVESTING ACTIVITIES:

Proceeds from sale of equipment		$ 40,000
Capital expenditures for equipment		(127,000)
Net cash used in investing activities		$ (87,000)

CASH FLOWS FROM FINANCING ACTIVITIES:

Proceeds from sale of treasury stock		$ 44,000
Cash dividend paid by parent company		(58,000)
Cash dividend paid to minority shareholder of subsidiary		(15,000)
Principal payment on note payable		(150,000)
Net cash used in financing activities		$(179,000)
Net increase in cash and cash equivalents		118,000
Cash and cash equivalents at beginning of year		$ 195,000
Cash and cash equivalents at end of year		$ 313,000

SUPPLEMENTAL DISCLOSURE OF NONCASH INVESTING AND FINANCING ACTIVITIES:

Issuance of common stock to purchase land for $215,000

Task-Based Simulation 2: Research

Solution

Source of answer for this question:

FASB ASC 230-10-50-1

Keyword: Cash Equivalents Policy

Financial Final Review

1 Securities Offering Registration Statements

When a company issues new securities, it is required to submit a registration statement to the SEC that includes disclosures about the securities being offered for sale, information similar to that filed in the annual filing, and audited financial statements.

2 Form 10-K

Form 10-K must be filed annually by U.S. registered companies (issuers). The filing deadline for Form 10-K is 60 days after the end of the fiscal year for large accelerated filers, 75 days after the end of the fiscal year for accelerated filers, and 90 days after the end of the fiscal year for all other registrants. These forms contain financial disclosures, including a summary of financial data, management's discussion and analysis (MD&A), and audited financial statements prepared using U.S. GAAP.

3 Form 10-Q

Form 10-Q must be filed quarterly by U.S. registered companies (issuers). The filing deadline for Form 10-Q is 40 days after the end of the fiscal quarter for large accelerated filers and accelerated filers, and 45 days after the end of the fiscal quarter for all other registrants. This form contains unaudited financial statements prepared using U.S. GAAP, interim period MD&A, and certain disclosures.

Question 3-1   FR-00846

The common stock price for Brevard Co. (a registered U.S. company) is $40 per share. The company has 6 million common shares outstanding. In order to meet the filing deadlines required by the SEC, Brevard must (after the fiscal period ends) file the following reports within:

	10-K	10-Q
1.	75 days	40 days
2.	75 days	45 days
3.	60 days	40 days
4.	60 days	45 days

---

4 Form 8-K

This form is filed to report major corporate events such as corporate asset acquisitions or disposals, changes in securities and trading markets, changes to accountants or financial statements, and changes in corporate governance or management.

5 Forms 3, 4, and 5

These forms are required to be filed by directors, officers, or beneficial owners of more than 10 percent of a class of equity securities of a registered company.

6 Regulation S-X

Regulation S-X outlines the form and content of financial statements to be included in SEC filings. Under Regulation S-X, annual financial statements filed with the SEC must be audited and must include balance sheets for the two most recent fiscal years and statements of income, changes in owners' equity, and cash flows for each of the three fiscal years preceding the date of the most recent audited balance sheet.

Question 6-1	FR-00773

Under Regulation S-X, an entity's annual financial statements filed with the SEC should include at least three of each of the following, *except the*:

1. Statement of changes in owners' equity.
2. Statement of cash flows.
3. Income statement.
4. Balance sheet.

1 Reporting Requirement

All public entities must present earnings per share on the face of the income statement.

- **Simple Capital Structure:** Has only common stock, or no other securities that can become common stock. An entity with a simple capital structure is required to present basic earnings per share (EPS).
- **Complex Capital Structure:** If securities that can be converted into common stock, inclusive of convertible preferred stock, convertible bonds, options, and warrants. All entities with complex capital structures must present basic and diluted per share amounts (assuming that there is dilution).

2 Basic EPS

$$\text{Basic EPS} = \frac{\text{Income available to common shareholders}}{\text{Weighted average number of common shares outstanding}}$$

The income available to common shareholders must be reduced by the dividends declared on noncumulative preferred stock, or by the dividends accumulated in the current period on any cumulative preferred stock whether or not those dividends have actually been declared.

To determine the weighted average number of shares outstanding, weight each total of shares outstanding by the amount of time that the total was outstanding. Stock dividends and stock splits are treated as if they had occurred at the beginning of the earliest period presented.

Question 2-1   FR-00443

The Burken Co. has one class of common stock outstanding and no other securities that are potentially convertible into common stock. During Year 10, 100,000 shares of common stock were outstanding. In Year 11, two distributions of additional common shares occurred: On April 1, 20,000 shares of treasury stock were sold, and on July 1, a 2-for-1 stock split was issued. Net income was $410,000 in Year 11 and $350,000 in Year 10. What amounts should Burken report as earnings per share in its Year 11 and Year 10 comparative income statements?

	Year 11	Year 10
1.	$1.78	$3.50
2.	$1.78	$1.75
3.	$2.34	$1.75
4.	$2.34	$3.50

? Related Questions

For related questions, go to the online question bank:

➤ FR-00326

➤ FR-00401

3 Diluted EPS

3.1 Convertible Securities

Diluted EPS is calculated taking into consideration any security (convertible preferred stock, convertible bonds, stock option or warrant, or contingent issuance of stock) that can be converted into common stock. Any conversion, exercise, or contingent issuance that has an antidilutive effect (increases EPS or decreases loss per share) is not included in the calculation. No antidilution is presented.

$$\text{Diluted EPS} = \frac{\substack{\text{Income available to common shareholders} \\ +\ \text{Interest on conversion of bonds (net of tax)}}}{\substack{\text{Weighted average number of common shares, assuming} \\ \text{all dilutive securities are converted to common stock}}}$$

3.2 Options and Warrants

Options and warrants are accounted for using the treasury stock method. An assumption is made that "in the money" (average market price > exercise price) options and/or warrants are exercised and that the proceeds from the exercise are used to buy back shares for the treasury. The incremental shares (difference between the shares "sold" and the shares "reacquired") are added to the denominator.

Example

A company has 1,000 stock options outstanding (for one share each), which are exercisable at $30 each. If the average market price is $50 per share, then the options are "in the money" and therefore dilutive. When the options are assumed to be exercised for the purposes of computing diluted EPS, it is assumed that the company will receive $30,000, which can be used to purchase 600 shares of stock ($30,000 / $50 share = 600 shares). The company will need to issue 400 new shares (1000 shares - 600 repurchased). The 400 newly issued shares will be added to the weighted average number of common shares outstanding when computing diluted EPS.

$$1,000 \text{ shares} - \left(\frac{1,000 \times 30 \text{ option price}}{50 \text{ average price}} \right) = \text{Shares added to denominator}$$

$$1,000 - 600 = \underline{400 \text{ shares}}$$

Question 3-1   FR-00416

Hutchins Company had 200,000 shares of common stock, 50,000 shares of convertible preferred stock, and $2,000,000 of 10% convertible bonds outstanding during the current year. The preferred stock was convertible into 40,000 shares of common stock.

During the current year, Hutchins paid dividends of $1.00 per share on the common stock and $2.00 per share on the preferred stock. Each $1,000 bond was convertible into 50 shares of common stock. The net income for the year was $1,000,000 and the income tax rate was 30%.

Diluted earnings per share for the current year was (rounded to the nearest penny):

1. $5.00
2. $3.35
3. $3.53
4. $3.06

? Related Questions

For related questions, go to the online question bank:

➤ FR-00431

➤ FR-00454

Task-Based Simulations

Task-Based Simulation 1: Research

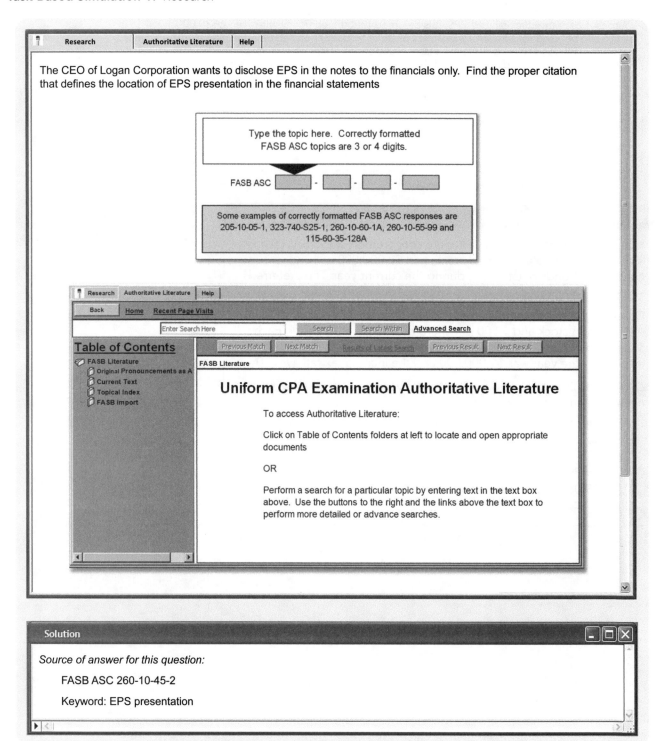

The CEO of Logan Corporation wants to disclose EPS in the notes to the financials only. Find the proper citation that defines the location of EPS presentation in the financial statements

Type the topic here. Correctly formatted FASB ASC topics are 3 or 4 digits.

FASB ASC ☐ - ☐ - ☐ - ☐

Some examples of correctly formatted FASB ASC responses are 205-10-05-1, 323-740-S25-1, 260-10-60-1A, 260-10-55-99 and 115-60-35-128A

Solution

Source of answer for this question:

FASB ASC 260-10-45-2

Keyword: EPS presentation

Task-Based Simulation 2: Research

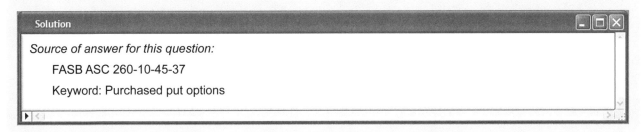

Solution

Source of answer for this question:

FASB ASC 260-10-45-37

Keyword: Purchased put options

Financial Final Review

1 Operating Segments

An operating segment is a part of an enterprise:

- that engages in business activities.
- whose operating results are regularly reviewed by the enterprise's chief operating decision maker.
- for which discrete financial information is available.

2 Reporting Segments

An operating segment is a reportable segment if it has at least 10 percent of the combined amounts of:

- revenue from sales to unaffiliated customers and intersegment transfers for all of the entities reported; or
- profit or loss; or
- assets.

If the segment does not meet the 10 percent limit, it is not separately disclosed unless all the reportable combined sales to unaffiliated customers is less than 75 percent of the total company sales revenue made to outsiders. If this limit is not achieved, additional segments must be disclosed despite their failure to satisfy one of the thresholds.

Question 2-1

FR-00318

The Houston Fellowship Corporation has three operating segments for which the following information was available:

	Beer	Wine	Pretzels
Sales to outsiders	$18,000	$24,000	$36,000
Intersegment sales	3,600	2,200	4,200
Total	$21,600	$26,200	$40,200

In addition, revenues generated at corporate headquarters were $4,000. What is the minimum amount of revenue that each of these operating segments must have to be considered a reportable segment?

1. $7,800
2. $9,200
3. $8,000
4. $8,800

Question 2-2

FR-00437

Selected financial results from Water Works Inc.'s five operating segments were as follows:

Segment	Total revenues	Total profit	Total assets
Rain	$ 100,000	$ 70,000	$ 300,000
Snow	130,000	30,000	350,000
Ice	600,000	300,000	700,000
Hail	95,000	15,000	190,000
Steam	400,000	220,000	550,000
	$1,325,000	$635,000	$2,090,000

The company had no intersegment sales. Which operating segment(s) is (are) deemed to be reportable segments?

1. Ice only.
2. Ice and Steam.
3. Ice, Steam, and Snow.
4. Ice, Steam, Snow, and Rain.

II | Selected Financial Statement Accounts

1 Accounts Receivable

Accounts receivable are reported at their net realizable value (AR—allowance for doubtful accounts).

There are two GAAP methods to compute bad debt expense using the allowance method. The direct write-off method is not GAAP.

1.1 Income Statement Approach

Bad debts are estimated as a percentage of net credit sales, resulting in bad debt expense for the period.

Allowance for DA	
Write-offs	Beginning balance
	Recoveries
	Bad debt expense (% of credit sales)
	Ending balance

1.2 Balance Sheet Approach

Bad debts are estimated as a percentage of ending accounts receivable or based on an aging of accounts receivable; emphasis is on the valuation of the receivables. This results in the ending balance for allowances for doubtful accounts and the bad debt expense is the "plug."

Allowance for DA	
Write-offs	Beginning balance
	Recoveries
	Bad debt expense (plug)
	Ending balance (based on A/R not expected to be collected)

Question 1-1

Fernandez Company had an accounts receivable balance of $150,000 on December 31, Year 2 and $175,000 on December 31, Year 3. The company wrote off $40,000 of accounts receivable during Year 3. Sales for the year Year 3 totaled $600,000, and all sales were on account.

The amount collected from customers on accounts receivable during Year 3 was:

1. $575,000
2. $531,000
3. $535,000
4. $600,000

Question 1-2

On its December 31, Year 2 balance sheet, Red Rock Candle Company reported accounts receivable of $855,000, net of an allowance for doubtful accounts of $45,000. On December 31, Year 3, Red Rock's balance sheet showed gross accounts receivable of $922,000 and Red Rock's income statement reported sales of $3,000,000. During the year, accounts receivable of $35,000 were written off and $18,000 were recovered. Based on past experience, 5% of Red Rock's ending accounts receivable are uncollectible. How much should Red Rock report as bad debt expense on its Year 3 income statement?

1. $18,100
2. $35,000
3. $46,100
4. $150,000

2 Pledging

A company may use its accounts receivable as collateral for loans. The company retains title to the receivables but pledges that it will use the proceeds to pay off the loans. Pledging requires note disclosure only.

3 Factoring

A company may sell its receivables to a factor either with or without recourse. "With recourse" means the seller retains the risk of any losses on collection. "Without recourse" means that the buyer assumes the risk of any losses on collection.

Question 3-1	FR-00377

Stanberry Company sold $500,000 of net accounts receivable to Cork Company for $450,000. The receivables were sold outright on a without recourse basis, and Stanberry Company retained no control over the receivables.

The Journal Entries to record the sale would be which of the following?

1.

DR	Cash	$500,000	
CR	Accounts receivable (net)		$500,000

2.

DR	Cash	$450,000	
DR	Loss on sale of accounts receivable	50,000	
CR	Accounts receivable (net)		$500,000

3.

DR	Cash	$450,000	
DR	Unrealized loss on sale of accounts receivable	50,000	
CR	Accounts receivable (net)		$500,000

4.

DR	Cash	$450,000	
DR	Due from Cork Company	50,000	
CR	Accounts receivable (net)		$500,000

1 Perpetual and Periodic Concepts

Inventory is property held for resale, property held in production (work-in-process), or raw materials consumed in the process of production. Just like the cost of any other asset, the cost of inventory includes all costs incurred in getting the inventory onto the premises and ready for sale or use.

Inventory is accounted for under either a *periodic method* or a *perpetual method*. With the perpetual method, a running total of the inventory is maintained as goods are purchased and sold and the cost of goods sold is updated as sales occur. With the periodic method, a running total is not maintained, and the cost of goods sold cannot be determined until the end of the period when the ending inventory is counted.

1.1 Periodic Inventory—Cost of Goods Sold

Beginning inventory	$XXX
Plus: Purchases	XXX
Equal: Cost of goods available for sale	XXX
Less: Ending inventory	(XXX)
Cost of goods sold	XXX

1.2 Goods in Transit

1.2.1 FOB Shipping Point

Title passes to the buyer when goods are shipped and in transit. Hence title passed when shipped, but no possession.

1.2.2 FOB Destination

Title passes to the buyer when goods are received. Hence, no title and no possession until received

B Inventory

Mixon Corporation, a manufacturer of small tools, provided the following information from its accounting records for the year ended December 31, Year 1:

Inventory at December 31, Year 1 (based on a physical count of goods in Mixon's plant at cost on December 31, Year 1)	$1,750,000
Accounts payable at December 31, Year 1	1,200,000
Net sales (sales less sales returns)	8,500,000

Additional information is as follows:

1. Included in the physical count were tools billed to a customer FOB shipping point on December 31, Year 1. These tools had a cost of $28,000 and were billed at $35,000. The shipment was on Mixon's loading dock at 5:00 PM on December 31, Year 1 waiting to be picked up by the common carrier.

2. Goods were in transit from a vendor to Mixon on December 31, Year 1. The invoice cost was $50,000, and the goods were shipped FOB shipping point on December 29, Year 1.

What would be the adjusted inventory at December 31, Year 1?

1. $1,750,000

2. $1,715,000

3. $1,700,000

4. $1,800,000

? Related Questions

For related questions, go to the online question bank:

➤ FR-00403

2 Inventory Valuation Methods

Under both IFRS and U.S. GAAP, the appropriate inventory valuation method can be applied to a single item, a category, or total inventory, provided that the method most clearly reflects periodic income.

2.1   U.S. GAAP

Under U.S. GAAP, inventory is valued at the lower-of-cost-or-market when using LIFO or the retail inventory method. Cost is determined using an appropriate inventory cost flow assumption. Market generally means current replacement cost, provided the current replacement cost does not exceed net realizable value (the "market ceiling") or fall below net realizable value reduced by normal profit margin (the "market floor"). In all other cases (not LIFO or retail), U.S. GAAP requires the lower of cost or net realizable value, the same as IFRS.

2.2   International Financial Reporting Standards (IFRS)

Under IFRS, inventory is valued at the lower-of-cost or net realizable value. Cost is determined using an appropriate inventory cost flow assumption. Net realizable value is net selling price less costs to complete and sell the inventory.

Question 2-1	FR-00373

Simmons, Inc. uses lower-of-cost-or-market to value its inventory. Data regarding an item in its inventory is as follows:

Cost	$26
Replacement cost	20
Selling price	30
Cost of completion	2
Normal profit margin	7

What is the lower-of-cost-or-market for this item?

1. $21
2. $20
3. $28
4. $26

? Related Questions

For related questions, go to the online question bank:

➤ FR-00388

3 Inventory Costing Methods

The common inventory cost flow methods are specific identification, FIFO, LIFO, and weighted average. LIFO is not permitted under IFRS.

3.1 FIFO

FIFO inventory consists of the most recent costs and the cost of goods sold consists of the older costs.

3.2 LIFO

LIFO inventory consists of the older costs and the cost of goods sold consists of the most recent costs.

In periods of rising prices, FIFO and LIFO will have opposite effects on inventory, cost of goods sold and net income. FIFO results in the highest inventory, and reports the lowest cost of goods sold and hence the highest net income. LIFO reports the lowest inventory, and reports the highest prices in cost of goods sold and hence the lowest net income. In periods of decreasing prices, the effects are of course the opposite.

On the CPA Exam, prices are generally rising, therefore:

> LIFO = Lowest ending inventory / Lowest net income
>
> FIFO = Highest ending inventory / Highest net income

Questions related to the effect of overstatement and understatement errors are common on the exam. Note that if ending inventory is overstated, then cost of goods is understated, and net income is overstated; if ending inventory is understated, the opposite is true. Errors in ending inventory have the same effect on net income (move in the same direction); errors in beginning inventory move in the opposite direction.

3.3 Weighted Average—Used With Periodic Inventory

$$\text{Weighted average cost per unit} = \frac{\text{Cost of goods available for sale}}{\text{Number of units available for sale}}$$

The weighted average cost per unit is used to determine both cost of goods sold and ending inventory.

3.4 Moving Average—Used With Perpetual Inventory

The unit cost changes each time there is a new purchase.

	Units	Units Cost	Total Costs	Total Units	Moving Average
Beginning inventory	100	$5	$500	100	$5.00
Purchases	200	$6	$1,700	300	$5.67

3.5 Dollar-Value LIFO

- Inventory under dollar-value LIFO is measured in dollars and is adjusted for changing price levels. When converting from FIFO to dollar-value LIFO, a price index is used.

- The company groups similar inventory items into "pools."

- Each pool is assigned a conversion index. It can be computed internally or obtained from external sources.

3.5.1 Calculation

- Internally computed price index formula:

$$\text{Price index} = \frac{\text{Ending inventory at current year dollar}}{\text{Ending inventory at base year dollar}}$$

- The LIFO layer added in the current year is multiplied by the price index and added to the dollar-value LIFO computation.

Date	At Base Year Cost	At Current Year Cost	At Dollar Value LIFO
1/1/Year 1	$50,000	$50,000	$50,000
Year 1 layer	10,000	40,000	?? (a)
12/31/Year 1	$60,000	$90,000	?? (b)

Step 1: $90,000/$60,000 = 3/2

Step 2: $10,000 × 3/2 = $15,000 (a)

Step 3: $50,000 + $15,000 = $65,000 (b)

3.6 Gross Profit Method

The gross profit method can be used to prepare interim financial statements. The gross profit percentage is known and is used to calculate cost of goods sold.

Sales	100%
CGS	80% (Plug)
Gross profit	20%

3.7 Conventional Retail Method

Converts inventory at retail to inventory at cost. This is accomplished via a cost/retail ratio. Markups are included in the ratio, whereas, markdowns are excluded, resulting in lower of cost or market.

	At Cost	At Retail	
Beginning inventory	$15,000	$ 35,000	
Purchases	$ 5,000	$ 12,000	
Markups	–	3,000	
Available for sale	$20,000	$ 50,000	= 40% Cost/retail ratio
Sales		$(30,000)	
Markdowns		(5,000)	
Ending inventory at retail		$ 15,000	
Ending inventory at LCM (15,000 × 40)	$ 6,000		

Question 3-1   FR-00432

The Loyd Company had 150 units of product Omega on hand at December 1, Year 1, costing $400 each. Purchases of product Omega during December were as follows:

Date	Units	Unit Cost
December 7	100	$440
December 14	200	$460
December 29	300	$500

Sales during December were 500 units. The cost of inventory at December 31, Year 1 under the FIFO method would be closest to:

1. $100,000
2. $104,000
3. $115,000
4. $125,000

Question 3-2   FR-00358

The Loyd Company had 150 units of product Omega on hand at December 1, Year 1 costing $400 each. Purchases of product Omega during December were as follows:

Date	Units	Unit Cost
December 7	100	$440
December 14	200	$460
December 29	300	$500

Sales during December were 500 units. The cost of inventory at December 31, Year 1 under the LIFO method would be:

1. $100,000
2. $104,000
3. $75,000
4. $125,000

Question 3-3   FR-00444

The Loyd Company had 150 units of product Omega on hand at December 1, Year 1 costing $400 each. Purchases of product Omega during December were as follows:

Date	Units	Unit Cost
December 7	100	$440
December 14	200	$460
December 29	300	$500

Sales during December were 500 units. The cost of inventory at December 31, Year 1 under the weighted average method would be closest to:

1. $100,000
2. $104,000
3. $115,000
4. $125,000

? Related Questions

For related questions, go to the online question bank:

➤ FR-00313
➤ FR-00343
➤ FR-00418
➤ FR-00455
➤ FR-00465

1 General Concepts

The cost of a fixed asset (or any other asset) is the cost to acquire the asset and place it in condition for its intended use. As an example, purchased equipment would include purchase price, freight in, installation, sale taxes, etc.

■ *Ordinary repairs* are expensed, not capitalized.

■ *Extraordinary repairs* should be capitalized if they increase the usefulness of the asset and should be recorded by decreasing accumulated depreciation if they increase the life of the asset.

■ Land is not a depreciable asset; land improvements are.

■ Sometimes, fixed assets are acquired in a "basket" purchase. The amount paid must be allocated to the various assets acquired, generally on a relative fair value or appraisal value basis.

2 Reporting Fixed Assets

2.1 U.S. GAAP

Under U.S. GAAP, the carrying value of a fixed asset is calculated as follows:

Carrying value = Historical cost − Accumulated depreciation − Impairment

2.2 IFRS

Under IFRS, fixed asset carrying value can be calculated using the cost model or the revaluation model. The cost model is the method used under U.S. GAAP. Under the revaluation model, fixed assets are revaluated to fair value by asset class at a specific point in time and then reported as follows:

$$\text{Carrying value (revaluation model)} = \text{Fair value on revaluation date} - \text{Subsequent accumulated depreciation} - \text{Subsequent impairment}$$

When fixed assets are revalued under IFRS, revaluation losses are reported on the income statement and revaluation gains are reported in other comprehensive income as revaluation surplus. When the fair value of a revalued asset differs materially from its carrying amount, a further revaluation is required.

Question 2-1 FR-00406

On June 30, Year 1, Bluebird Inc. purchased a $750,000 tract of land for a new regional office. Costs related to purchasing the property and preparing the land for construction included:

Legal fees	$32,000
Title guarantee insurance	15,000
Cost to clear timber from land	18,000
Proceeds from sale of timber	7,000
Excavation costs for office building	20,000

In its December 30, Year 1 balance sheet, Boyd should report a balance in the land account of:

1. $797,000
2. $808,000
3. $815,000
4. $828,000

? Related Questions

For related questions, go to the online question bank:

➤ FR-00316

3 Interest on Self-Constructed Assets

Interest on self-constructed assets is capitalized based on the weighted average of the accumulated expenditures multiplied by an appropriate interest rate and cannot exceed actual interest costs. Interest on inventory routinely manufactured is not capitalized.

Question 3-1 FR-00421

On January 1, Year 1, Bluebird Inc. borrowed $10 million at a rate of 9% for 5 years and began construction of its new regional office building. Bluebird has no other debt. During Year 1, Bluebird's weighted average accumulated construction expenditures totaled $3,750,000. What should Bluebird report as interest expense on its income statement for Year 1?

1. $337,500
2. $500,000
3. $562,500
4. $900,000

4 Depreciation

Generally, the depreciation methods on the CPA Exam include *straight-line*, *sum-of-the-years-digits*, and *declining balance methods*. Depreciation is a rational and systematic cost allocation process closely tied to properly matching revenue and expenses. Under IFRS, the depreciation method used must match the expected pattern of fixed asset consumption. This is not required under U.S. GAAP.

4.1 Component Depreciation

Component depreciation is required under IFRS. Separate significant components of a fixed asset with different lives should be recorded and depreciated separately. The carrying amount of parts or components that are replaced should be derecognized.

4.2 Depreciation Methods

Depreciation is caused by physical factors such as wear, tear, and use.

4.2.1 Straight-Line

$$\frac{\text{Cost} - \text{Salvage value}}{\text{Estimated useful life}} = \text{Depreciation expense}$$

4.2.2 Units-of-Production (Productive Output)

$$\frac{\text{Cost} - \text{Salvage value}}{\text{Total estimated units or hours}} = \frac{\text{Depreciation}}{\text{rate}} \times \frac{\text{Units produced or}}{\text{hours used in a period}} = \frac{\text{Depreciation}}{\text{expense}}$$

4.2.3 Sum-of-Years'-Digits

$$\text{Depreciation rate} = \frac{\text{Remaining life}}{\text{SYD}}$$

The *numerator* is the remaining life of the asset at the beginning of the current year.

The *denominator* is the sum of the digits for the number of years of asset life (3-year life = 1 + 2 + 3 = 6):

$$(\text{Cost} - \text{Salvage value}) \times \frac{\text{Remaining life}}{\text{SYD}} = \text{Depreciation expense}$$

Financial Final Review   **II   C-3**

4.2.4 Declining Balance

The salvage value is not considered upfront; it is considered at the end.

The asset should never be depreciated below the estimated salvage value.

$$BV \times Rate = \text{Depreciation for the period}$$

$$Rate = \frac{100\%}{N} = R \; \frac{\text{If double} = 2R}{\text{If } 150\% = 1.5R}$$

$N = \text{Useful life}$

Question 4-1   FR-00376

McDonnell Company purchased a machine on January 1, Year 1 for $250,000. The machine was estimated to have a useful life of 10 years, with a salvage value of $50,000. During Year 3, it became apparent that the machine would not be usable past December 31, Year 5 and that the salvage value at that point would be $0.

What would be the accumulated depreciation at December 31, Year 3? Assume the company uses the straight-line method.

1. $100,000
2. $60,000
3. $110,000
4. $70,000

? Related Questions

For related questions, go to the online question bank:

➤ FR-00346

➤ FR-00361

➤ FR-00435

➤ FR-00776

1 Exchanges Having Commercial Substance (U.S. GAAP)

An exchange has commercial substance if the future risk, timing or amount of cash flows change as a result of the transaction. A fair value approach is used.

- Gains/Losses are always recognized on exchanges having commercial substance.

- Gains/Losses are the difference between the FV and BV of the old asset.

- The fair value of assets given up is assumed to be equal to the fair value of assets received, including any cash given or received in the transaction.

New asset (FV of old asset plus cash given, if any)	$XXX	
Accumulated depreciation of asset given up	XXX	
Cash received (if any)	XXX	
Loss (if any)	XXX	
Old asset at historical cost		$XXX
Cash given (if any)		XXX
Gain (if any)		XXX

Question 1-1 FR-00391

Pate paid $50,000 and gave a plot of undeveloped land with a carrying amount of $320,000 and a fair value of $450,000 to Bizzell Co. in exchange for a plot of undeveloped land with a fair value of $500,000. The land was carried on Bizzell's books at $350,000. The exchange is one that has commercial substance under U.S. GAAP.

At what amount is the land received from Pate recorded on Bizzell's books?

1. $370,000

2. $320,000

3. $500,000

4. $450,000

2 Exchanges Lacking Commercial Substance (U.S. GAAP)

If projected cash flows after the exchange are not expected to change significantly, then the exchange lacks commercial substance and a book value approach is used.

■ All losses are recognized on exchanges lacking commercial substance.

■ Gains are recognized based on the nature of the transaction:

- No boot received = No gain

- Boot given = No gain

- Boot received < 25% = Recognize gain in proportion to boot received

- Boot ≥ 25% of total consideration = Monetary exchange
  (Both parties to exchange recognize all gains and losses)

Question 2-1   FR-00458

Which of the following statements regarding nonmonetary exchanges is/are correct under U.S. GAAP?

I.   A fair value approach is used to record an exchange that lacks commercial substance.

II. An exchange is considered to have commercial substance if the future risk, timing, or amount of cash flows changes as a result of the transaction.

III. In all nonmonetary exchanges, it is assumed that the fair value given up is equal to the fair value received.

IV. In exchanges having commercial substance, the gain or loss on the exchange is calculated by comparing the book value of the asset given to the fair value of the asset received.

    1. I only.

    2. II only.

    3. II and III.

    4. II, III, and IV.

---

3 Exchanges of Similar Assets and Dissimilar Assets (IFRS)

Under IFRS, nonmonetary exchanges are characterized as exchanges of similar assets and exchanges of dissimilar assets. Exchanges of dissimilar assets are regarded as exchanges that generate revenue and are accounted for in the same manner as exchanges having commercial substance under U.S. GAAP. Exchanges of similar assets are not regarded as exchanges that generate revenue and no gains are recognized.

1 Debt Securities

1.1 Investments in Debt Securities

Under U.S. GAAP, there are three debt securities portfolio classifications: trading, available-for-sale, and held-to-maturity.

1.1.1 Trading Securities

Trading debt securities are intended for active trading. The portfolio itself is carried at cost and is reported at fair value in the financial statements through the use of a valuation account. Unrealized gains or losses are reported on the income statement.

DR	Unrealized loss	$XXX	
CR	Trading debt securities		$XXX
	OR		
DR	Trading debt securities	$XXX	
CR	Unrealized gain		$XXX

1.1.2 Available-for-Sale (AFS) Securities

AFS debt securities are carried at cost and are reported at fair value in the financial statements through the use of a valuation account. Unrealized gains or losses are reported in other comprehensive income (the "U" in **PUFER**).

DR	Unrealized loss	$XXX	
CR	Available-for-sale debt securities		$XXX
	OR		
DR	Available-for-sale debt securities	$XXX	
CR	Unrealized gain		$XXX

1.1.3 Held-to-Maturity (HTM) Securities

The HTM classification is appropriate when the investor has the ability and intent to hold the debt securities to maturity. The portfolio itself is reported in the financial statements at amortized cost.

1.2 Debt Impairment

An impairment loss must be recorded when the decline in fair value below the adjusted or amortized cost of any debt security classified as either available-for-sale or held-to-maturity is other than temporary. The cost basis of the individual security is written down to fair value as the new cost basis and the amount of the write-down is accounted for as a *realized* loss and included in earnings.

1.3 Realized Gains/Losses

Realized gains/losses are recognized in net income when a debt security is sold or impaired.

Trading Debt Securities		
DR Cash	$XXX	
CR Trading debt securities		$XXX
CR Realized gain		XXX
OR		
DR Cash	XXX	
DR Realized loss	XXX	
CR Trading debt securities		XXX

Available-for-Sale Debt Securities		
Facts:		
Cost	$100	
FV 1/01/Year 1	120	
Sold 9/15/Year 1	150	
DR Cash	$150	
DR Unrealized gain (PUFER)	20	
CR Available-for-sale debt securities		$120
CR Realized gain		50

1.4 Summary of Investments in Debt Securities

Summary of Investments in Debt Securities				
Classification	*Balance Sheet*	*Reported*	*Unrealized Gain/Loss*	*Realized Gain/Loss*
Trading stocks and bonds	Current or non-current	Fair value at balance sheet date	Income statement	Income statement
Available-for-sale stocks and bonds	Current or non-current	Fair value at balance sheet date	Other comprehensive income PUFER	Realized gain/loss in income statement Unrealized gain/loss is reversed
Held-to-maturity bonds	Current or non-current	Amortized cost	None	Not applicable

Question 1-1   FR-00339

The following data pertains to Tyne Co.'s investments in marketable debt securities:

Related Questions

For related questions, go to the online question bank:

➤ FR-00309

➤ FR-00324

➤ FR-00354

➤ FR-00369

➤ FR-00384

➤ FR-00429

		Market Value	
	Cost	12/31/Y2	12/31/Y1
Trading	$150,000	$155,000	$100,000
Available-for-sale	150,000	130,000	120,000

What amount should Tyne report as unrealized gain (loss) in its Year 2 income statement?

1. $55,000
2. $50,000
3. $60,000
4. $65,000

Question 1-2   FR-00399

Money for Nothing Enterprises ("MNE") held the following available-for-sale debt securities during Year 2:

	Cost	Market Value 12/31/Y1	Sales Price	Market Value 12/31/Y2
Alpha Corp.	$50,000	$53,000	$57,000	--
Beta Corp.	35,000	30,000		$38,000
Omega Corp.	21,000	27,000		24,000

What will MNE report as unrealized gain on available-for-sale securities on its Year 2 statement of comprehensive income (ignore taxes)?

1. $2,000
2. $3,000
3. $6,000
4. $8,000

Question 1-3   FR-00414

Money for Nothing Enterprises ("MNE") held the following available-for-sale debt securities during Year 2:

	Cost	Market Value 12/31/Y1	Sales Price	Market Value 12/31/Y2
Alpha Corp.	$50,000	$53,000	$57,000	--
Beta Corp.	35,000	30,000		$38,000
Omega Corp.	21,000	27,000		24,000

What will MNE report as accumulated other comprehensive income on its 12/31/Y2 balance sheet (ignore taxes)?

1. $2,000
2. $3,000
3. $6,000
4. $8,000

2 Investments in Equity Securities

2.1   Investments in Equity Securities

Equity investments are typically carried at fair value through net income (FVTNI), with unrealized gains/losses included in earnings as they occur. For equity investments that do not have a readily determinable fair value, the practicability exception allows an entity to measure an investment at cost plus/minus observable price changes of identical or similar investments, less impairment.

2.2   Equity Impairment

When a qualitative assessment indicates that equity investments measured using the practicability exception are impaired, the cost basis of the security is written down to fair value and the amount of the write-down is accounted for as a realized loss and included in earnings.

2.3   Realized Gains/Losses

Realized gains/losses equal to the sale price relative to the adjusted cost are booked on the income statement.

3 Equity Method

The equity method must be used if the investor has significant influence over the investee. Even if the investor owns less than 20 percent of the stock of an investee company, but exercises significant influence, the equity method must be used.

With the equity method, income/loss from the investee is the pro rata share of the investee's income/loss. The carrying amount of the investment is reduced by the pro rata share of the dividends paid by the investee.

FV adjustment is the difference between the FV and BV of the assets and/or liabilities of the investee. FV adjustments for non-current assets other than land are subject to depreciation (e.g., equipment).

Investment		Income	
Cost	% of cash dividends	FV adjustment	% of net income
% of net income	FV adjustment	Depreciation	
	Depreciation		

Under both U.S. GAAP and IFRS, joint ventures are accounted for using the equity method.

Question 3-1   FR-00438

On January 1, Year 1, Red Crown, Inc. purchased 25 percent of Red Hand Co.'s outstanding common shares and 40 percent of Red Leaf Co.'s nonvoting preferred stock. Red Crown plans to hold the investments on a long-term basis. Red Hand reported net income of $300,000 for Year 1 and paid common stock dividends of $100,000. Red Leaf reported net income of $450,000 and paid preferred dividends of $200,000. On its December 31, Year 1 income statement, what amount of income from these investments should Red Crown report?

1. $105,000
2. $155,000
3. $205,000
4. $255,000

? Related Questions

For related questions, go to the online question bank:

➤ FR-00334

➤ FR-00349

➤ FR-00364

E   Investments

Task-Based Simulations

Task-Based Simulation 1: Definition

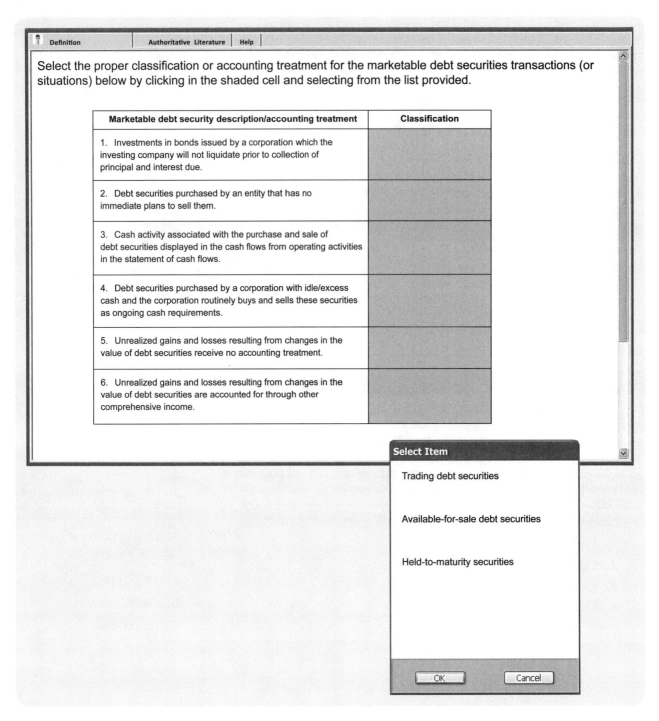

Definition | Authoritative Literature | Help

Select the proper classification or accounting treatment for the marketable debt securities transactions (or situations) below by clicking in the shaded cell and selecting from the list provided.

Marketable debt security description/accounting treatment	Classification
1. Investments in bonds issued by a corporation which the investing company will not liquidate prior to collection of principal and interest due.	
2. Debt securities purchased by an entity that has no immediate plans to sell them.	
3. Cash activity associated with the purchase and sale of debt securities displayed in the cash flows from operating activities in the statement of cash flows.	
4. Debt securities purchased by a corporation with idle/excess cash and the corporation routinely buys and sells these securities as ongoing cash requirements.	
5. Unrealized gains and losses resulting from changes in the value of debt securities receive no accounting treatment.	
6. Unrealized gains and losses resulting from changes in the value of debt securities are accounted for through other comprehensive income.	

Select Item

Trading debt securities

Available-for-sale debt securities

Held-to-maturity securities

[OK]   [Cancel]

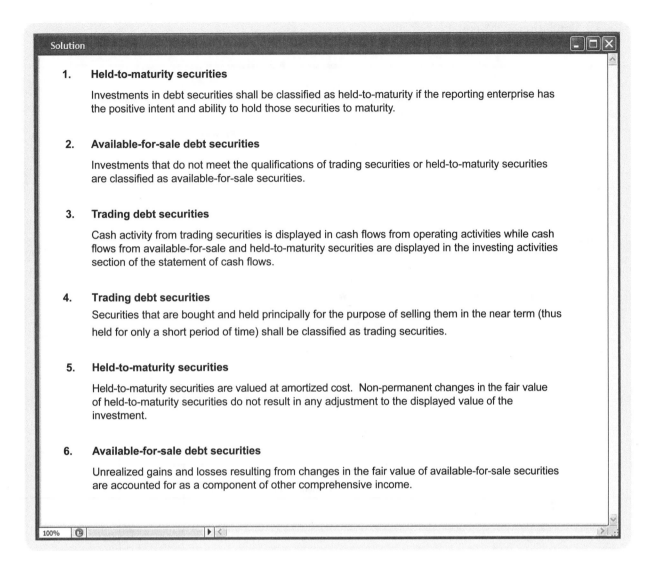

Solution

1. **Held-to-maturity securities**

   Investments in debt securities shall be classified as held-to-maturity if the reporting enterprise has the positive intent and ability to hold those securities to maturity.

2. **Available-for-sale debt securities**

   Investments that do not meet the qualifications of trading securities or held-to-maturity securities are classified as available-for-sale securities.

3. **Trading debt securities**

   Cash activity from trading securities is displayed in cash flows from operating activities while cash flows from available-for-sale and held-to-maturity securities are displayed in the investing activities section of the statement of cash flows.

4. **Trading debt securities**

   Securities that are bought and held principally for the purpose of selling them in the near term (thus held for only a short period of time) shall be classified as trading securities.

5. **Held-to-maturity securities**

   Held-to-maturity securities are valued at amortized cost. Non-permanent changes in the fair value of held-to-maturity securities do not result in any adjustment to the displayed value of the investment.

6. **Available-for-sale debt securities**

   Unrealized gains and losses resulting from changes in the fair value of available-for-sale securities are accounted for as a component of other comprehensive income.

100%

E Investments

Task-Based Simulation 2: Marketable Securities

| Marketable Securities | Authoritative Literature | Help |

The following data has been provided relative to the debt investment portfolio of the Zarbo Corporation. Use this information as the data for your marketable securities task solution.

	Cost	Fair Value 12/31/Year 1	Activity in Year 2 Purchases	Activity in Year 2 Sales	Fair Value 12/31/Year 2
Held-to-maturity securities					
Arbor Corporation	–	–	55,000	–	45,000
Trading debt securities					
Delphi Corporation	100,000	120,000	–	–	105,000
Available-for-sale debt securities					
Gorman Corporation	125,000	75,000	–	65,000	–
Jubilee Creations	125,000	140,000	–	–	130,000

Additional notes:

- Securities of the Arbor Corporation were purchased at par.
- Delphi, Gorman, and Jubilee debt securities were purchased during Year 1.

For each of the securities listed below, enter the amount requested in the shaded cell.

1. Compute the carrying amount of each security at December 31, Year 2.	
Held-to-maturity securities	
Arbor Corporation	
Trading debt securities	
Delphi Corporation	
Available-for-sale debt securities	
Gorman Corporation	
Jubilee Creations	
2. Compute the amount of recognized gain or loss on the income statement as a result of the debt securities transactions.	
Available-for-sale debt securities	
Gorman Corporation	
3. Compute the amount of unrealized gain or loss on the income statement as a result of the debt securities transactions.	
Trading debt securities	
Delphi Corporation	
4. Compute the amount of unrealized gain or loss in other comprehensive income as a result of the debt securities transactions for Year 1.	
Available-for-sale debt securities	
Gorman Corporation	
Jubilee Creations	
5. Compute the ending balance for accumulated other comprehensive income for Year 2.	
Other comprehensive income ending balance for Year 2	

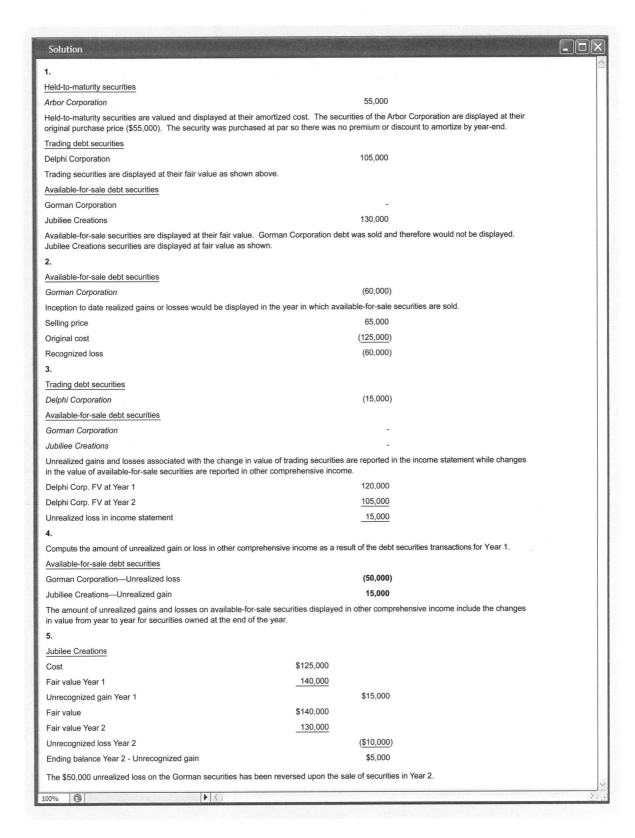

Solution

1.

Held-to-maturity securities

Arbor Corporation   55,000

Held-to-maturity securities are valued and displayed at their amortized cost. The securities of the Arbor Corporation are displayed at their original purchase price ($55,000). The security was purchased at par so there was no premium or discount to amortize by year-end.

Trading debt securities

Delphi Corporation   105,000

Trading securities are displayed at their fair value as shown above.

Available-for-sale debt securities

Gorman Corporation   -

Jubiliee Creations   130,000

Available-for-sale securities are displayed at their fair value. Gorman Corporation debt was sold and therefore would not be displayed. Jubilee Creations securities are displayed at fair value as shown.

2.

Available-for-sale debt securities

Gorman Corporation   (60,000)

Inception to date realized gains or losses would be displayed in the year in which available-for-sale securities are sold.

Selling price   65,000

Original cost   (125,000)

Recognized loss   (60,000)

3.

Trading debt securities

Delphi Corporation   (15,000)

Available-for-sale debt securities

Gorman Corporation   -

Jubiliee Creations   -

Unrealized gains and losses associated with the change in value of trading securities are reported in the income statement while changes in the value of available-for-sale securities are reported in other comprehensive income.

Delphi Corp. FV at Year 1   120,000

Delphi Corp. FV at Year 2   105,000

Unrealized loss in income statement   15,000

4.

Compute the amount of unrealized gain or loss in other comprehensive income as a result of the debt securities transactions for Year 1.

Available-for-sale debt securities

Gorman Corporation—Unrealized loss   **(50,000)**

Jubiliee Creations—Unrealized gain   **15,000**

The amount of unrealized gains and losses on available-for-sale securities displayed in other comprehensive income include the changes in value from year to year for securities owned at the end of the year.

5.

Jubilee Creations

Cost $125,000

Fair value Year 1   140,000

Unrecognized gain Year 1 $15,000

Fair value $140,000

Fair value Year 2   130,000

Unrecognized loss Year 2   ($10,000)

Ending balance Year 2 - Unrecognized gain $5,000

The $50,000 unrealized loss on the Gorman securities has been reversed upon the sale of securities in Year 2.

E   Investments

Task-Based Simulation 3: Research

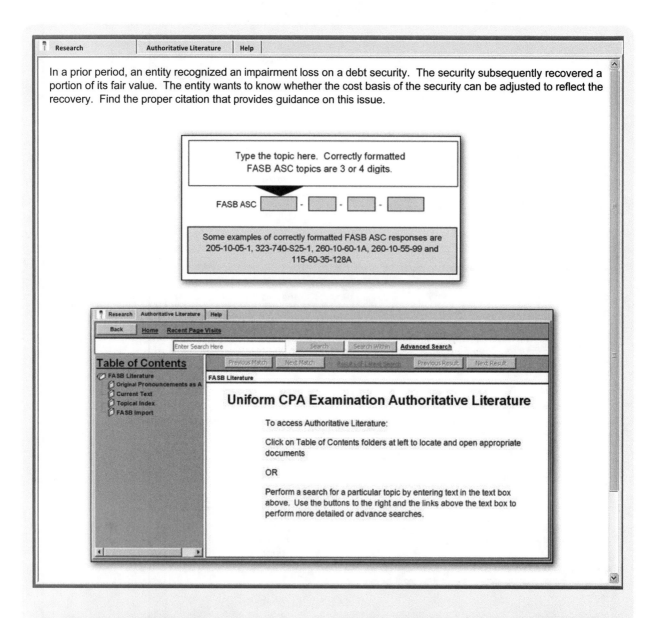

In a prior period, an entity recognized an impairment loss on a debt security. The security subsequently recovered a portion of its fair value. The entity wants to know whether the cost basis of the security can be adjusted to reflect the recovery. Find the proper citation that provides guidance on this issue.

Type the topic here. Correctly formatted FASB ASC topics are 3 or 4 digits.

FASB ASC ☐ - ☐ - ☐ - ☐

Some examples of correctly formatted FASB ASC responses are 205-10-05-1, 323-740-S25-1, 260-10-60-1A, 260-10-55-99 and 115-60-35-128A

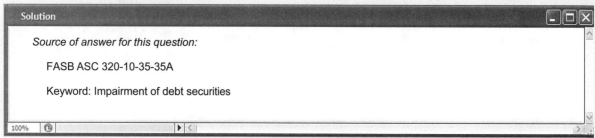

Solution

Source of answer for this question:

FASB ASC 320-10-35-35A

Keyword: Impairment of debt securities

---

1 Intangible Assets

1.1 Types of Intangible Assets

Patents, copyrights, franchises, trademarks, and goodwill are common intangible assets.

- Purchased intangibles are recorded at cost.

- Under U.S. GAAP, internally developed intangibles are expensed when incurred because research and development costs cannot be capitalized.

- Under IFRS, research costs related to internally developed intangibles must be expensed, but development costs can be capitalized if certain criteria are met.

- Costs of developing, maintaining, or restoring intangible assets that are not specifically identifiable, or have indeterminate lives, such as goodwill, are expensed when incurred.

1.2 Amortization

Under U.S. GAAP, intangible assets are reported at cost less amortization (finite life intangibles only) and impairment.

1.2.1 Finite Life Intangibles

For intangible assets with finite lives, the cost of the asset less its residual value, is amortized over its useful life, generally using the straight-line method. Goodwill cannot be amortized, but is subject to the impairment test.

1.2.2 Indefinite Life Intangibles

Intangible assets that have no legal or economic lives are considered to have indefinite useful lives. These intangible assets are not amortized but are reviewed for impairment periodically.

1.3 IFRS

Under IFRS, intangible assets are reported using the cost model (same as U.S. GAAP) or the revaluation model.

1.3.1 Revaluation Model

Under the revaluation model, revalued intangible assets are reported at fair value on the revaluation date less subsequent amortization and impairment. Revaluation losses are reported on the income statement and revaluation gains are generally reported in other comprehensive income.

Question 1-1   FR-00436

During Year 1, Innovative Technologies Corp. spent $900,000 developing a product which was granted a patent on June 30, Year 1. The company paid $20,000 in legal and other fees related to the patent registration process. On January 1, Year 2, the company paid $76,000 in legal fees related to the successful defense of the patent in a patent-infringement lawsuit brought by the company's main competitor. The patent's legal life is 17 years and its estimated economic life is 10 years. What will Innovative Technologies report as amortization expense related to the patent on its December 31, Year 2, income statement if the company uses U.S. GAAP?

1. $1,000
2. $2,000
3. $9,500
4. $10,000

Question 1-2   FR-00347

In a business combination consummated on January 1, Year 1, Wright acquired an intangible asset with an acquisition cost of $5,000,000, a fair value at December 31, Year 1 of $6,000,000, and a finite life of 50 years and also another intangible asset with an acquisition cost of $3,000,000 and a fair value of $2,500,000 at December 31, Year 1, for which a life cannot be determined.

What amount of intangible amortization should Wright recognize for the year ended December 31, Year 1?

1. $0
2. $100,000
3. $150,000
4. $500,000

? Related Questions

For related questions, go to the online question bank:

➤ FR-00423

➤ FR-00764

➤ FR-00765

1 Requirement

The carrying amounts of intangibles (including goodwill) and fixed assets held for use and to be disposed of need to be reviewed at least annually or whenever events or changes in circumstances indicate that the carrying amount may not be recoverable. The process used to determine impairment depends on the type of asset (i.e., intangible or fixed).

2 Impairment of Intangible Assets Other Than Goodwill

The impairment of an intangible asset is recorded by reducing the cost basis of the intangible asset (credit intangible asset) and recording an impairment loss. If the intangible asset is not totally impaired and the intangible asset has a finite life, then the new cost basis is amortized over the remaining life.

2.1 Impairment Test (U.S. GAAP)

2.1.1 Intangible Assets With Finite Lives

When testing an intangible asset with a finite life for impairment, the future cash flows expected to result from the use of the asset and its eventual disposition need to be estimated when testing for impairment. Under U.S. GAAP, if the sum of *undiscounted* expected (future) cash flows is less than the carrying amount, an impairment loss needs to be recognized.

2.1.2 Intangible Assets With Indefinite Lives

When testing an intangible asset with an indefinite life for impairment, the test for recoverability is performed by comparing the fair value of the asset to its carrying value because it is difficult, if not impossible, to estimate future cash flows. If the fair value is less than the carrying amount, an impairment loss needs to be recognized.

2.1.3 Impairment Loss Calculation

The impairment loss is calculated as the amount by which the carrying amount exceeds the fair value of the asset. U.S. GAAP does not permit the reversal of impairment losses unless the asset is held for disposal.

2.2 Impairment Test (IFRS)

Under IFRS, an impairment loss for a long-lived asset other than goodwill is calculated by comparing the carrying value of the asset to the asset's recoverable amount. IFRS define the recoverable amount as the greater of the asset's fair value less costs to sell and the asset's value in use. Value in use is the present value of the future cash flows expected from the intangible asset. IFRS allow the reversal of impairment losses.

Question 2-1   FR-00766

On December 31, an entity analyzed a finite life trademark with a net carrying value of $750,000 for impairment. The entity determined the following:

Fair value	$700,000
Undiscounted future cash flows	$740,000

What is the impairment loss that will be reported on the December 31 income statement under U.S. GAAP?

1. $0
2. $10,000
3. $40,000
4. $50,000

Question 2-2   FR-00767

On December 31, an entity analyzed a finite life trademark with a net carrying value of $750,000 for impairment. The entity determined the following:

Fair value (less costs to sell)	$700,000
Present value of future cash flows	$710,000

What is the impairment loss that will be reported on the December 31 income statement under IFRS?

1. $0
2. $10,000
3. $40,000
4. $50,000

3 Impairment of Goodwill

3.1 Goodwill Impairment (U.S. GAAP)

Under U.S. GAAP, goodwill impairment is calculated on the reporting unit level. A reporting unit is an operating segment, or one level below an operating segment. The goodwill of one reporting unit may be impaired, while the goodwill for other reporting units may or may not be impaired. The evaluation of goodwill impairment is a two-step process.

3.1.1   Step 1

Identify potential impairment by comparing the fair value of each reporting unit with its carrying amount, including goodwill.

1. Assign assets acquired and liabilities assumed to the various reporting units. Assign goodwill to the reporting units.

2. Determine the fair values of the reporting units and of the assets and liabilities of those reporting units.

3. If the fair value of a reporting unit is less than its carrying amount, there is potential goodwill impairment. The impairment is assumed to be due to the reporting unit's goodwill since any impairment in the other assets of the reporting unit will already have been determined and adjusted for (other impairments are evaluated before goodwill).

4. If the fair value of a reporting unit is more than its carrying amount, there is no goodwill impairment and Step 2 is not necessary.

3.1.2   Step 2

Measure the amount of goodwill impairment loss by comparing the implied fair value of the reporting unit's goodwill with the carrying amount of that goodwill.

1. Allocate the fair value of the reporting unit to all assets and liabilities of the unit. Any fair value that cannot be assigned to specific assets and liabilities is the implied goodwill of the reporting unit.

2. Compare the implied fair value of the goodwill to the carrying value of the goodwill. If the implied fair value of the goodwill is less than its carrying amount, recognize a goodwill impairment loss. Once the goodwill impairment loss has been fully recognized, it cannot be reversed.

3.1.3   Assessing Qualitative Factors

Under U.S. GAAP, the goodwill and indefinite life intangible asset impairment tests have been simplified by allowing companies to test qualitative factors to determine whether it is necessary to perform the relevant quantitative impairment tests.

The quantitative impairment tests are not necessary if, after assessing the relevant qualitative factors, an entity determines that *it is not more likely than not* that the fair value of the reporting unit or indefinite life intangible asset is less than its carrying amount. If the qualitative assessment indicates that there is a greater than fifty percent chance that the fair value of the reporting unit or indefinite life intangible asset is less than its carrying amount, then the entity must perform the quantitative impairment test.

3.2 Goodwill Impairment (IFRS)

Under IFRS, goodwill impairment testing is done at the cash-generating unit (CGU) level. A cash-generating unit is defined as the smallest identifiable group of assets that generates cash inflows that are largely independent of the cash inflows from other assets or groups of assets. The goodwill impairment test is a one-step test in which the carrying value of the CGU is compared to the CGU's recoverable amount, which is the greater of the CGU's fair value less costs to sell and its value in use. Value in use is the present value of the future cash flows expected from the CGU. An impairment loss is recognized to the extent that the carrying value exceeds the recoverable amount. The impairment loss is first allocated to goodwill and then allocated on a pro rata basis to the other assets of the CGU.

Question 3-1	FR-00768

On December 31, Star Corp. had a reporting unit that had a book value of $950,000, including goodwill of $130,000. As part of the company's annual review of goodwill impairment, Star determined that the fair value of the reporting unit was $890,000. Star assigned $840,000 of the reporting units fair value to its assets and liabilities other than goodwill. What is the goodwill impairment loss to be reported on December 31 under U.S. GAAP?

1. $50,000
2. $60,000
3. $80,000
4. $110,000

4 Impairment of Fixed Assets

When a fixed asset is totally impaired, the obsolete asset and related accumulated depreciation are removed from the accounts, and a loss is recognized for the difference. When a fixed asset is partially impaired, the asset should be written down to a new cost basis. The cost is then depreciated over the remaining life.

4.1 Impairment Test (U.S. GAAP)

Fixed assets are reviewed for impairment at least annually. Under U.S. GAAP, the impairment test is a two-step test that is similar in concept to the two-step impairment test for goodwill. The details of the accounting treatment are actually slightly different for long-term assets to be held and used than for long-term assets to be disposed of.

4.1.1 Step 1

The first step of the impairment test is a screening test to determine if the asset is impaired. In the first step, the total future undiscounted cash flows expected from the use of the asset is compared to the carrying amount of the asset; if the total undiscounted cash flows is less than the carrying amount, there is an impairment loss. If not, there is no impairment loss and the second step of the impairment test is not needed.

4.1.2 Step 2

The second step of the impairment test measures the amount of the impairment loss by the difference between the fair value of the asset and the carrying amount of the asset. The asset is written down to its fair value, and an impairment loss is recognized in income from continuing operations.

4.1.3 Income Statement Presentation

Income statement presentation depends on whether the assets are to be held and used or are to be disposed of.

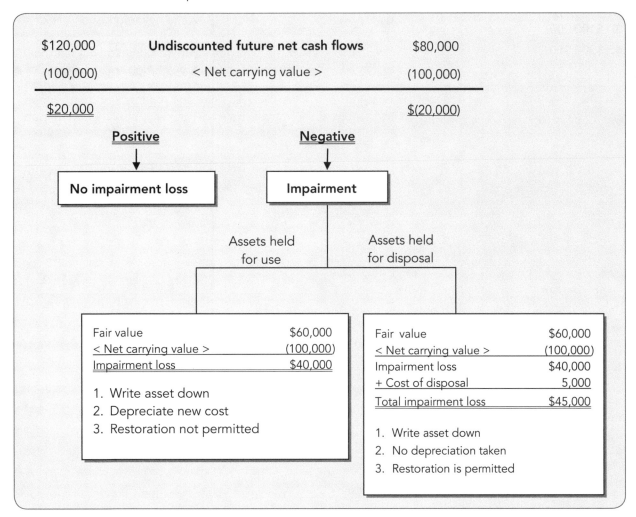

4.2 Impairment Test (IFRS)

Under IFRS, impairment exists if the carrying value of the fixed asset exceeds the higher of 1) fair value less costs to sell; and 2) value in use (present value of expected future cash flows). Restoration is permitted under IFRS for both fixed assets held for sale and fixed assets held for use.

Question 4-1 — FR-00331

Sumrall Corporation owns machinery that was purchased 20 years ago. The machinery, which originally cost $2,000,000, has been depreciated using the straight-line method using a 40-year useful life and no salvage value and has a current carrying amount of $1,000,000 and a current fair value of $800,000. Sumrall estimates that the machinery has a remaining useful life of 20 years and will provide net cash inflow of $45,000 per year.

Sumrall should record an impairment loss associated with the machinery of:

1. $0 since there is no impairment.
2. $150,000
3. $100,000
4. $200,000

? Related Questions

For related questions, go to the online question bank:

➤ FR-00447

➤ FR-00774

1 Asset Retirement Obligation

1.1 Definition

An asset retirement obligation (ARO) is a legal obligation associated with the retirement of a tangible long-lived asset that results from the acquisition, construction, development and/or normal operation of a long-lived asset.

- An ARO qualifies for recognition when it meets the definition of a liability.

- Uncertainty about whether performance will be required is factored into the measurement of the liability.

1.2 Measurement of Amounts

- An entity records an asset (asset retirement cost—ARC) and a liability (asset retirement obligation—ARO) equal to the fair value of the asset retirement obligation.

- Accretion expense is the increase in the ARO liability due to the passage of time.

- Depreciation expense decreases the ARC asset reported on the balance sheet.

Question 1-1   FR-00838

Dig Inc. has several natural gas containment systems that must be disposed of in four years at an estimated cost of $200,000. The company plans to book an asset retirement obligation using straight-line depreciation and a 7 percent accretion rate.

After four years, the combination of cumulative accretion and accumulated depreciation will be closest to:

	Accretion	*Depreciation*
1.	$47,421	$200,000
2.	$47,421	$152,579
3.	$152,579	$47,421
4.	$200,000	$47,421

? Related Questions

For related questions, go to the online question bank:

➤ FR-00839

2 Other Liabilities and Debt Covenants

2.1 Current Liabilities

Current liabilities are obligations that mature within one year or the operating cycle, whichever is longer. Current liabilities are valued at their settlement values. The most common current liabilities are:

- Trade accounts payable
- Refundable deposits
- Sales, use and property taxes payable
- Accrued salaries, wages and bonuses
- Unpaid payroll deductions and employer's share of payroll taxes

2.2 Notes Payable

- Notes payable must be recorded at present value at the date of issuance.
- When a note contains either no interest or an unreasonable rate of interest, the present value of the obligation is shown at the appropriate market interest rate. The difference between the face value of the note and its present value is a discount or premium to be amortized over the life of the note using the effective interest method.
  - The market rate of interest should approximate the rate that would have been if negotiated by an independent lender.

2.3 Debt Covenants

Debt covenants prohibit certain actions by debtors that might negatively affect the position of the creditor. When covenants are violated, the loan is in technical default. The creditor and borrower generally work out concessions that may include a higher interest rate to be paid by the borrower.

Question 2-1   FR-00841

An employee earns $5,000 in gross pay per month. In additional to benefits and health care deductions, the employee also has 15 percent withheld for federal and state income taxes, as well as 7.65 percent for Social Security/Medicare taxes. His employer also pays 7.65 percent for its portion of Social Security/Medicare.

Assuming the employer in a given month has not remitted payments to the taxing authority yet, which of the following statements is most accurate?

1. $382.50 will be booked as a payable for the employee portion.
2. $382.50 will be booked as an expense for the employee portion.
3. $1,132.50 will be booked as a payable for the employee portion.
4. $1,132.50 will be booked as an expense for the employer portion.

? Related Questions

For related questions, go to the online question bank:

➤ FR-00840

1 Bonds Payable

1.1 Bond Terminology

A bond indenture is a contract that specifies the terms between the bond issuer and the bondholders.

Among the elements of the contract:

- **Face Value:** The total dollar amount of the bond. Bonds are generally sold in denominations of $1,000 and are quoted in 100s.
- **Stated/Nominal/Coupon Rate:** The interest to be paid to the bondholders.
- **Life of the Bond:** The number of periods from the bond date to the maturity date.
- Frequency of interest payments (annual, semiannual).

1.2 Issuance of Bonds

The selling price of a bond is equal to the *present value* of the future cash payments related to the bond, including both the principal and interest payments using the *effective rate* of interest. The effective/market rate is the rate of interest for bonds of similar risk and maturity on the date the bonds are sold. The effective market rate of interest on a bond is also referred to as the yield.

1.2.1 Bonds Issued at a Discount

A discount results when the market/effective rate exceeds the stated/coupon rate because investors will pay less than the bond's face value (e.g., 97, 98, 99). Under U.S. GAAP, the discount is amortized over the contractual life of the bonds. Under IFRS, the discount is amortized over the expected life of the bonds.

1.2.2 Bonds Issued at a Premium

A premium results when the market/effective rate is lower than the stated/coupon rate because investors are willing to pay more than the bond's face value (e.g., 101, 102, 103). Under U.S. GAAP, the premium is amortized over the contractual life of the bonds. Under IFRS, the premium is amortized over the expected life of the bonds.

1.2.3 Bonds Issued at Par

If bonds are issued at par, the stated rate of interest equals the effective rate of interest.

1.2.4 Bond Issuance Costs

Under both IFRS and U.S. GAAP, bond issuance costs are presented on the balance sheet as a direct reduction of the carrying amount of the bond, similar to bond discounts. When bonds are issued, the bond proceeds are recorded net of the bond issuance costs. Bond issuance costs are amortized as interest expense over the life of the bond using the effective interest method.

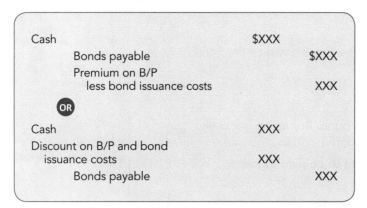

Cash	$XXX	
Bonds payable		$XXX
Premium on B/P		
less bond issuance costs		XXX
OR		
Cash	XXX	
Discount on B/P and bond		
issuance costs	XXX	
Bonds payable		XXX

1.3   Issuance of Bonds Between Interest Dates

When bonds are issued between interest dates, the amount of interest that has accrued since the last interest payment is added to the price of the bonds and is reimbursed at the next interest payment date to the purchaser. (The purchaser gets the full interest payment regardless of how long he/she has held the bond.)

Cash	$XXX	
Discount on B/P	XXX	
Bonds payable		$XXX
Interest expense (or payable)		XXX

1.4   Amortization of Premiums and Discounts

The carrying amount of a bond is the bond's face value plus the unamortized premium or minus the unamortized discount (and minus any bond issuance costs, as discussed above). At the maturity of a bond, the carrying amount of the bond is equal to the face.

There are two methods to amortize bond discounts, bond issuance costs, or bond premium:

1. **Straight-Line Method:** Tolerated under U.S. GAAP when the difference between this method and the effective interest amortization method is immaterial; prohibited under IFRS.

2. **Effective Interest Amortization Method:** U.S. GAAP/IFRS.

1.4.1 Straight-Line Method

The straight-line method amortizes the premium or discount equally over the life of the bonds.

1.4.2 Effective Interest Method

With the effective interest method, each interest payment is divided into an interest and principal component. The interest component is equal to the carrying amount of the bond at the beginning of the period times the effective interest rate. The difference between the interest component and the interest payment is the amortization of the premium or discount (including any bond issuance costs), and is used to adjust the carrying amount of the bond by decreasing the unamortized premium or discount.

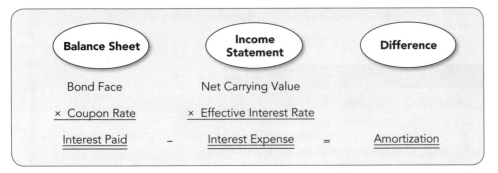

Date	Cash Interest 4%*	Interest Expense 5%**	Amortized Discount	Unamortized Discount	Carrying Amount
1/1/Year 1				50,000	950,000
6/30/Year 1	40,000	47,500	7,500	42,500	957,500
12/31/Year 1	40,000	47,875	7,875	34,625	965,375

*(1,000,000 × 0.04)

**(950,000 × 0.05)

Interest expense	$47,500	
Discount on B/P		$7,500
Cash		40,000

OR

Interest expense	XXX	
Premium on B/P	XXX	
Cash		XXX

I   Long-Term Debt

1.5   Retirement of Bonds

Corporations can call or retire bonds prior to maturity. Bonds are retired as a percentage of face value (e.g., 98, 101).

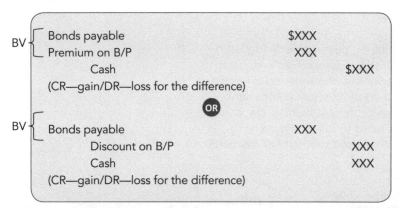

BV {
Bonds payable $XXX
Premium on B/P   XXX
     Cash $XXX
(CR—gain/DR—loss for the difference)

OR

BV {
Bonds payable   XXX
     Discount on B/P   XXX
     Cash   XXX
(CR—gain/DR—loss for the difference)

Question 1-1   FR-00427

On January 1, Year 1, Congo.com issued $1,000,000, 9% 10-year bonds (interest paid annually) to yield 8%. The present value of $1 at 9% for 10 years is 0.4224 and the present value of an ordinary annuity of $1 at 9% for 10 years is 6.4177. The present value of $1 at 8% for 10 years is 0.4632 and the present value of an ordinary annuity of $1 at 8% for 10 years is 6.7101. Which of the following is closest to the selling price of the bond?

1. $920,000
2. $1,000,000
3. $1,040,800
4. $1,067,100

Question 1-2   FR-00307

On July 1, Year 1, Cobb Company issued 9% bonds in the face amount of $1,000,000 which mature in ten years. The bonds were issued for $939,000 to yield 10%, resulting in a bond discount of $61,000. Cobb uses the effective interest method of amortizing bond discount. Interest is payable annually on June 30.

At June 30, Year 3, Cobb's unamortized bond discount should be:

1. $52,810
2. $57,100
3. $48,800
4. $43,000

? Related Questions

For related questions, go to the online question bank:

➤ FR-00322
➤ FR-00337
➤ FR-00352
➤ FR-00367
➤ FR-00440
➤ FR-00452
➤ FR-00462
➤ FR-00791
➤ FR-00852
➤ FR-00853

2 Imputing Interest

Notes receivable and notes payable contain an interest element. Money is not loaned for free or for a below-market interest rate. Notes are recorded at present value when the interest rate is not stated or when the stated interest rate is unreasonably low. The difference between the face amount of the note and the present value of the note is recorded as a discount and amortized over the life of the note.

3 Troubled Debt Restructuring

A troubled debt restructuring is one in which the creditor allows the debtor certain concessions such as reduced interest rates, extension of maturity dates, reduction of the face amount of the debt, and reduction of the amount of accrued interest as a result of the debtor's financial difficulty.

3.1 Accounting by the Debtor

3.1.1 Transfer of Assets

■ Recognize gain/loss on:

FV Asset Transferred

< NBV Asset Transferred >

Gain / Loss

■ Recognize gain on:

Carrying Amount of the Payable

< FV Asset Transferred >

Gain

3.1.2 Transfer of Equity

■ Recognize gain on:

> Carrying Amount of the Payable
>
> < FV Equity Transferred >
> _____
>
> Gain

3.1.3 Modification of Terms

In a modification, the debtor accounts for the effects prospectively and does not change the carrying amount or show a gain unless the carrying amount exceeds the total future cash payments specified by the new terms.

3.2 Accounting by the Creditor

A loan restructured in a troubled debt restructuring is accounted for by the creditor as an impaired loan. Bad debt expense is recognized for the difference between the loan amount and the fair value of whatever has been received and/or the present value of expected cash to be received, discounted at the loan's historical effective interest rate.

Question 3-1   FR-00842

Ansley Inc. (which uses IFRS) has debt on its books with a current value of $425,000. For the first time in its history, the company receives debt modifications that will result in future cash flows totaling $280,000.

As a result of the modifications, the company will most likely:

1. Handle the change prospectively, and keep the carrying value the same.
2. Handle the change prospectively, and lower the carrying value over time.
3. Book a gain in current operations and reduce the carrying value of the liability.
4. Book a reduction in interest expense and reduce the carrying value of the liability.

? Related Questions

For related questions, go to the online question bank:

➤ FR-00843

---

1 Capital Stock

1.1 Common Stock

Common stock (CS) normally has a par (or stated) value, for instance, CS $1 par value issued at $5 per share.

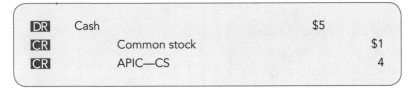

DR	Cash	$5	
CR	Common stock		$1
CR	APIC—CS		4

1.2 Preferred Stock

Preferred stock (PS) may be cumulative, noncumulative, or participating as to the payment of dividends and generally has a preferred claim to assets on liquidation of the business. PS $10 par value is issued at $30.

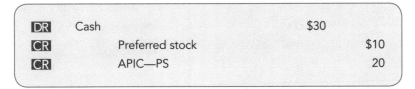

DR	Cash	$30	
CR	Preferred stock		$10
CR	APIC—PS		20

1.2.1 Cumulative

Cumulative preferred stockholders receive current dividends and all dividends in arrears (unpaid from prior years) before dividends are paid to common stockholders.

1.2.2 Participating

Any amounts available for dividend distribution after both preferred and common stockholders receive a specified payment based on the same percentage is divided between preferred and common stockholders on a pro rata basis.

1.2.3 Mandatorily Redeemable

Mandatorily redeemable preferred stock is classified as a liability because it has a maturity date, similar to debt instruments.

1.3 Shares Authorized, Issued, and Outstanding

- **Authorized:** Legal number of shares available for sale (maximum).

- **Issued:** Number of shares sold.

- **Outstanding:** Shares issued less treasury shares. Only outstanding shares are entitled to dividends.

Question 1-1   FR-00371

On September 1, Year 1, Royal Corp., a newly formed company, had the following stock issued and outstanding:

- Common stock, no par, $1 stated value, 5,000 shares originally issued for $15 per share.

- Preferred stock, $10 par value, 1,500 shares originally issued for $25 per share.

Royal's September 1, Year 1, statement of stockholders' equity should report:

	Common Stock	Preferred Stock	Additional Paid-In Capital
1.	$5,000	$15,000	$92,500
2.	5,000	37,500	70,000
3.	75,000	37,500	0
4.	75,000	15,000	22,500

? Related Questions

For related questions, go to the online question bank:

➤ FR-00464

2 Treasury Stock

Treasury stock (TS) is stock that has been issued and then repurchased by the issuer. Treasury stock is reported as a contra account to equity. There are two methods used to account for treasury stock under U.S. GAAP: the cost method and the par value method.

2.1 Cost Method

Under the cost method, treasury stock is recorded at cost. The total cost of a treasury share is deducted from the total of the stockholders' equity on the balance sheet. When the TS is reissued for less than its acquisition price the loss is recognized by debiting APIC—treasury stock. Retained earnings is debited if there is not a sufficient balance in the APIC—TS account. When TS is reissued for more than its acquisition price the gain is recognized by crediting APIC—treasury stock.

2.2 Par Value Method

Under the par value method, treasury stock is recorded at par value, and APIC is reduced for the amount of additional paid-in capital that was initially recognized on issuance. The total cost of the TS (par value) is deducted from the common stock account on the balance sheet. When treasury stock is reacquired for less than the original issue price (gain), APIC—treasury stock is recognized. When TS is reacquired for more than the original issue price (loss), any APIC—treasury stock is eliminated and then retained earnings is reduced.

2.3 Gains and Losses

Gains and losses on treasury stock transactions are not reported on the income statement. A company cannot report income dealing in its own stock. Treasury stock is not an asset. Treasury stock does not vote and does not receive dividends.

2.4   Summary Chart

Summary Chart of Journal Entries

1. Original Issue

10,000 shares of $10 par value, CS are sold for $15 per share

Income taxes paid

Cash	150,000	
Common stock		100,000
APIC—CS		50,000

	Cost Method			Par Value Method		
2. Buy Back Below						
200 shares repurchased for $12 per share	Treasury stock	2,400		Treasury stock	2,000	
	Cash		2,400	APIC—CS	1,000	
				Cash		2,400
				APIC—TS		600
3. Reissue Above Cost						
100 shares repurchased for $12 are resold for $15	Cash	1,500		Cash	1,500	
	Treasury stock		1,200	Treasury stock		1,000
	APIC—TS		300	APIC—CS		500
4. Reissue Below Cost						
100 shares repurchased for $12 are resold for $3	Cash	300		Cash	300	
	APIC—TS	300		APIC—TS	600	
	Retained earnings	600		Retained earnings	100	
	Treasury stock		1,200	Treasury stock		1,000

Note: Retained earnings may be debited, but never credited in treasury stock transactions.

Question 2-1   FR-00472

On January 1, Year 1, Black Dog Corp. began operations and issued 30,000 shares of $5 par common stock for $9/share. On June 30, the company bought back 10,000 shares for $8/share. Then, on September 15, the company resold 5,000 shares for $12/share. What amount of total additional paid-in capital should Black Dog report on its December 31, Year 1 balance sheet if Black Dog uses the cost method to account for its treasury stock?

1. $20,000
2. $120,000
3. $140,000
4. $165,000

? Related Questions

For related questions, go to the online question bank:

➤ FR-00356

➤ FR-00386

➤ FR-00478

3 Dividends and Stock Splits

3.1 Cash Dividends

Cash dividends may be declared on common and/or preferred stock.

Relevant dates for cash dividends are:

▪ **Declaration Date:**

> **DR** Retained earnings
> **CR**   Dividends payable

▪ **Record Date:** The date the stockholders must own the stock in order to receive the dividend declared.

No entry

▪ **Payment Date:** The date the dividends are actually disbursed.

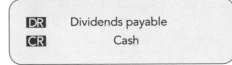

> **DR** Dividends payable
> **CR**   Cash

3.2 Property Dividends

Property dividends are distributions of noncash assets, such as inventories and investment securities. Property dividends are recorded at *fair value*.

3.3 Stock Dividends

A stock dividend of less than 20–25 percent of the outstanding capital stock is recorded at fair value (small dividend). A stock dividend of greater than 20–25 percent of the capital stock is recorded at par value (large dividend).

3.4 Liquidating Dividends

A liquidating dividend is a dividend in excess of retained earnings.

3.5 Stock Splits

In a stock split, the number of shares outstanding is increased, and the par value is decreased. (In a reverse split, the opposite is true.) There is no change in the total book value of shares outstanding and a memo entry is used to acknowledge a stock split.

Note

Recipient of stock dividends and stock splits recognize no income. The basis of each share of stock is adjusted accordingly.

3.6 Stock Rights/Warrants

Stock rights/warrants give the holder the right to acquire shares of stock on the payment of a defined amount. A memo entry is made when the rights are issued.

Question 3-1 — FR-00311

Boone Corporation's outstanding capital stock at December 15 consisted of the following:

- 30,000 shares of 5% cumulative preferred stock, par value $10 per share, fully participating as to dividends. No dividends were in arrears.
- 200,000 shares of common stock, par value $1 per share.

On December 15, Boone declared dividends of $100,000. What was the amount of dividends payable to Boone's common stockholders?

1. $10,000
2. $34,000
3. $40,000
4. $47,500

? Related Questions

For related questions, go to the online question bank:

➤ FR-00481
➤ FR-00484

4 Retained Earnings

Retained earnings (or deficits) are cumulative earnings (or losses) during the life of the corporation that have not been paid as dividends. A portion of retained earnings may be appropriated (restricted) for legal reasons or as a discretionary action of management. The appropriated retained earnings is distinguished from the unappropriated retained earnings account in the balance sheet.

Retained Earnings
Beginning retained earnings
+ Net income/loss
− Dividends (cash, property, and stock) declared
± Prior period adjustments
± Accounting changes (cumulative effect)
− Treasury stock (when necessary)
+ Adjustment from quasi-reorganization
Ending retained earnings

Task-Based Simulations

Task-Based Simulation 1: Retained Earnings

| Retained Earnings | Authoritative Literature | Help |

Kansas Inc. is a publicly held company whose shares are traded in the over-the-counter market. The stockholders' equity accounts at December 31, Year 1, of the prior year had the following balances:

Preferred stock, $100 par value, 6% cumulative; 5,000 shares authorized; 2,000 issued and outstanding	$ 200,000
Common stock, $1 par value, 150,000 shares authorized; 100,000 issued and outstanding	100,000
Additional paid-in capital	800,000
Retained earnings	1,586,000
Total stockholders' equity	$2,686,000

Transactions during Year 2 and other information relating to the stockholders' equity accounts were as follows:

- February 1, Year 2—Issued 13,000 shares of common stock to Ram Co. in exchange for land. On the date issued, the stock had a market price of $11 per share. The land had a carrying value on Ram's books of $135,000, and an assessed value for property taxes of $90,000.

- March 1, Year 2—Purchased 5,000 shares of its own common stock to be held as treasury stock for $14 per share. Kansas uses the cost method to account for treasury stock. Transactions in treasury stock are legal in the state of incorporation.

- May 10, Year 2—Declared a property dividend of marketable securities held by Kansas to common shareholders. The securities had a carrying value of $600,000; fair value on relevant dates were:

Date of declaration (May 10, Year 2)	$720,000
Date of record (May 25, Year 2)	758,000
Date of distribution (June 1, Year 2)	736,000

- October 1, Year 2—Reissued 2,000 shares of treasury stock for $16 per share.
- November 4, Year 2—Declared a cash dividend of $1.50 per share to all common shareholders of record November 15. The dividend was paid on November 25.
- December 20, Year 2—Declared the required annual cash dividend on preferred stock for Year 2. The dividend was paid on January 5, Year 3.
- January 16, Year 3—Before closing the accounting records for Year 2, Kansas became aware that no amortization had been recorded for the prior year for a patent purchased on July 1, Year 1. The patent was properly capitalized at $320,000 and had an estimated useful life of eight years when purchased. The company's income tax rate is 30%. The appropriate correcting entry was recorded on the same day.
- Adjusted net income for Year 2 was $838,000.

Calculate the following amounts as they would be reported on the Year 2 *Statement of Retained Earnings*. Enter the appropriate values in the shaded cells.

✗ ✔ fx	
Prior period adjustment.	
Preferred dividends.	
Common dividends—cash.	
Common dividends—property.	

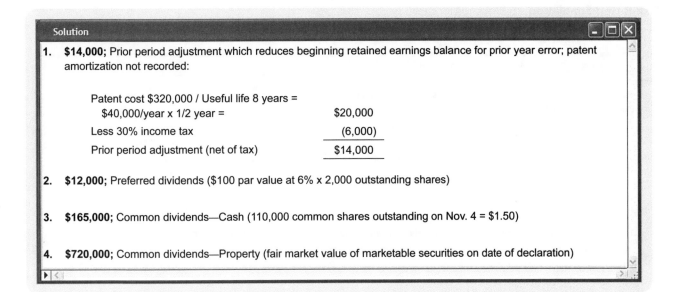

Solution

1. **$14,000;** Prior period adjustment which reduces beginning retained earnings balance for prior year error; patent amortization not recorded:

Patent cost $320,000 / Useful life 8 years =	
$40,000/year x 1/2 year =	$20,000
Less 30% income tax	(6,000)
Prior period adjustment (net of tax)	$14,000

2. **$12,000;** Preferred dividends ($100 par value at 6% x 2,000 outstanding shares)

3. **$165,000;** Common dividends—Cash (110,000 common shares outstanding on Nov. 4 = $1.50)

4. **$720,000;** Common dividends—Property (fair market value of marketable securities on date of declaration)

J Equity

Task-Based Simulation 2: Stockholder's Equity

Stockholders' Equity	Authoritative Literature	Help

Kansas Inc. is a publicly held company whose shares are traded in the over-the-counter market. The stockholders' equity accounts at December 31, Year 1, of the prior year had the following balances:

Preferred stock, $100 par value, 6% cumulative; 5,000 shares authorized; 2,000 issued and outstanding	$ 200,000
Common stock, $1 par value, 150,000 shares authorized; 100,000 issued and outstanding	100,000
Additional paid-in capital	800,000
Retained earnings	1,586,000
Total stockholders' equity	$2,686,000

Transactions during Year 2 and other information relating to the stockholders' equity accounts were as follows:

- February 1, Year 2—Issued 13,000 shares of common stock to Ram Co. in exchange for land. On the date issued, the stock had a market price of $11 per share. The land had a carrying value on Ram's books of $135,000, and an assessed value for property taxes of $90,000.

- March 1, Year 2—Purchased 5,000 shares of its own common stock to be held as treasury stock for $14 per share. Kansas uses the cost method to account for treasury stock. Transactions in treasury stock are legal in the state of incorporation.

- May 10, Year 2—Declared a property dividend of marketable securities held by Kansas to common shareholders. The securities had a carrying value of $600,000; fair value on relevant dates were:

Date of declaration (May 10, Year 2)	$720,000
Date of record (May 25, Year 2)	758,000
Date of distribution (June 1, Year 2)	736,000

- October 1, Year 2—Reissued 2,000 shares of treasury stock for $16 per share.
- November 4, Year 2—Declared a cash dividend of $1.50 per share to all common shareholders of record November 15. The dividend was paid on November 25.
- December 20, Year 2—Declared the required annual cash dividend on preferred stock for Year 2. The dividend was paid on January 5, Year 3.
- January 16, Year 3—Before closing the accounting records for Year 2, Kansas became aware that no amortization had been recorded for the prior year for a patent purchased on July 1, Year 1. The patent was properly capitalized at $320,000 and had an estimated useful life of eight years when purchased. The company's income tax rate is 30%. The appropriate correcting entry was recorded on the same day.
- Adjusted net income for Year 2 was $838,000.

Calculate the following amounts as they would be reported on the Year 2 *Statement of Stockholders' Equity*. Enter the appropriate values in the shaded cells.

✖ ✔ *fx*	
Number of common shares issued at December 31, Year 2.	
Amount of common stock issued.	
Additional paid-in capital, including treasury stock transactions.	
Treasury stock.	

Solution

1. 113,000

Date	Transaction	Issued	Outstanding		Months		Weighted Average
End of prior year	Balance	100,000	100,000	x	1	=	100,000
2/1/Year 2	Shares for land	13,000	13,000				
		113,000	113,000	x	1	=	113,000
3/1/Year 2	Purchase treasury stock	-	(5,000)				
		113,000	108,000	x	7	=	756,000
10/1/Year 2	Reissue treasury stock	-	2,000				
	Balance	113,000	110,000	x	3	=	330,000
	Total				12		1,299,000
	Weighted average						108,250

Alternative solution:

Date	Transaction	Outstanding		Months		Weighted Average
End of prior year	Balance	100,000	x	12/12	=	100,000
2/1/Year 2	Shares for land	13,000				
		113,000	x	11/12	=	11,916
3/1/Year 2	Purchase treasury stock	(5,000)				
		108,000	x	10/12	=	(4,166)
10/1/Year 2	Reissue treasury stock	2,000				
	Balance	110,000	x	3/12	=	500
	Weighted average					108,250

2. $113,000

Balance (100,000 shares x $1 par)	$100,000
Land for shares (13,000 shares x $1)	13,000
	$113,000

3. $934,000

Beginning balance, 12/31/Year 1		$800,000
Land for shares (13,000 shares x $10)		130,000
2,000 shares treasury stock sold × $16	$32,000	
Less cost of treasury stock (2,000 × $14)	(28,000)	
Excess (2,000 × $2)		4,000
		$934,000

4. $42,000

5,000 treasury shares × $14 cost	$ 70,000
(2,000) treasury shares × $14 cost	(28,000)
3,000 treasury shares × $14 cost	$ 42,000

1 The Five-Step Approach

Revenue is recognized when the good or service is transferred to the customer and the performance obligation is satisfied. The amount of revenue to be recognized should reflect the expected consideration that the entity is entitled to receive.

The five-step approach should be implemented by an entity in order to properly recognize revenue. The steps are as follows:

- **Step 1:** Identify the contract with the customer—a contract is an agreement between parties that creates enforceable rights or obligations.

- **Step 2:** Identify the separate performance obligations in the contract—a performance obligation is a promise to transfer either a good or a service to a customer.

- **Step 3:** Determine the transaction price—the transaction price is the amount of consideration that an entity is entitled to receive in exchange for transferring goods and/or services to a customer.

- **Step 4:** Allocate the transaction price to the separate performance obligations—if a contract contains more than one performance obligation, the overall transaction price will need to be allocated to each separate obligation.

- **Step 5:** Recognize revenue when or as the entity satisfies each performance obligation—revenue is recognized when the performance obligation is satisfied either at a point in time or over time through transferring the good/service to the customer.

2 Specific Applications Within Revenue Recognition

There are unique aspects to revenue recognition that are applicable in many distinct scenarios, as described below:

- Incremental costs to obtain a contract

  Costs to obtain a contract are treated as assets if the entity expects to recover them. Costs are treated as expenses if they are borne regardless of whether the contract is obtained.

- Costs to fulfill a contract

  Costs to fulfill a contract are treated as an asset if they relate directly to the contract, they generate/enhance the entity's resources, and they are expected to be recovered.

■ **Principal vs. agent**

A principal has control over the good/service prior to transfer and will recognize revenue equal to expected gross consideration. An agent does not have control and will recognize revenue equal to a fee/commission.

■ **Repurchase agreements**

Repurchase agreements are contracts where an entity sells an asset and promises or has the option to repurchase the asset later. An obligation to repurchase is a forward, a right to repurchase at an entity's option is a call option, and a right to repurchase at the customer's option is a put option.

■ **Bill-and-hold arrangements**

Bill-and-hold arrangements allow revenue to be recognized prior to the customer receiving the product as long as there is a substantive reason for holding the product, the entity cannot use or redirect the product, and the product is separately identified and ready for transfer to the purchasing customer.

■ **Consignment**

Consignment arrangements exist when an entity provides a product to a dealer to be held until it is ultimately sold to a third-party customer. Revenue is recognized either upon ultimate sale to a customer or after the expiration of a defined period of time.

■ **Warranties**

Warranties are treated as separate performance obligations distinct from the product covered in the contract if the warranty is not required by law, if the coverage period is lengthy, and if there are no specific tasks required regarding compliance assurance.

■ **Right to return**

When a customer has a right to return, the selling entity should book revenue for the amount of consideration it expects to receive, a refund liability, and an asset related to subsequent product recovery.

3 Long-Term Construction Contracts

3.1 Completed Contract Method

The completed contract method is used when a long-term construction contract does not meet the criteria for recognizing revenue over time.

DR	Construction in progress	$XXX	
CR	Cash/accounts payable		$XXX
DR	Accounts receivable	XXX	
CR	Progress billings		XXX

Losses (100 percent) for the completed contract method are recognized in full as they are discovered. The completed contract method is prohibited under IFRS.

3.2 Percentage of Completion Method

When a long-term construction contract meets the criteria for recognizing revenue over time, it is appropriate to use the percentage-of-completion method if the entity can reasonably estimate profitability and can provide a reasonable measure of progress toward completion. Revenue/income is recognized based on the ratio of the cost incurred to date to the total estimated cost. Under IFRS, if the final outcome of the project cannot be reliably measured, then the cost recovery method is required.

Losses for the percentage of completion method are recognized in full as they are discovered (e.g., 100 percent).

DR	Construction in progress	$XXX	
CR	Cash/accounts payable		$XXX
DR	Accounts receivable	XXX	
CR	Progress billings		XXX
DR	Construction in progress	XXX	
CR	Current gross profit		XXX

Calculation of Current Gross Profit		
Step 1	Total Gross Profit	Contract Price (Total Estimated Cost) Gross Profit
Step 2	% Completed	Cost to Date Total Estimated Cost
Step 3	Gross Profit Earned to Date	Step 1 × Step 2
Step 4	Current Gross Profit	Gross Profit Earned to Date (Gross Profit Previously Recognized) Current Gross Profit

Question 3-1

Big Wheel Construction had the following two construction projects which began in Year 1:

	Project 1	Project 2
Contract price	$690,000	$425,000
Costs incurred during Year 1	200,000	225,000
Estimated costs to complete	400,000	225,000
Billed to customers during Year 1	230,000	175,000
Received from customers during Year 1	100,000	150,000

What amount of gross profit (loss) would Big Wheel report on its Year 1 income statement?

	Percentage of Completion	Completed Contract
1.	$ 5,000	$(12,500)
2.	5,000	(25,000)
3.	17,500	(12,500)
4.	17,500	(25,000)

? **Additional Questions**

For additional questions, go to the online question bank:

➤ FR-00317

➤ FR-00392

1 Defined Benefit Pension Plans

Defined benefit plans define the benefits to be paid to employees based on factors such as years of service and compensation levels at retirement.

Defined contribution plans specify the amount of the employer's contributions to the plan; employee retirement benefits are determined based on the value of such contributions upon retirement.

1.1 Pension Obligations

1.1.1 Projected Benefit Obligation

The projected benefit obligation (PBO) is the actuarial present value of all benefits attributed by the plan's benefit formula. The PBO is used in the calculation of funded status, service cost, and interest cost and is computed using future salary levels.

1.1.2 Accumulated Benefit Obligation

The accumulated benefit obligation (ABO) is the actuarial present value of benefits attributed by a formula using current and past salary levels.

1.1.3 Defined Benefit Obligation

Under IFRS, the pension liability is called the defined benefit obligation (DBO). The DBO is very similar to the U.S. GAAP PBO.

1.2 Pension Plan Funded Status

Pension plans are accounted for on the accrual basis. Defined benefit pension plans are reported on the balance sheet based on funded status:

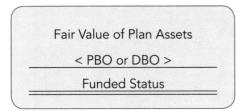

Fair Value of Plan Assets

< PBO or DBO >

Funded Status

1.2.1 U.S. GAAP

Under U.S. GAAP, companies are required to aggregate all *overfunded* (fair value of plan assets > PBO) pension plans and report them as a non-current asset on the balance sheet. All *underfunded* (fair value of plan assets < PBO) pension plans should also be aggregated and reported as a current liability, a non-current liability, or both. A pension plan is reported as a current liability to the extent that the benefits payable in the next 12 months exceed the fair value of the plan's assets.

1.2.2 IFRS

Under IFRS, the funded status (DBO – fair value of plan assets) of the pension plan is reported on the balance sheet as the net defined benefit liability (asset). A liability is reported if the plan is underfunded (DBO > fair value of plan assets) and an asset is reported if the plan is overfunded (DBO < fair value of plan assets). IFRS do not specify whether an entity should classify the net defined benefit liability (asset) as current or non-current.

1.3   Reporting Changes in Funded Status in OCI

1.3.1 U.S. GAAP

Under U.S. GAAP, a change in the funded status of a pension plan due to pension net losses or gains or prior service cost is reported in the period incurred as a component of accumulated other comprehensive income, net of tax. Any unrecognized net transition obligation (or asset) is also reported in accumulated other comprehensive income.

1.3.2 IFRS

Under IFRS, prior (past) service cost is reported as a component of service cost on the income statement in the period incurred. Pension gains and losses are reported in other comprehensive income in the period incurred and are not reclassified (amortized) to the income statement.

To report net loss or prior service cost:

DR	Other comprehensive income
CR	Pension benefit asset/liability
DR	Deferred tax asset
CR	Deferred tax benefit—OCI

To report net gain or net transition asset:

DR	Pension benefit asset/liability
CR	Other comprehensive income
DR	Deferred tax expense—OCI
CR	Deferred tax liability

1.4 Pension Reclassification Adjustments

Pension net gains or losses, prior service cost, and net transition assets or obligations remain in accumulated other comprehensive income until recognized in net periodic pension cost through amortization.

Reclassification adjustment to record amortization of net loss, prior service cost, or net transition obligation to net periodic pension cost:

DR	Net periodic pension cost	
CR		Other comprehensive income
DR	Deferred tax benefit—OCI	
CR		Deferred tax benefit—income statement

Reclassification adjustment to record amortization of net gain or net transition asset to net periodic pension cost:

DR	Other comprehensive income	
CR		Net periodic pension cost
DR	Deferred tax expense—income statement	
CR		Deferred tax expense—OCI

1.5 Pension Plan Contributions

An employer's contribution to its defined benefit pension plan(s) increases the pension benefit asset (overfunded pension plans) or decreases the pension benefit liability (underfunded pension plans).

Journal entry to record pension plan contribution:

DR	Pension benefit asset/liability	
CR		Cash

1.6 Pension Expense Components (SIRAGE)

Under U.S. GAAP, the amount of the net periodic pension cost is calculated using the following six components:

+	**S**ervice cost (current)
+	**I**nterest cost (on the projected benefit obligation)
–	**R**eturn on plan assets (expected or actual)
+	**A**mortization of unrecognized prior service cost
±	(**G**ains) and losses
±	Amortization of **E**xisting net (asset) or obligation

Prior service cost, gains and losses, and existing net obligations or assets are amortized and charged to net periodic pension cost over a specified period of time.

Under U.S. GAAP, service cost is reported as an operating expense on the income statement in the same line with other compensation costs. The other components of net periodic pension cost are presented on the income statement, separately or in total, below income from operations.

Under IFRS, defined benefit cost includes service cost and net interest on the defined benefit liability (asset). The components of defined benefit cost are generally reported separately on the income statement; there is no requirement that these amounts be aggregated and presented as one amount.

Question 1-1   FR-00325

Do It Right Inc.'s actuary provided the company with the following information regarding its defined benefit pension plan for the year ended December 31, Year 7:

Fair value of plan assets	$5,580,000
Accumulated benefit obligation	3,400,000
Projected benefit obligation	4,930,000
Unrecognized prior service cost	400,000
Unrecognized transition obligation	275,000
Unrecognized net gain	140,000
Expected benefit obligation - Year 8	250,000

The company reported net periodic pension cost of $310,000 on its income statement and made a $500,000 contribution to the pension plan during Year 7. The company's effective tax rate is 40%. What amount should Do It Right record as a pension asset/liability on the December 31, Year 7, balance sheet under U.S. GAAP?

1. $650,000 current liability.
2. $2,180,000 non-current liability.
3. $650,000 non-current asset.
4. $2,180,000 current asset.

Question 1-2   FR-00310

The following information pertains to Burnel Corporation's defined benefit pension plan for Year 1:

Service cost	$160,000
Actual and expected gain on plan assets	35,000
Unexpected loss on pension plan assets related to a Year 1 disposal of a subsidiary	40,000
Amortization of unrecognized prior service cost	5,000
Annual interest on pension obligation	50,000

What is Burnel's total net periodic pension cost for the period?

1. $250,000
2. $220,000
3. $210,000
4. $180,000

? Related Questions

For related questions, go to the online question bank:

➤ FR-00340
➤ FR-00355
➤ FR-00370
➤ FR-00385
➤ FR-00400
➤ FR-00415
➤ FR-00430
➤ FR-00442
➤ FR-00753

2 Postretirement Benefits Other Than Pensions

2.1 Postretirement Benefits

Postretirement benefits include:

- Health care insurance
- Life insurance
- Welfare benefits
- Tuition assistance

2.2 Financial Statement Reporting

Postretirement benefits must be reported on the balance sheet (funded status and OCI components), income statement (**SIRAGE**), and footnotes in the same manner as pensions if:

- the obligation is attributable to employees' services already rendered;
- the employees' rights accumulate or vest;
- payment is probable; and
- the amount of benefits can be reasonably estimated.

Postretirement benefits must be accrued during the period the employee works, called the "attribution period" (date hired to date fully vested).

The calculation of the funded status of a postretirement benefit plan is done using the APBO (accumulated postretirement benefit obligation), which is the present value of future benefits that have vested as of the measurement date:

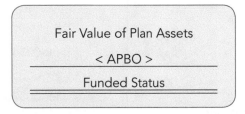

Fair Value of Plan Assets

< APBO >

Funded Status

Question 2-1   FR-00854

Churchill Inc. is a public company operating under U.S. GAAP that offers its former employees postretirement benefits. Which of the following statements is most accurate regarding Churchill's nonpension benefits?

1. The EPBO for the benefits will be equal to or greater than the APBO as a result of any nonvested benefits.

2. Although the assumed health care trend rate is critical to the company's estimates, it is not a required disclosure.

3. Any differences between the expected and actual returns must be recognized in the income statement in the period incurred.

4. The cost associated with retiree benefits may be accrued before services are rendered, as long as they can be reasonably estimated.

? Related Questions

For related questions, go to the online question bank:

➤ FR-00855

---

3 Stock Options

Compensatory stock options should be valued at the fair value of the options issued. The compensation expense is allocated over the service period.

3.1 Determining Fair Value

Either a Black-Scholes model or a lattice model, a type of binomial model, can be used to determine the fair value of the option. The statement requires the use of a valuation technique or model that returns the best estimate of the fair value of the option. Fair value will be given on the CPA Exam.

The models that estimate the value of stock based compensation should consider the following variables:

- The exercise price
- The expected life of the option
- The current price of the stock
- The expected volatility of the stock
- The expected dividends on the stock
- The risk-free rate of return for the expected term of the option

3.2 Accounting for Stock Options

Example
Accounting for Stock Options

On January 1, Year 1, Green Co. granted options exercisable after December 31, Year 2, to purchase 50,000 shares of $1 par common stock for $8 per share. Using an acceptable valuation model, the options had a total fair value of $50,000. The options are to serve as compensation for services during Year 1 and Year 2.

Journal Entry: January 1, Year 1—No entry required

Journal Entry: To allocate compensation cost to Year 1 operations

DR	Compensation expense	$25,000	
CR	Additional paid-in capital—stock options		$25,000

Journal Entry: To allocate compensation cost to Year 2 operations

DR	Compensation expense	25,000	
CR	Additional paid-in capital—stock options		25,000

On January 1, Year 3, all options are exercised.
Journal Entry: To record the exercise of the options

DR	Cash (50,000 × $8)	400,000	
DR	Additional paid in capital—stock options	50,000	
CR	Common stock (50,000 × $1 par)		50,000
CR	Additional paid in capital in excess of par (common stock)		400,000

Question 3-1   FR-00341

On January 1, Year 1, Sweeney Company granted an employee options to purchase 100 shares of Sweeney's common stock at $40 per share. The options became exercisable on December 31, Year 1, after the employee had completed one year of service, and were exercised on that date. Market prices of the stock and fair values of the options were as follows:

	Market Price	Fair Value
January 1, Year 1	$50	$61
December 31, Year 1	$65	$75

What amount should Sweeney recognize as compensation cost for Year 1?

1. $0
2. $2,100
3. $4,000
4. $6,100

Task-Based Simulations

Task-Based Simulation: Stock Options

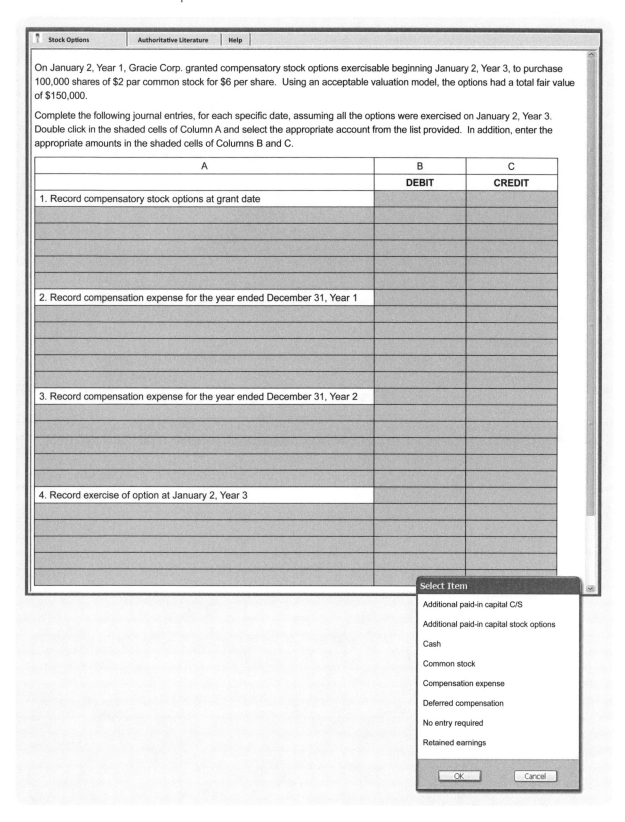

| Stock Options | Authoritative Literature | Help |

On January 2, Year 1, Gracie Corp. granted compensatory stock options exercisable beginning January 2, Year 3, to purchase 100,000 shares of $2 par common stock for $6 per share. Using an acceptable valuation model, the options had a total fair value of $150,000.

Complete the following journal entries, for each specific date, assuming all the options were exercised on January 2, Year 3. Double click in the shaded cells of Column A and select the appropriate account from the list provided. In addition, enter the appropriate amounts in the shaded cells of Columns B and C.

A	B	C
	DEBIT	**CREDIT**
1. Record compensatory stock options at grant date		
2. Record compensation expense for the year ended December 31, Year 1		
3. Record compensation expense for the year ended December 31, Year 2		
4. Record exercise of option at January 2, Year 3		

Select Item

Additional paid-in capital C/S

Additional paid-in capital stock options

Cash

Common stock

Compensation expense

Deferred compensation

No entry required

Retained earnings

| OK | Cancel |

L Compensation and Benefits

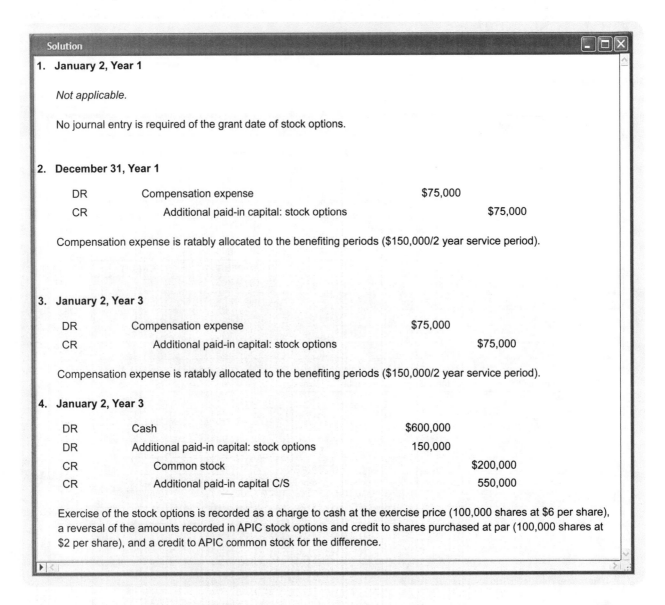

Solution

1. **January 2, Year 1**

   Not applicable.

   No journal entry is required of the grant date of stock options.

2. **December 31, Year 1**

DR	Compensation expense	$75,000	
CR	Additional paid-in capital: stock options		$75,000

   Compensation expense is ratably allocated to the benefiting periods ($150,000/2 year service period).

3. **January 2, Year 3**

DR	Compensation expense	$75,000	
CR	Additional paid-in capital: stock options		$75,000

   Compensation expense is ratably allocated to the benefiting periods ($150,000/2 year service period).

4. **January 2, Year 3**

DR	Cash	$600,000	
DR	Additional paid-in capital: stock options	150,000	
CR	Common stock		$200,000
CR	Additional paid-in capital C/S		550,000

   Exercise of the stock options is recorded as a charge to cash at the exercise price (100,000 shares at $6 per share), a reversal of the amounts recorded in APIC stock options and credit to shares purchased at par (100,000 shares at $2 per share), and a credit to APIC common stock for the difference.

1 Interperiod Tax Allocation

1.1 Total Income Tax Expense

Total income tax expense or benefit for the year is the sum of:

- Current income tax expense/benefit; and
- Deferred income tax expense/benefit.

1.2 Current Income Tax Expense

Current income tax expense/benefit is equal to the taxable income for the current year, multiplied by the current tax rate.

1.3 Deferred Income Tax Expense

Deferred income tax expense/benefit is equal to temporary differences multiplied by the future tax rate, or the change in deferred tax liability or asset account on the balance sheet from the beginning of the current year to the end of the current year (called the "balance sheet approach").

1.4 Summary

Thus, total income tax expense/benefit can be depicted as follows:

Question 1-1 FR-00425

Two independent situations are described below. Each situation has future deductible amounts and/or future taxable amounts produced by temporary differences:

Situation	1	2
Taxable income	$40,000	$80,000
Amounts at year-end:		
Future deductible amounts	5,000	10,000
Future taxable amounts	0	5,000
Balances at beginning of year:		
Deferred tax asset	1,000	4,000
Deferred tax liability	0	1,000

The enacted tax rate is 40% for both situations. Determine the income tax expense for the year.

	Situation 1	Situation 2
1.	$16,000	$32,000
2.	15,000	33,000
3.	11,000	30,000
4.	20,000	28,000

Related Questions

For related questions, go to the online question bank:

➤ FR-00380

➤ FR-00395

2 Permanent and Temporary Differences

There are two types of differences between pretax GAAP financial income and taxable income: permanent and temporary.

2.1 Permanent Differences

Permanent differences do not affect the deferred tax computation. They only affect the current tax computation. These differences affect only the period in which they occur. They do not affect future financial or taxable income.

Permanent differences are items of revenue and expense that either:

■ Enter into pretax GAAP financial income, but never enter into taxable income (e.g., interest income on state or municipal obligations, life insurance, proceeds/expense).

■ Enter into taxable income, but never enter into pretax GAAP financial income (e.g., dividends received deduction).

2.2　Temporary Differences

Temporary differences are the differences between the tax basis of an asset or liability and its reported amount in the financial statement that will result in taxable or deductible amounts in future years when the reported amount of the asset or liability is recovered or settled, respectively.

There are four basic causes of temporary differences, which reverse in future periods.

1. Revenues or gains that are included in taxable income, after they have been included in financial accounting income, which results in a deferred tax liability (e.g., sales on account).

2. Revenues or gains that are included in taxable income, before they are included in financial accounting income, which results in a deferred tax asset (e.g., rents collected in advance).

3. Expenses or losses deducted from taxable income, after they have been deducted for financial accounting income, which results in a deferred tax asset (e.g., warranty expense).

4. Expenses or losses deducted for taxable income, before they are deducted from financial accounting purposes, which results in a deferred tax liability (e.g., accelerated tax depreciation).

3 Deferred Tax Liability

A deferred tax liability is a future payable. Current financial income is greater than current taxable income.

3.1　Expense First

■ Depreciation expense greater for tax than for book

3.2　Revenue Later

■ Prepaid expenses (cash basis for tax)

■ Installment sales (used for tax purposes)

■ Contractor accounting

4 Deferred Tax Assets

A deferred tax asset is a future receivable. Current financial income is less than current taxable income.

M Income Taxes

4.1 Revenue First

- Unearned rent (taxable income before book income)
- Unearned interest (taxable income before book income)

4.2 Expense Later

- Bad debt expense (allowance for GAAP and direct write-off for tax)
- Estimated liability/warranty expense (allowance for GAAP and direct write-off for tax)

Question 4-1   FR-00410

Two independent situations are described below. Each situation has future deductible amounts and/or future taxable amounts produced by temporary differences:

Situation	1	2
Taxable income	$40,000	$80,000
Amounts at year-end:		
Future deductible amounts	5,000	10,000
Future taxable amounts	0	5,000
Balances at beginning of year:		
Deferred tax asset	1,000	4,000
Deferred tax liability	0	1,000

The enacted tax rate is 40% for both situations. Determine the deferred tax asset balance at year-end.

	Situation 1	Situation 2
1.	$5,000	$10,000
2.	3,000	8,000
3.	1,000	3,000
4.	2,000	4,000

---

5 Valuation Allowance

5.1   U.S. GAAP

Deferred tax assets are created by transactions that defer the tax benefits of expenses or transactions that recognize tax income before book income. If it is more likely than not that part or all of a deferred tax asset will not be realized, a valuation allowance should be recognized to reduce the amount of the deferred tax asset.

5.2   IFRS

IFRS prohibits the use of a valuation allowance. Under IFRS, a deferred tax asset is recognized when it is probable that sufficient taxable profit will be available against which the temporary difference can be utilized.

6 Balance Sheet Presentation

6.1   U.S. GAAP and IFRS

Under both U.S. GAAP and IFRS, deferred tax assets and deferred tax liabilities are reported as non-current on the balance sheet. Deferred tax assets and deferred tax liabilities may be netted if the entity has a legally enforceable right to offset current tax assets against current tax liabilities and the deferred tax assets and deferred tax liabilities relate to income taxes levied by the same tax authorities.

Question 6-1   FR-00461

At the end of Year 6, the tax effects of temporary differences reported in Apple Company's year-end financial statements were as follows:

	Deferred tax assets (liabilities)
Accelerated tax depreciation	$(120,000)
Warranty expense	80,000
NOL carryforward	200,000
	$ 160,000

A valuation allowance was not considered necessary. Apple anticipates that $40,000 of the deferred tax liability will reverse in Year 7, that actual warranty costs will be incurred evenly in Year 8 and Year 9, and that the NOL carryforward will be used in Year 7. On Apple's December 31, Year 6 balance sheet, what amount should be reported as a non-current deferred tax asset under U.S. GAAP?

1. $160,000
2. $200,000
3. $240,000
4. $280,000

7 Operating Loss

A net operating loss (NOL) occurs when tax-deductible expenses exceed taxable revenues. In this case the corporation pays no income taxes and it may select one of two options under the U.S. Internal Revenue Code (IRC): (1) carry the NOL back 2 years (to the earlier year first then to the second) and then carry any remaining NOL forward up to 20 years; or (2) carry the NOL forward up to 20 years. The NOL offsets taxable income. An NOL carryback results in a refund of taxes paid in prior years.

Carryback benefit:

> **DR** Income tax refund receivable
> **CR**   Benefit due to loss carryback (income tax expense)

Carryforward benefit:

> **DR** Deferred Tax Asset
> **CR**   Benefit due to loss carryforward (income tax expense)

Question 7-1   FR-00470

The pretax financial income and taxable income of Zeus Corporation were the same for the following years (i.e., there were no permanent or temporary differences):

	Income	Tax Rate
Year 4	$ 20,000	30%
Year 5	15,000	25%
Year 6	(100,000)	25%
Year 7	70,000	40%

What amount of income tax benefit will Zeus Corporation record in Year 6 under U.S. GAAP, assuming that Zeus elects to use the 2-year carryback/20-year carryforward option?

1. $25,000
2. $26,000
3. $35,750
4. $37,750

> **? Related Questions**
>
> For related questions, go to the online question bank:
>
> ➤ FR-00477

M Income Taxes

Task-Based Simulations

Task-Based Simulation: Tax Reconciliation

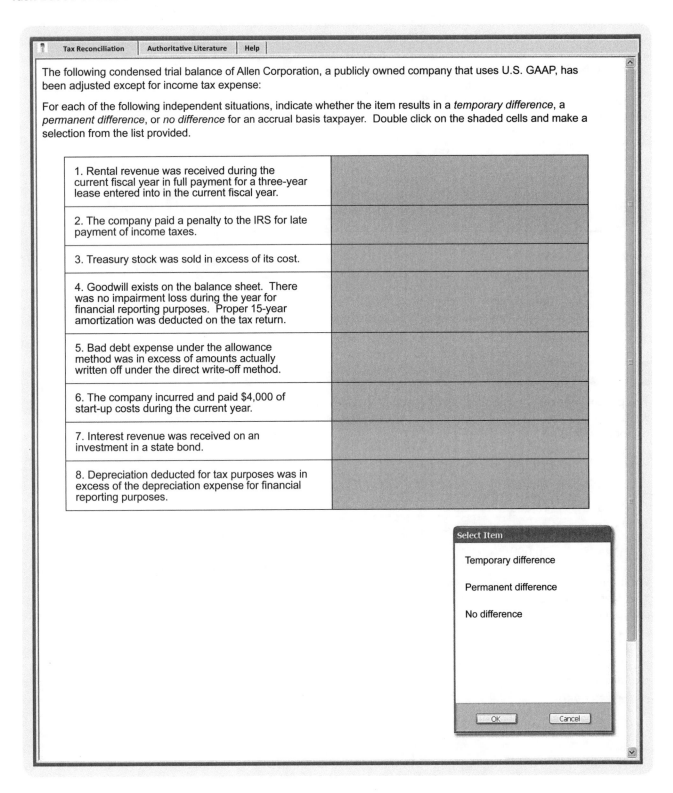

| Tax Reconciliation | Authoritative Literature | Help |

The following condensed trial balance of Allen Corporation, a publicly owned company that uses U.S. GAAP, has been adjusted except for income tax expense:

For each of the following independent situations, indicate whether the item results in a *temporary difference*, a *permanent difference*, or *no difference* for an accrual basis taxpayer. Double click on the shaded cells and make a selection from the list provided.

1. Rental revenue was received during the current fiscal year in full payment for a three-year lease entered into in the current fiscal year.	
2. The company paid a penalty to the IRS for late payment of income taxes.	
3. Treasury stock was sold in excess of its cost.	
4. Goodwill exists on the balance sheet. There was no impairment loss during the year for financial reporting purposes. Proper 15-year amortization was deducted on the tax return.	
5. Bad debt expense under the allowance method was in excess of amounts actually written off under the direct write-off method.	
6. The company incurred and paid $4,000 of start-up costs during the current year.	
7. Interest revenue was received on an investment in a state bond.	
8. Depreciation deducted for tax purposes was in excess of the depreciation expense for financial reporting purposes.	

Select Item

Temporary difference

Permanent difference

No difference

OK   Cancel

Solution

1. **Temporary difference**

   The rent revenue received in advance is deferred and not immediately recognized as revenue for financial reporting purposes. For tax purposes, it is reported as income in the year received.

2. **Permanent difference**

   Although the penalty is an expense for financial reporting purposes, it is never deductible on a tax return.

3. **No difference**

   Treasury stock sold in excess of cost is added to paid in capital and is not reported as a gain for either financial reporting or tax purposes.

4. **Temporary difference**

   Goodwill is amortized over 15 years for tax purposes and subject to an impairment test for financial reporting purposes.

   Note: Many students incorrectly label this a permanent difference. However, the theory is that over time, goodwill will eventually be written off as impaired for financial reporting purposes.

5. **Temporary difference**

   The allowance method should be used for financial reporting purposes, while the direct write-off method is required for tax purposes. This is a temporary difference because bad debts are fully written off under both methods.

6. **No difference**

   The start-up costs will be expensed in the current year for both financial and tax reporting purposes. Generally this is a temporary difference because start-up costs are always expensed for financial reporting purposes, while tax rules allow the deduction of $5,000 in the year the costs are incurred and then a 180-month amortization of the remainder. However, since the question indicates that the start-up costs were $4,000, the costs will be fully expensed for tax and financial purposes.

7. **Permanent difference**

   State bond interest income is reported as revenue for financial reporting purposes but is tax-exempt.

8. **Temporary difference**

   Tax law and GAAP use different depreciation schedules. Over time, the depreciation will be the same.

Financial Final Review

III | Select Transactions

A Accounting Changes and Error Corrections

B Business Combinations

C Contingencies

D Derivatives and Hedge Accounting

E Foreign Currency Transactions and Translation

F Leases

G Research and Development

H Software Costs

I Subsequent Events

J Fair Value Measurements

1 Changes in Accounting Estimate (Prospective Approach)

Under the prospective approach, adjustments for changes in accounting estimate are made in the current and future accounting periods. They do not affect previous periods. Examples include:

- Change in useful life
- Change in salvage value
- Settlement of litigation

When a change in accounting principle is inseparable from a change in accounting estimate, it should be reported as a change in accounting estimate.

Question 1-1   FR-00327

Gonzales Company purchased a machine on January 1, Year 1 for $600,000. On the date of acquisition, the machine had an estimated useful life of six years with no salvage value. The machine was being depreciated on a straight-line basis. On January 1, Year 4, Gonzales determined that the machine had an estimated life of eight years from the date of acquisition. An accounting change was made in Year 4.

What is the amount of the depreciation expense that should be recorded for the year ended Year 4?

1. $75,000
2. $100,000
3. $60,000
4. $0

? Related Questions

For related questions, go to the online question bank:

➤ FR-00387

2 Changes in Accounting Principle

2.1 General Rule (Retrospective Application)

Any change from one generally accepted accounting principle to another generally accepted accounting principle is recognized using the retrospective approach by adjusting beginning retained earnings for the cumulative effect of the change, net of tax. Prior period financial statements are restated (IDA).

2.1.1 Cumulative Effect

The cumulative effect of a change in accounting principle is computed as of the beginning of the earliest year presented, regardless of the actual date of the change, by applying the new principle to the item to be changed since inception. The difference between the two principles is the catch-up amount for all prior affected periods. It includes direct effects and only those indirect effects that are entered into the accounting records.

2.1.2 IFRS

Under IFRS, when an entity applies an accounting principle retroactively or makes a retrospective restatement of items in the financial statements, the entity must (at a minimum) present three balance sheets (end of current period, end of prior period, and beginning of prior period) and two of each of the other financial statements (current period and prior period). The cumulative effect adjustment would be shown as an adjustment of the beginning retained earnings on the balance sheet for the beginning of the prior period. U.S. GAAP does not have a three balance sheet requirement.

2.2 Exceptions to the General Rule (Prospective Application)

2.2.1 Impractical to Estimate

If it is considered impractical to accurately calculate this cumulative effect adjustment, then the change is handled prospectively (like a change in estimate). An example of a change handled in this manner is a change in inventory cost flow assumption to LIFO (U.S. GAAP only). Since a cumulative effect adjustment to LIFO would require the reestablishment and recalculation of old inventory layers, it is considered impractical to try and rebuild those old cost layers.

2.2.2 Change in Depreciation Method

A change in the method of depreciation, amortization, or depletion is considered to be both a change in accounting principle and a change in estimate. These changes should be accounted for as changes in estimate and are handled prospectively. The new depreciation method should be used as of the beginning of the year of change in estimate and should start with the current book value of the underlying asset. No adjustment should be made to retained earnings.

Question 2-1   FR-00342

On December 31, Year 10, Brown Company changed its inventory valuation method from the weighted average method to FIFO for financial statement purposes. The change will result in an $800,000 decrease in the beginning inventory at January 1, Year 10. The tax rate is 30%.

The cumulative effect of this accounting change for the year ended December 31, Year 10 in the statement of retained earnings is:

1. $0
2. $800,000
3. $240,000
4. $560,000

Question 2-2   FR-00312

On January 1, Year 1, Schreiber Company purchased a $300,000 machine with a five-year useful life and no salvage value. The machine was depreciated by an accelerated method for book and tax purposes. The machine's carrying amount was $120,000 on December 31, Year 2. On January 1, Year 3, Schreiber changed to the straight-line method for financial statement purposes. Schreiber's income tax rate is 40%.

Assuming that Schreiber can justify the change, in its Year 3 statement of retained earnings, what amount should Schreiber report as the cumulative effect of this change?

1. $60,000
2. $36,000
3. $0
4. $24,000

Related Questions

For related questions, go to the online question bank:

➤ FR-00357

➤ FR-00402

➤ FR-00417

3 Changes in Accounting Entity (Retrospective Application)

Include changes in the companies that make up the consolidated or combined financial statements from year to year. Hence, if five-year comparative statements are presented, all these statements would be restated as though all the companies were always combined. The concept of a change in accounting entity is not discussed in IFRS.

4 Error Corrections (Restatement Approach)

Error corrections require retroactive restatement by adjusting the beginning balance of retained earnings, net of tax, in the earliest year presented. If the error occurred in a year presented, the error is corrected in those prior financial statements.

Under IFRS, when it is impracticable to determine the cumulative effect of an error, the entity is required to restate information prospectively from the earliest date that is practicable. U.S. GAAP does not have an impracticality exemption for error corrections.

Gracie Company **Statement of Retained Earnings (Partial)** *For the Year Ended December 31, Year 1*	
Beginning balance (as previously reported)	$28,000,000
Prior period adjustments:	
Correction of error (net of tax benefit of $1,800,000)	(2,700,000)
Cumulative effect of accounting change (net of tax expense of $2,000,000)	3,000,000
Beginning balance (restated)	$28,300,000

Question 4-1   FR-00372

Lore Co. changed from the cash basis of accounting to the accrual basis of accounting during the current year. The cumulative effect of this change should be reported in Lore's current year financial statements as a:

1. Prior period adjustment resulting from the correction of an error.
2. Prior period adjustment resulting from the change in accounting principle.
3. Component of income from continuing operations.
4. Component of nonoperating gains.

5 Summary of Accounting Changes and Necessary Treatments

Accounting Changes	Example(s)	Income Statement	Statement of Retained Earnings
From one GAAP/IFRS principle to another GAAP/IFRS principle	▪ Adopt a new standard ▪ Change methods of inventory costing—FIFO to Average		**Retrospective application**, compute **cumulative** effect and report **net of tax** by adjusting beginning retained earnings of earliest year presented
Changes in principle—**Exceptions** (require prospective treatment)	▪ From any inventory valuation method to LIFO (U.S. GAAP only) ▪ Change depreciation methods —SL to SYD	▪ **Prospective application**, the beginning inventory of the year of change is the first LIFO layer ▪ Apply new depreciation method to remaining book value as of the beginning of the year	
Changes in entity	▪ Consolidation of a subsidiary not previously included in consolidated FS ▪ Report consolidated FS in place of individual statements		▪ **Retrospective** adjustments (plus or minus) **net of tax**, against the beginning balance of the retained earnings under the caption of "Prior Period Adjustments" ▪ Restate all financial statements presented
Neither a change in principle nor a change in estimate	▪ Change from fair value method to equity method because an increase in ownership now qualifies as equity method investment. Adopt the equity method as of the date the investment qualifies for equity method.	If the investment was previously accounted for as an available-for-sale security, recognize in earnings the unrealized holding gain or loss from accumulated other comprehensive income.	Because the cost of acquiring the additional interest in the investee is added to the carrying value of the previously held investment, retroactive adjustments are not required.
Correction of errors	▪ From cash to accrual ▪ Errors made in prior statements		▪ **Retroactive adjustments** (plus or minus) **net of tax**, against the beginning balance of the retained earnings under the caption of "Prior Period Adjustments" ▪ Restate all financial statements presented that are affected
Changes in estimate	▪ Depreciation method ▪ Useful life of depreciable asset ▪ Residual value ▪ Bad debt % ▪ Loss accruals	▪ **Prospective application**, account for in the current statement "above the line" ▪ **No cumulative effect**	

A Accounting Changes and Error Corrections

Task-Based Simulations

Task-Based Simulation 1: Accounting Treatments

	Accounting Treatments	Authoritative Literature	Help

On January 1, Year 2, Riggs Corporation hired a new controller. During the year, the controller working with Riggs' outside accountants and president, made changes to existing accounting policies, instituted new accounting policies, and corrected several errors in prior year accounting. Riggs uses U.S. GAAP and does not present comparative financial statements.

For each of the transactions below, identify the classification of the transaction by double-clicking in the shaded cells under "Classification" and selecting from the list provided. Also, identify the general accounting treatment required for each transaction's classification by double-clicking in the shaded cells under "Treatment" and selecting from the list provided. The available treatments are:

Retrospective application

Include the *cumulative effect* of the adjustment resulting from an accounting change in the Year 2 financial statements as an adjustment to beginning retained earnings.

Restatement approach

Adjust the Year 2 beginning retained earnings if the error affects a period prior to Year 2.

Prospective application

Report Year 2 and future financial statements on a new basis, but do *not* adjust the beginning retained earnings.

Transaction	Classification	Treatment
1. Riggs manufactures heavy equipment to customer specifications on a contract basis. On the basis that it is preferable, accounting for these long-term contracts was switched from the completed-contract method to the percentage-of-completion method.		
2. As a result of a production breakthrough, Riggs determined that manufacturing equipment previously depreciated over 15 years should be depreciated over 20 years.		
3. The equipment that Riggs manufactures is sold with a five-year warranty. Because of a production breakthrough, Riggs reduced its computation of warranty costs from 3% of sales to 1% of sales.		
4. Riggs changed from FIFO to average cost to account for its raw materials and work in process inventories.		
5. Riggs sells extended service contracts on its products. Because related services are performed over several years, in Year 2 Riggs changed from the cash method to the accrual method of recognizing income from these service contracts.		
6. During Year 2, Riggs determined that an insurance premium paid and entirely expensed in Year 1 was for the period January 1, Year 1, through January 1, Year 3.		
7. Riggs changed its method of depreciating office equipment from an accelerated method to the straight-line method to more closely reflect costs in later years.		
8. Riggs instituted a pension plan for all employees in Year 2 and adopted U.S. GAAP Standards relating to employer's accounting for pensions. Riggs had not previously had a pension plan.		
9. During Year 2, Riggs increased its investment in Brunner, Inc. from a 10% interest, purchased in Year 1, to 30%, and acquired a seat on Brunner's board of directors. As a result of its increased investment, Riggs changed its method of accounting for investment in subsidiary from the fair value method to the equity method.		
10. Based on improved collection procedures, Riggs changed the percentage of credit sales used to determine the allowance for uncollectible accounts from 2% to 1%.		

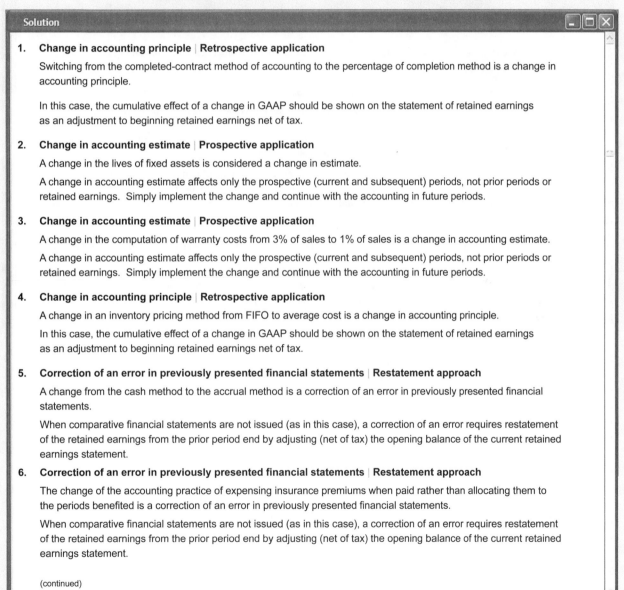

Solution

1. **Change in accounting principle | Retrospective application**

    Switching from the completed-contract method of accounting to the percentage of completion method is a change in accounting principle.

    In this case, the cumulative effect of a change in GAAP should be shown on the statement of retained earnings as an adjustment to beginning retained earnings net of tax.

2. **Change in accounting estimate | Prospective application**

    A change in the lives of fixed assets is considered a change in estimate.

    A change in accounting estimate affects only the prospective (current and subsequent) periods, not prior periods or retained earnings. Simply implement the change and continue with the accounting in future periods.

3. **Change in accounting estimate | Prospective application**

    A change in the computation of warranty costs from 3% of sales to 1% of sales is a change in accounting estimate.

    A change in accounting estimate affects only the prospective (current and subsequent) periods, not prior periods or retained earnings. Simply implement the change and continue with the accounting in future periods.

4. **Change in accounting principle | Retrospective application**

    A change in an inventory pricing method from FIFO to average cost is a change in accounting principle.

    In this case, the cumulative effect of a change in GAAP should be shown on the statement of retained earnings as an adjustment to beginning retained earnings net of tax.

5. **Correction of an error in previously presented financial statements | Restatement approach**

    A change from the cash method to the accrual method is a correction of an error in previously presented financial statements.

    When comparative financial statements are not issued (as in this case), a correction of an error requires restatement of the retained earnings from the prior period end by adjusting (net of tax) the opening balance of the current retained earnings statement.

6. **Correction of an error in previously presented financial statements | Restatement approach**

    The change of the accounting practice of expensing insurance premiums when paid rather than allocating them to the periods benefited is a correction of an error in previously presented financial statements.

    When comparative financial statements are not issued (as in this case), a correction of an error requires restatement of the retained earnings from the prior period end by adjusting (net of tax) the opening balance of the current retained earnings statement.

    (continued)

A Accounting Changes and Error Corrections

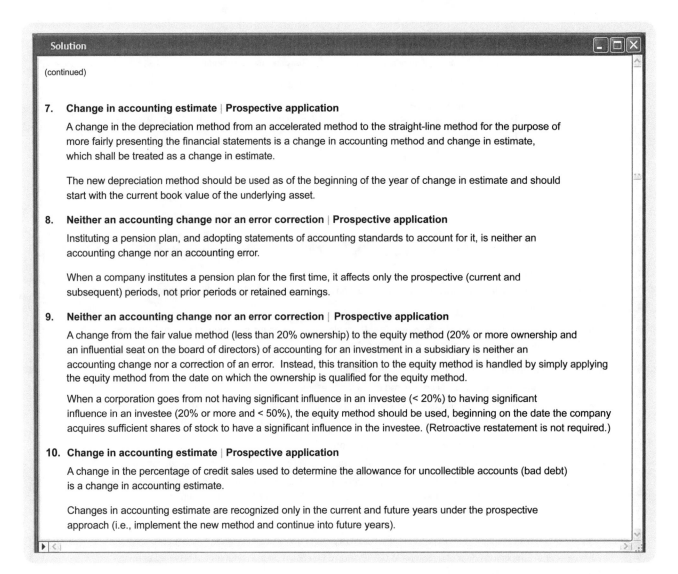

Solution

(continued)

7. **Change in accounting estimate | Prospective application**

   A change in the depreciation method from an accelerated method to the straight-line method for the purpose of more fairly presenting the financial statements is a change in accounting method and change in estimate, which shall be treated as a change in estimate.

   The new depreciation method should be used as of the beginning of the year of change in estimate and should start with the current book value of the underlying asset.

8. **Neither an accounting change nor an error correction | Prospective application**

   Instituting a pension plan, and adopting statements of accounting standards to account for it, is neither an accounting change nor an accounting error.

   When a company institutes a pension plan for the first time, it affects only the prospective (current and subsequent) periods, not prior periods or retained earnings.

9. **Neither an accounting change nor an error correction | Prospective application**

   A change from the fair value method (less than 20% ownership) to the equity method (20% or more ownership and an influential seat on the board of directors) of accounting for an investment in a subsidiary is neither an accounting change nor a correction of an error. Instead, this transition to the equity method is handled by simply applying the equity method from the date on which the ownership is qualified for the equity method.

   When a corporation goes from not having significant influence in an investee (< 20%) to having significant influence in an investee (20% or more and < 50%), the equity method should be used, beginning on the date the company acquires sufficient shares of stock to have a significant influence in the investee. (Retroactive restatement is not required.)

10. **Change in accounting estimate | Prospective application**

    A change in the percentage of credit sales used to determine the allowance for uncollectible accounts (bad debt) is a change in accounting estimate.

    Changes in accounting estimate are recognized only in the current and future years under the prospective approach (i.e., implement the new method and continue into future years).

Task-Based Simulation 2: FIFO

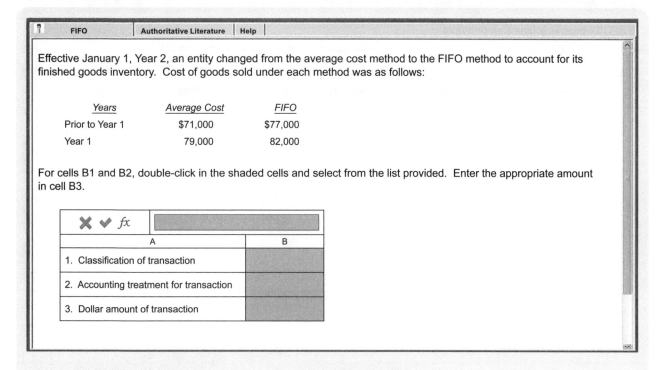

Effective January 1, Year 2, an entity changed from the average cost method to the FIFO method to account for its finished goods inventory. Cost of goods sold under each method was as follows:

Years	Average Cost	FIFO
Prior to Year 1	$71,000	$77,000
Year 1	79,000	82,000

For cells B1 and B2, double-click in the shaded cells and select from the list provided. Enter the appropriate amount in cell B3.

	A	B
1.	Classification of transaction	
2.	Accounting treatment for transaction	
3.	Dollar amount of transaction	

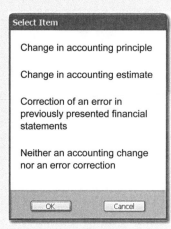

Select Item

Change in accounting principle

Change in accounting estimate

Correction of an error in previously presented financial statements

Neither an accounting change nor an error correction

OK   Cancel

Select Item

Retrospective application

Restatement approach

Prospective application

OK   Cancel

A Accounting Changes and Error Corrections

1. **Change in accounting principle**

   A change in the cost method used to account for inventory is a change in accounting principle.

2. **Retrospective application**

   A change in the cost method used to account for inventory is accounted for using a retrospective application (cumulative effect).

3. **$9,000**

Years	Average Cost	FIFO	Change
Prior to Year 1	$71,000	$77,000	$6,000
Year 1	79,000	82,000	3,000
			$9,000

Task-Based Simulation 3: Straight-line Depreciation

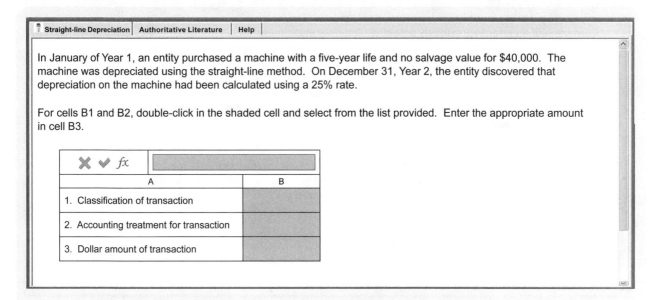

In January of Year 1, an entity purchased a machine with a five-year life and no salvage value for $40,000. The machine was depreciated using the straight-line method. On December 31, Year 2, the entity discovered that depreciation on the machine had been calculated using a 25% rate.

For cells B1 and B2, double-click in the shaded cell and select from the list provided. Enter the appropriate amount in cell B3.

	A	B
1.	Classification of transaction	
2.	Accounting treatment for transaction	
3.	Dollar amount of transaction	

Select Item

Change in accounting principle

Change in accounting estimate

Correction of an error in previously presented financial statements

Neither an accounting change nor an error correction

[OK]   [Cancel]

Select Item

Retrospective application

Restatement approach

Prospective application

[OK]   [Cancel]

A   Accounting Changes and Error Corrections

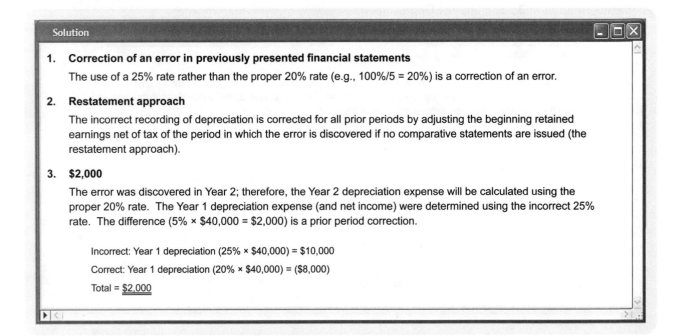

Solution

1. **Correction of an error in previously presented financial statements**

   The use of a 25% rate rather than the proper 20% rate (e.g., 100%/5 = 20%) is a correction of an error.

2. **Restatement approach**

   The incorrect recording of depreciation is corrected for all prior periods by adjusting the beginning retained earnings net of tax of the period in which the error is discovered if no comparative statements are issued (the restatement approach).

3. **$2,000**

   The error was discovered in Year 2; therefore, the Year 2 depreciation expense will be calculated using the proper 20% rate. The Year 1 depreciation expense (and net income) were determined using the incorrect 25% rate. The difference (5% × $40,000 = $2,000) is a prior period correction.

   Incorrect: Year 1 depreciation (25% × $40,000) = $10,000

   Correct: Year 1 depreciation (20% × $40,000) = ($8,000)

   Total = $2,000

Task-Based Simulation 4: Research

1 Consolidation

Consolidated financial statements are prepared when a parent-subsidiary relationship has been formed. An investor is considered to have parent status when more than 50 percent of the voting stock of the investee has been acquired. Do not consolidate when subsidiary is in legal reorganization or bankruptcy (parent does not control the subsidiary).

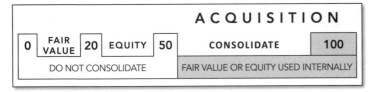

2 Acquisition Method

In a business combination accounted for as an acquisition, the subsidiary may be acquired for cash, stock, debt securities, etc. The investment is valued at the fair value of the consideration given or the fair value of the consideration received, whichever is the more clearly evident. The accounting for an acquisition begins at the date of acquisition.

2.1 Acquisition Costs

The following is a summary of the accounting for costs related to an acquisition business combination:

- Direct out-of-pocket costs are expensed as incurred. (Debit: Expense)

- Stock registration and issuance costs are a direct reduction of the value of the stock issued. (Debit: Paid-in capital account)

- Indirect costs are expensed as incurred. (Debit: Expense)

- Bond issuance costs are presented as a reduction of the cash proceeds of the bond issue, and are amortized according to the effective interest method (Debit bond discount + Bond issuance costs *or* Credit premium – Bond issuance costs).

2.2   Acquisition Method Summary

Assets	Fair value
Liabilities	Fair value
Retained earnings	Parent only
Income	After acquisition date
Goodwill	Yes (subject to impairment adjustment)
Noncontrolling interest	Yes (up to 49%)
Investment in subsidiary	Eliminated
Intercompany transactions	Eliminate 100%

2.3   Consolidating Workpaper Eliminating Journal Entry

The year-end consolidating journal entry known as the consolidating workpaper eliminating journal entry (EJE) is:

DR	Common stock—subsidiary	$XXX	
DR	APIC—subsidiary	XXX	
DR	Retained earnings—subsidiary	XXX	
CR	Investment in subsidiary		$XXX
CR	Noncontrolling interest		XXX
DR	Balance sheet adjusted to fair value	XXX	
DR	Identifiable intangible asset fair value	XXX	
DR	Goodwill	XXX	

The consolidated balance sheet will report the equity of the parent company only. The parent's investment in the subsidiary is eliminated.

2.4   Noncontrolling Interest

Noncontrolling interest is recognized in the consolidated financial statements when the parent company owns less than 100 percent of the subsidiary. Noncontrolling interest on the balance sheet is the noncontrolling shareholder's share of the fair value of the subsidiary. Under U.S. GAAP, the noncontrolling interest included in equity on the balance sheet is calculated as:

Noncontrolling interest (BS) = Fair value of subsidiary × Noncontrolling interest percentage

Noncontrolling interest must be recognized as a line-item deduction on the income statement for the portion of the subsidiary's net income not allocated to the parent company:

> Noncontrolling interest in net income of subsidiary = Subsidiary net income × Noncontrolling interest percentage

Comprehensive income attributable to the noncontrolling interest is presented on the consolidated statement of comprehensive income. A reconciliation at the beginning and end of the period of the carrying amount of the equity attributable to the noncontrolling interest is shown on the consolidated statement of changes in equity.

Under IFRS, noncontrolling interest (and goodwill) can be calculated using either the full goodwill method, which is the method required under U.S. GAAP, or the partial goodwill method. Under the partial goodwill method, noncontrolling interest on the balance sheet is calculated as:

> Noncontrolling interest (BS) = Fair value of subsidiary's net assets × Noncontrolling interest percentage

2.5   Fair Value Adjustment/Goodwill

The difference between the fair value of the subsidiary and the book value of the subsidiary net assets should be allocated as follows:

1. Balance sheet adjustment of the subsidiary's assets and liabilities from book value to fair value.

2. Identifiable intangible assets recorded at fair value.

3. Goodwill is excess. Under U.S. GAAP, goodwill is calculated as follows (full goodwill method):

> Goodwill = Fair value of subsidiary – Fair value of subsidiary's net assets

IFRS permits the use of the full goodwill method or the partial goodwill method. Under the partial goodwill method, goodwill is calculated as follows:

> Goodwill = Acquisition cost – Fair value of subsidiary's net assets acquired

Goodwill recognized in a business combination is not amortized. Instead, it is tested for impairment, and a loss is recognized in income from continuing operations if the goodwill is impaired.

2.6   Gain

When a subsidiary is acquired for less than the fair value of 100 percent of the underlying assets acquired, the acquisition cost is first allocated to the fair value of 100 percent of the balance sheet accounts and the fair value of 100 percent of the identifiable intangible assets acquired. This creates a negative balance in the acquisition cost account, which is recognized as a gain in the period of the acquisition.

2.7   Eliminate 100% of Intercompany Transactions

2.7.1   Payable/Receivable

In a consolidated balance sheet, all intercompany payables and receivables are eliminated.

DR	Account payable	$XXX
CR	Accounts receivable	$XXX

2.7.2   Inventory

Affiliated companies often sell inventory to one another. Intercompany sales and intercompany cost of goods sold should be eliminated. This entry is made if the books are open. Any intercompany profit from the intercompany inventory transaction must also be eliminated against the purchaser's ending inventory and cost of goods sold.

DR	Intercompany Sales (selling affiliate)	$XXX
CR	Intercompany COGS (selling affiliate)	$XXX
CR	COGS (purchasing affiliate)	XXX
CR	Inventory (purchasing affiliate)	XXX

2.7.3   Fixed Assets

The gain or loss on the intercompany sale of a depreciable asset is unrealized from a consolidated financial statement perspective until the asset is sold to an outsider. A working paper eliminating entry in the period of the intercompany sale eliminates the intercompany gain/loss and adjusts the asset and the accumulated depreciation to their original balances on the date of sale. The excess depreciation on the gain must also be eliminated.

DR	Gain	$XXX
CR	Equipment	$XXX
CR	Accumulated depreciation	XXX
DR	Accumulated depreciation	XXX
CR	Depreciation expense (RE)	XXX

2.7.4 Bonds

If one member of the consolidated group acquires an affiliate's debt from an outsider, the debt is considered to be retired and a gain/loss is recognized. This gain/loss on extinguishment of debt is calculated as the difference between the price paid to acquire the debt and the book value of the debt. This gain/loss is not reported on either company's books, but is recorded on the consolidated income statement through an elimination entry. All intercompany account balances are also eliminated; e.g., bond interest payable and bond interest receivable.

DR	Bond interest payable	$XXX	
CR	Bond interest receivable		$XXX
DR	Bonds payable	XXX	
DR	Premium on bonds payable	XXX	
DR	Loss	XXX	
CR	Investment in bonds		XXX
CR	Discount on bonds payable		XXX
CR	Gain		XXX

Question 2-1   FR-00394

On December 31, Saxon Corporation was merged into Philadelphia Corporation. In the business combination, Philadelphia issued 200,000 shares of its $10 par value common stock, with a market price of $18 a share, for all of Saxon's common stock. The stockholders' equity section of each company's balance sheet immediately before the combination was:

	Philadelphia	Saxon
Common Stock	$3,000,000	$1,500,000
Additional paid-in capital	1,300,000	150,000
Retained earnings	2,500,000	850,000
	$6,800,000	$2,500,000

In the December 31 consolidated balance sheet, additional paid-in capital should be reported at:

1. $950,000
2. $1,300,000
3. $1,450,000
4. $2,900,000

Question 2-2   FR-00778

On January 1, Year 1, Sunshine Corporation acquired an 80% ownership interest in Grey Sky Enterprises by purchasing 400,000 of Grey Sky's 500,000 voting common shares outstanding for $10,000,000. Additional information regarding Grey Sky as of January 1, Year 1, follows:

	Book Value	Fair Value
Net assets	$11,200,000	$11,500,000

On the acquisition date, what is the noncontrolling interest that will be reported on the consolidated balance sheet of Sunshine Corporation under the IFRS partial goodwill method?

1. $1,200,000
2. $1,500,000
3. $2,300,000
4. $2,500,000

Question 2-3   FR-00460

Pico Corp. owns 100% of Sepulveda Inc.'s common stock. During Year 1, Pico sold inventory to Sepulveda for $400,000, which was 25% above cost. Sepulveda sold half of the inventory purchased from Pico in Year 1. At year-end, before consolidation, Pico reported inventory of $390,000 and Sepulveda reported inventory of $480,000. All other inventory transactions for both companies were with outside customers and suppliers. At December 31, Year 1, what should Pico Corp. report as consolidated inventory on its balance sheet?

1. $670,000
2. $830,000
3. $870,000
4. $910,000

? Related Questions

For related questions, go to the online question bank:

➤ FR-00379
➤ FR-00409
➤ FR-00424
➤ FR-00450
➤ FR-00469
➤ FR-00476
➤ FR-00777
➤ FR-00779
➤ FR-00780

3 Variable Interest Entities (VIEs)

3.1 Definition

A variable interest entity is a corporation, partnership, trust, LLC or other legal structure used for business purposes that either does not have equity investors with voting rights or lacks the sufficient financial resources to support its activities.

3.2   Primary Beneficiary

The primary beneficiary is the entity that has the power to direct the activities of a variable interest entity that most significantly impact the entity's economic performance, and:

■ absorbs the expected VIE losses; or

■ receives the expected VIE residual returns.

3.3   U.S. GAAP Consolidation Rule

Under U.S. GAAP, the primary beneficiary of a variable interest entity must consolidate the variable interest entity.

Under U.S. GAAP, all consolidation decisions are evaluated first under the VIE model. If consolidation is not required under the VIE model, then the investor (parent) company determines whether consolidation is necessary under the voting interest model (consolidate when ownership is more than 50 percent of the investee's voting stock, as previously covered).

3.4   IFRS Consolidation Rule

IFRS focus on the accounting for special purpose entities. A special purpose entity (SPE) is a specific type of VIE created by a sponsoring company to hold assets or liabilities, often for structured financing purposes (e.g., sales of receivables, synthetic leases, securitization of loans).

Under IFRS, a sponsoring company controls, and must consolidate, an SPE when the company:

■ is benefited by the SPE's activities.

■ has decision-making powers that allow it to benefit from the SPE.

■ absorbs the risks and rewards of the SPE.

■ has a residual interest in the SPE.

Question 3-1   FR-00856

An investor (company) will most likely avoid consolidating a potential variable interest entity (VIE) if:

1. The investor absorbs at least 50 percent of the VIE's expected gains.
2. The VIE requires significant financial support from the investor.
3. Current VIE equity holders do not have substantive voting rights.
4. The investor does not absorb over half of the VIE's expected losses.

? Related Questions

For related questions, go to the online question bank:

➤ FR-00857

1 Contingent Losses

The recognition and presentation of loss contingencies depends on the classification of the contingency.

- **Probable:** Likely to occur. An adjusting entry and a note disclosure are required.

  - **Range:** If a range of amounts is given, adjust for the smaller amount and disclose the difference in the notes to the financial statements.

- **Reasonably Possible:** A note disclosure is required.

- **Remote:** Ignore (unless guarantee of indebtedness of others, then disclose).

2 Contingent Gains

Contingent gains that are probable or reasonably possible may be disclosed.

Question 2-1   FR-00475

Far Out Producers is involved in two product liability lawsuits and a third lawsuit that the company brought against a competitor for patent infringement. At December 31, Year 1, the company's attorneys informed management of the following:

- It is probable that Far Out will lose one of the product liability lawsuits, although the actual settlement could be as low as $800,000 and as high as $2,000,000.

- It is possible that the company could lose $1,000,000 in the second product liability lawsuit.

- It is probable that Far Out will win $500,000 in the patent infringement case.

What should Far Out report on its December 31, Year 1 balance sheet for these contingencies?

   1. $300,000 contingent liability.

   2. $800,000 contingent liability.

   3. $1,800,000 contingent liability.

   4. $3,000,000 contingent liability.

? Related Questions

For related questions, go to the online question bank:

➤ FR-00378

---

1 Financial Instruments

1.1 Financial Instruments Are:

- Cash, foreign currency, and demand deposits.
- Ownership interest in an entity (stock, partnership, LLC).
- Contracts that both:
  - Impose on one entity a contractual obligation or duty.
  - Convey to the second entity a contractual right to do the opposite.
- Derivatives.

1.2 Disclosure

Fair value must be disclosed for all financial instruments for which it is practicable to estimate that value together with the related carrying amounts.

Disclosure of concentrations of credit risk is required. Credit risk is the possibility of loss from the failure of another party to perform according to the terms of a contract. Disclosure of market risk is encouraged but not required under U.S. GAAP. Under IFRS, disclosure of market risk is required.

Question 1-1   FR-00382

Which of the following must be disclosed for most financial instruments?

	Carrying Value	Fair Value
1.	No	No
2.	No	Yes
3.	Yes	No
4.	Yes	Yes

? Related Questions

For related questions, go to the online question bank:

➤ FR-00397

---

2   Derivatives and Hedging

2.1   Definition

Derivatives derive their value from other securities. A derivative must have all three of the following characteristics:

1. One or more underlyings, and one or more notional amounts or payment provisions (or both); and

2. No initial net investment (or smaller than would be expected); and

3. Its terms require or permit a net settlement.

   - An underlying is a specified price, rate, or other variable, e.g., $10 a bushel.

   - A notional amount is a specified unit of measure on which the derivative is valued, e.g., 10,000 bushels.

   - The value or settlement amount is the amount determined by the multiplication of the notional amount and the underlying, e.g., 10,000 bushels × $10 per unit = $100,000.

   - Examples of common derivatives are forward contracts, futures, swaps, and options.

   - Derivatives are reported as assets or liabilities and are measured at fair value just like other financial instruments.

2.2   Hedging Instruments

2.2.1   No Hedge Designation

No hedge designation. Just speculation. Changes in fair value are fully included in income.

2.2.2   Fair Value Hedge

A fair value hedge hedges an exposure to changes in fair value of a recorded asset or liability or recognized firm commitment. Changes in fair value are included in income but are offset by changes in the fair value of the hedged item.

2.2.3   Cash Flow Hedge

A cash flow hedge hedges an exposure to variability in the cash flows of a recognized asset or a forecasted transaction. Changes in fair value of the ineffective portion of a cash flow hedge are included in income; changes in fair value of the effective portion of a cash flow hedge are included in the stockholders' equity as part of other comprehensive income (OCI) until the related cash flows are realized.

Accounting for Hedges: Reporting Gains and Losses	
Type of Hedge Instrument	*Accounting for Changes in Fair Value*
No hedge designation	Income Statement
Fair value hedge	Income Statement offset by changes in fair value of the hedged item
Cash flow hedge **In**effective portion	**In**come Statement
Cash flow hedge **E**ffective portion (PUF**E**)	In OCI then in Accumulated OCI in **E**quity

Question 2-1   FR-00471

Which of the following statements regarding the accounting for derivatives is correct?

I. A derivative must have one or more underlyings or one or more notional amounts, require little or no net investment, and permit or require a net settlement.

II. Derivatives are always reported on the balance sheet as assets at fair value.

III. If a derivative is speculative (no hedge designation), changes in fair value are reported on the income statement.

IV. If a derivative is used as a fair value hedge, then changes in fair value are reported in other comprehensive income.

    1. III only.

    2. I and III

    3. I, II, III.

    4. I, II, III, IV.

? Related Questions

For related questions, go to the online question bank:

➤ FR-00412

1 Foreign Currency Translation

Foreign currency translation is the conversion of a financial statement of a foreign subsidiary into financial statements expressed in the reporting currency of the parent company. The method used to convert the financial statements depends on the functional currency of the subsidiary.

1.1 Remeasurement Method

Foreign currency remeasurement is the restatement of foreign financial statements from the foreign currency to the entity's functional currency in the following situations:

- The reporting currency is the functional currency.
- The entity's books of record must be restated in the entity's functional currency prior to translating the financial statements from the functional currency to the reporting currency.

Remeasurement starts with the balance sheet and converts monetary items using current/year-end exchange rates and nonmonetary items using historical exchange rates. The income statement is then converted using a weighted average exchange rate for all items except those related to the balance sheet (depreciation, amortization, and cost of goods sold). Balance sheet related items are converted using the appropriate historical rate. A gain or loss is plugged to net income to get the required balance needed to adjusted retained earnings so that the balance sheet balances. Remeasurement gains and losses are included in income.

1.2 Translation Method

Foreign currency translation is the restatement of financial statements denominated in the functional currency to the reporting currency.

Translation starts with the income statement and converts all elements using a weighted average exchange rate. Translated net income is transferred to retained earnings. Assets and liabilities on the balance sheet are then converted using the current/year-end exchange rate, common stock/APIC are converted using historical exchange rates, retained earnings is rolled forward, and then a gain or loss is plugged to OCI to make the balance sheet balance. Translation gains and losses are part of other comprehensive income (**PUFE**).

Question 1-1   FR-00449

Which of the following statements regarding the process of foreign currency translation is/are correct?

I.   After the translation process is complete, a subsidiary's financial statements must be adjusted to conform to U.S. GAAP.

II. The process of translation is done to convert financial statements from a functional currency to the reporting currency.

III. The process of remeasurement is done when the local currency of a subsidiary is different than the functional currency.

IV. Translation gains and losses are reported on the income statement, while gains and losses from remeasurement are reported in other comprehensive income.

1. I and IV.

2. II and III.

3. I, II, and III.

4. II, III, and IV.

2 Foreign Currency Transactions

Foreign currency transactions are transactions with a foreign entity (e.g., buying from and selling to) denominated in (to be settled in) a foreign currency.

Foreign exchange transaction gains and losses must be computed at a given balance sheet date on all recorded transactions denominated in foreign currencies that have not be settled.

On 12/1/Yr 1, Green company purchased goods on credit for 100,000 pesos. Green paid for the goods on 3/1/Yr 2. The exchange rates were:

Date	Rate
12/1/Yr 1	$0.10
12/31/Yr 1	$0.08
3/1/Yr 2	$0.09

The journal entries related to this foreign currency transaction are:

12/1/Yr 1	Transaction Date		
Purchases (100,000 pesos × 0.10 exchange rate)		$10,000	
Accounts payable			$10,000

12/31/Yr 1	Balance Sheet Date		
Accounts Payable [100,000 pesos × ($0.10 − $0.08)]		$2,000	
Foreign exchange transaction gain			$2,000

3/1/Yr 2	Settlement Date		
Accounts Payable ($10,000 original balance − $2,000 adjustment)		$8,000	
Foreign exchange transaction loss [100,000 × ($0.08 − $0.09)]		1,000	
Cash (100,000 pesos × $0.09)			$9,000

*Transaction gains and losses are included in income from continuing operations.

Question 2-1 FR-00459

On November 1, Year 1, Western Traders sold goods to an Italian company for 25,000 euros. Western was paid by the company in Euros on February 15, Year 2. The exchange rates to convert euros to dollars were:

11/1/Y1	$1.19/euro
12/31/Y1	$1.16/euro
2/15/Y2	$1.23/euro

How much should Western report as a foreign exchange gain or loss on its December 31, Year 1 and Year 2 financial statements?

	Year 1	Year 2
1.	$750 gain	$1,000 loss
2.	$750 gain	$1,750 loss
3.	$750 loss	$1,000 gain
4.	$750 loss	$1,750 gain

? Related Questions

For related questions, go to the online question bank:

➤ FR-00333

➤ FR-00348

1 Operating Leases

No risks or rewards have been transferred to the lessee. The lessor has the rights to the asset and continues to depreciate the asset. Operating leases are considered off-balance sheet financing because the use of an asset is provided without any corresponding liability being recognized (although there is an economic and legal obligation to pay).

1.1 Straight-Line Method

For an operating lease, the lessee records rent expense over the lease term. The lessor records rent revenue. The lessee must take the total rent expense to be paid for the entire lease term inclusive of a lease bonus or exclusive of free rent and divide it evenly over the entire lease term—straight-line method. The lessor must do the same when recording rent revenue.

1.2 Leasehold Improvements

Leasehold improvements should be amortized over the lease term or the asset/improvement life, whichever is shorter.

Question 1-1   FR-00336

On December 1, Year 1, Tom V. Company entered into an operating lease for office space for its executives for 10 years at a monthly rental of $200,000, increasing to $400,000 halfway through the lease. On that date, Tom V. paid the landlord the following amounts:

First month's rent	$ 200,000
Last month's rent	400,000
Installation of new carpet	600,000
	$1,200,000

The entire amount was charged to rent expense in Year 1. What amount should Tom V. have charged to expense for the year?

1. $1,200,000
2. $300,000
3. $200,000
4. $305,000

> **? Related Questions**
>
> For related questions, go to the online question bank:
>
> ➤ FR-00426

---

2 Capital (Finance) Leases

A capital lease (U.S. GAAP) or finance lease (IFRS) transfers substantially all of the benefits and risks of ownership of property to the lessee. It is an installment purchase in the form of a lease. If a lease does not meet the requirements of a capital (finance) lease, it is an operating lease.

2.1 Capital (Finance) Lease Accounting—Lessee

Under U.S. GAAP, a lessee must capitalize a leased asset if one of the following four conditions is met:

1. **O**wnership transfers at end of lease (upon the final payment or a required buyout).

2. **W**ritten option for bargain purchase (called a bargain purchase option).

3. **N**inety percent (90%) rule. The present value of the minimum lease payments is at least 90 percent of the FV of the leased asset.

4. **S**eventy-five percent (75%) rule. The life of the lease is at least 75 percent of the asset's economic life.

Under IFRS, a lease is classified as a finance lease if the lease transfers substantially all the risks and rewards of ownership to the lessee.

2.1.1 Capitalized Amount

The capitalized amount is the lesser of the fair value of the asset at the inception of the lease or the present value of the minimum lease payments.

Minimum lease payments include:

- Required payments (present value of annuity)
- Bargain purchase option, if any (present value of $1)
- Residual value guaranteed by the lessee, if any (present value of $1)

Minimum lease payments exclude:

- Executory costs (insurance, maintenance and taxes)

Under IFRS, initial direct costs paid by the lessee are added to the amount recognized as a finance lease asset.

2.1.2 Interest Rate

Use the lower (lesser) of:

1. Implicit rate (if known by lessee)
2. Lessee's incremental borrowing rate

2.1.3 Effective Interest Method

Once the asset is capitalized and the liability is recognized, the liability must be paid off over the term of the lease. Lease payments are separated into an interest component and a principal component using the effective interest method of amortization. The interest component for a period is the carrying amount of the lease at the beginning of the period times the interest rate that was used to capitalize the lease. The remainder of the lease payment is the principal component. The greater portion of the payment at the beginning of the lease term is interest.

Date	Lease Payment	Interest Expense (10%)	Principle Reduction	Lease Liability
12/31/Y1				$50,000
12/31/Y1	$10,000		$10,000	40,000
12/31/Y2	10,000	$4,000	6,000	34,000
12/31/Y3	10,000	3,400	6,600	27,400

12/31/Y1	Capital (Finance) Lease	$50,000	
	Lease Obligation		$50,000
12/31/Y1	Lease Obligation	10,000	
	Cash		10,000
12/31/Y2	Interest Expense	4,000	
	Lease Obligation	6,000	
	Cash		10,000

2.1.4 Depreciation Period

◼ U.S. GAAP

Criteria	Depreciation Period
Ownership transfers	Asset life
Written bargain option	Asset life
Ninety (90%) rule	Lease term
Seventy-five (75%) rule	Lease term

◼ IFRS

The depreciation period is the shorter of the lease term and the useful life of the asset. If there is a reasonable certainty that the lessee will own the leased asset after the lease term, then the leased asset should be depreciated over its useful life.

     Financial Final Review

2.2   Direct Financing/Sales-Type (Finance) Lease—Lessor

2.2.1   U.S. GAAP

Direct Financing Lease: The lessor receives interest income only.

Sales-Type Lease: The lessor receives gross profit plus interest income.

For the lessor to account for the lease as a direct financing lease or a sales-type lease under U.S. GAAP, two conditions must be met in addition to one of the four classification criteria for a capital lease (**OWNS**):

- The collectibility of the lease payments must be reasonably predictable.

- Performance by the lessor is substantially complete. If any costs have yet to be incurred they are predictable.

2.2.2   IFRS

A lessor classifies a lease as a finance lease if the lease transfers substantially all the risks and rewards of ownership to the lessee. A sales-type lease is referred to as a finance lease of an asset by a manufacturer or dealer lessor. A direct-financing lease is simply referred to as a finance lease.

Question 2-1	FR-00306

On December 31, Year 1, Eve Company leased a machine under a capital (finance) lease for a period of ten years, contracting to pay $50,000 on signing the lease and $50,000 annually on December 31 of each of the next nine years.

The present value at December 31, Year 1 of the ten lease payments discounted at 10% was $338,000. At December 31, Year 2, Eve's total capital (finance) lease liability is:

1. $303,980
2. $266,800
3. $259,200
4. $243,000

Question 2-2 | FR-00396

Tom Co. leased equipment it had manufactured to Jerry Corp. on January 1, Year 1, for a ten-year period expiring December 31, Year 10. Equal payments under the lease are $450,000 and are due on January 1 of each year. The first payment was made on January 1, Year 1. The list selling price of the equipment is $3,300,000 and its carrying value on Tom's books is $2,950,000. The lease is appropriately accounted for as a sales-type (finance) lease. The present value of the lease payments at an imputed interest rate of 9% (Tom's incremental borrowing rate) is $3,150,000. What amount of profit on the sale should Tom Co. report for the year ended December 31, Year 1?

1. $0
2. $150,000
3. $200,000
4. $350,000

? Related Questions

For related questions, go to the online question bank:

➤ FR-00321

➤ FR-00366

➤ FR-00381

3 Sale-Leasebacks

A sale-leaseback is a transaction where the lessee sells an asset to another party and subsequently leases it back. The leaseback will either qualify as a capital (finance) lease or as an operating lease.

3.1 U.S. GAAP

Under U.S. GAAP, the accounting for gains on a sale-leaseback is dependent on the rights to remaining use of property retained by the seller/lessee:

3.1.1 "Substantially All" Rights Retained (Greater Than 90%)

If the present value of the rent payments is equal to or greater than 90 percent of the fair value of the asset, defer all gains and amortize over the leaseback period.

3.1.2 Rights Retained Are Less Than "Substantially All" but Greater Than "Minor" (Between 90%–10%)

If the present value of the minimum lease payments is greater than 10 percent and less than 90 percent of the fair value of the asset, a portion of the gain is deferred for an amount up to the present value of the minimum lease payments and the excess is recognized immediately.

3.1.3 "Minor" Portion of Rights Retained (Less Than 10%/No Deferral)

If the present value of the rental payments is 10 percent or less of the fair value of the asset, or if the leaseback period is 10 percent or less of the asset's remaining life, the (operating) leaseback is considered a minor leaseback and the transaction is accounted for as two separate transactions, a sale with full gain or loss recognized immediately and a separate lease.

3.2   IFRS

Under IFRS, the accounting for gains is dependent on the classification of the lease as operating or finance.

3.2.1   Finance Lease

Gains are deferred and amortized over the lease term.

3.2.2   Operating Lease

Gains (and losses) are recognized based on the relationship between the leased asset's carrying amount, fair value, and selling price. If the sales price is equal to fair value (general rule), any profit or loss is recognized immediately (no deferral).

Question 3-1   FR-00411

On December 31, Year 1, Smalltime Airlines sold Big Bucks Company two airplanes and simultaneously leased them back. Additional information pertaining to the sale-leasebacks follows:

	Plane #1	Plane #2
Sales price	$500,000	$900,000
Carrying amount, 1/1/Y1	$200,000	$300,000
Lease term	8 years	3 years
Annual lease payments	$ 80,000	$200,000

The implicit rate in both leases is 10%. The present value of an annuity due of $1 at 10% for eight years is 5.868 and the present value of an annuity due of $1 at 10% for three years is 2.736.

In its December 31, Year 1, balance sheet, what amount should Smalltime Airlines report as deferred gain on these transactions under U.S. GAAP?

1. $52,800
2. $300,000
3. $547,200
4. $847,200

Related Questions

For related questions, go to the online question bank:

➤ FR-00351

➤ FR-00792

➤ FR-00793

Task-Based Simulations

Task-Based Simulation 1: Operating Lease

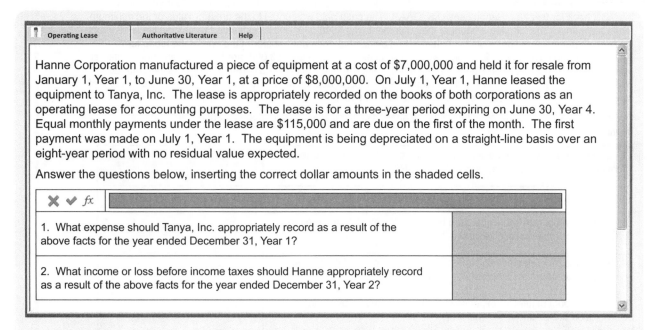

| Operating Lease | Authoritative Literature | Help |

Hanne Corporation manufactured a piece of equipment at a cost of $7,000,000 and held it for resale from January 1, Year 1, to June 30, Year 1, at a price of $8,000,000. On July 1, Year 1, Hanne leased the equipment to Tanya, Inc. The lease is appropriately recorded on the books of both corporations as an operating lease for accounting purposes. The lease is for a three-year period expiring on June 30, Year 4. Equal monthly payments under the lease are $115,000 and are due on the first of the month. The first payment was made on July 1, Year 1. The equipment is being depreciated on a straight-line basis over an eight-year period with no residual value expected.

Answer the questions below, inserting the correct dollar amounts in the shaded cells.

✖ ✔ *fx*

1. What expense should Tanya, Inc. appropriately record as a result of the above facts for the year ended December 31, Year 1?

2. What income or loss before income taxes should Hanne appropriately record as a result of the above facts for the year ended December 31, Year 2?

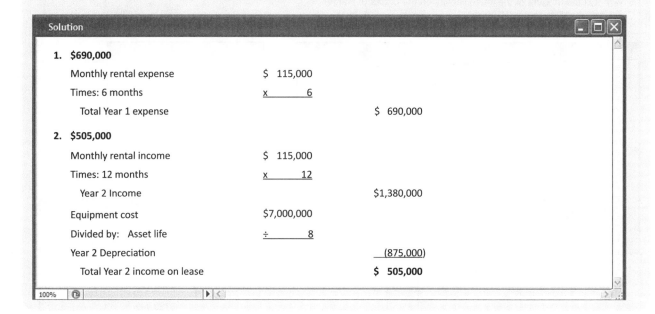

Solution

1. **$690,000**

Monthly rental expense	$ 115,000	
Times: 6 months	x 6	
Total Year 1 expense		$ 690,000

2. **$505,000**

Monthly rental income	$ 115,000	
Times: 12 months	x 12	
Year 2 Income		$1,380,000
Equipment cost	$7,000,000	
Divided by: Asset life	÷ 8	
Year 2 Depreciation		(875,000)
Total Year 2 income on lease		$ 505,000

100%

F Leases

Task-Based Simulation 2: Sale/Leaseback

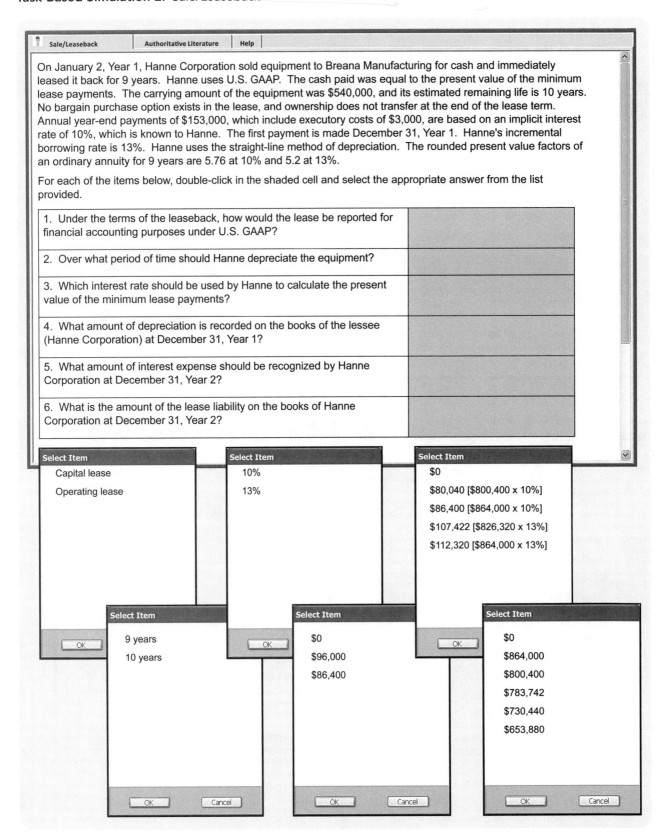

| Sale/Leaseback | Authoritative Literature | Help |

On January 2, Year 1, Hanne Corporation sold equipment to Breana Manufacturing for cash and immediately leased it back for 9 years. Hanne uses U.S. GAAP. The cash paid was equal to the present value of the minimum lease payments. The carrying amount of the equipment was $540,000, and its estimated remaining life is 10 years. No bargain purchase option exists in the lease, and ownership does not transfer at the end of the lease term. Annual year-end payments of $153,000, which include executory costs of $3,000, are based on an implicit interest rate of 10%, which is known to Hanne. The first payment is made December 31, Year 1. Hanne's incremental borrowing rate is 13%. Hanne uses the straight-line method of depreciation. The rounded present value factors of an ordinary annuity for 9 years are 5.76 at 10% and 5.2 at 13%.

For each of the items below, double-click in the shaded cell and select the appropriate answer from the list provided.

1. Under the terms of the leaseback, how would the lease be reported for financial accounting purposes under U.S. GAAP?	
2. Over what period of time should Hanne depreciate the equipment?	
3. Which interest rate should be used by Hanne to calculate the present value of the minimum lease payments?	
4. What amount of depreciation is recorded on the books of the lessee (Hanne Corporation) at December 31, Year 1?	
5. What amount of interest expense should be recognized by Hanne Corporation at December 31, Year 2?	
6. What is the amount of the lease liability on the books of Hanne Corporation at December 31, Year 2?	

Select Item
- Capital lease
- Operating lease

OK

Select Item
- 10%
- 13%

OK

Select Item
- $0
- $80,040 [$800,400 x 10%]
- $86,400 [$864,000 x 10%]
- $107,422 [$826,320 x 13%]
- $112,320 [$864,000 x 13%]

OK

Select Item
- 9 years
- 10 years

OK   Cancel

Select Item
- $0
- $96,000
- $86,400

OK   Cancel

Select Item
- $0
- $864,000
- $800,400
- $783,742
- $730,440
- $653,880

OK   Cancel

Solution

1. **Capital Lease**

    The sale-leaseback transaction is classified as a capital lease because the term of 9 years is greater than 75% of the equipment's estimated remaining economic life (10 years). [Note that the present value of the minimum lease payments is also greater than 90% of the fair value of the property as determined by the cash sale, discussed below.]

    Recall the following mnemonic to determine if a lease qualifies as a capital lease (only one criterion need be met to classify the lease as capital):

    Ownership   Ownership transfers at the end of the lease
    Written   A written bargain purchase option exists
    Ninety   Ninety   percent (90%) of the FMV of the leased property ≤ to the present value of the minimum lease payments
    Seventy-five   At least seventy-five percent (75%) of the asset's economic life is committed in the lease term

2. **9 years**

    Hanne should depreciate the asset over the lease term of 9 years because the lease qualified as a capital lease only under the 75% and the 90% rules. If there is no transfer of ownership and the lease term also does not contain a bargain purchase option, the asset cannot be depreciated over its estimated remaining life. Recall the following rules:

Ownership	=	Depreciate over asset life (legal form)
Written	=	Depreciate over asset life (legal form)
Ninety % FMV	=	Depreciate over lease term (substance over form)
Seventy-five % Life	=	Depreciate over lease term (substance over form)

3. **10%**

    Breana's rate (the lessor's rate) of 10% should be used to calculate the present value of the minimum lease payments (and thus the asset value) because that rate is *lower* than Hanne's (the lessee's) incremental borrowing rate of 13% and Breana's rate is *known* to Hanne.

4. **$96,000**

    To arrive at PVMLP:

Annual lease payments	$153,000
Executory costs	(3,000)
Net amount	$150,000 x 5.76 = $864,000

    $864,000 / 9 = $96,000

    The asset is depreciated over 9 years, as indicated in the answer to item 2.

5. **$80,040**

    Note that the question asks for the interest expense for Year 2. We must calculate the liability balance at the beginning of Year 2 in order to calculate interest expense for Year 2:

    Step 1
Lease liability at 1/2/Year 1	$864,000
Times 10%	x 10%
Year 1 interest expense	**$ 86,400**

    Step 2
Year 1 lease payment	$153,000
Less: Executory costs	(3,000)
Less: Year 1 interest expense	(86,400)
Year 1 lease principal reduction	**$ 63,600**

    Step 3
Lease liability at 1/2/Year 1	$864,000
Less: Year 1 principal reduction	(63,600)
Lease liability at 12/31/Year 1	$800,400
Times 10%	x 10%
Year 2 interest expense	**$ 80,040**

6. **$730,440**

    Using the information obtained in item 5, above, following is the calculation for the lease liability at December 31, Year 2:

Year 2 lease payment	$153,000
Less: Executory costs	(3,000)
Less: Year 2 interest expense	(80,040)
Year 2 lease principal reduction	**$ 69,960**
Lease liability at 12/31/Year 1	$800,400
Less: Year 2 lease principal reduction	(69,960)
Lease liability at 12/31/Year 2	**$730,440**

    [Note that all of the other answer options consider the liability at various year-ends using either the 10% rate or the 13% rate.]

F Leases

Task-Based Simulation 3: Research

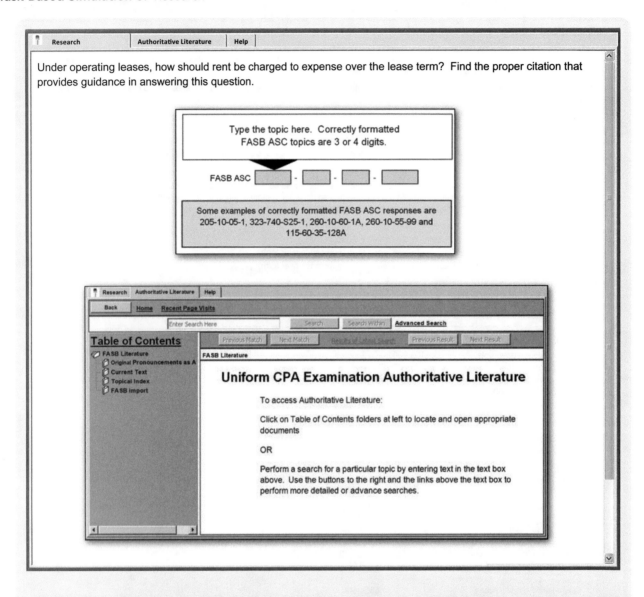

Under operating leases, how should rent be charged to expense over the lease term? Find the proper citation that provides guidance in answering this question.

Type the topic here. Correctly formatted FASB ASC topics are 3 or 4 digits.

FASB ASC ☐ - ☐ - ☐ - ☐

Some examples of correctly formatted FASB ASC responses are 205-10-05-1, 323-740-S25-1, 260-10-60-1A, 260-10-55-99 and 115-60-35-128A

Uniform CPA Examination Authoritative Literature

To access Authoritative Literature:

Click on Table of Contents folders at left to locate and open appropriate documents

OR

Perform a search for a particular topic by entering text in the text box above. Use the buttons to the right and the links above the text box to perform more detailed or advance searches.

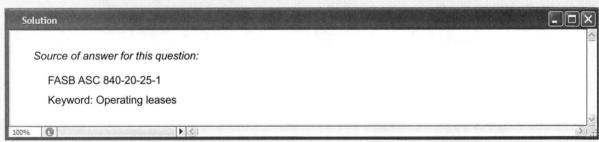

Solution

Source of answer for this question:

FASB ASC 840-20-25-1

Keyword: Operating leases

Research and Development

1 U.S. GAAP

Under U.S. GAAP, research and development costs must be expensed in the period incurred. In general, items to be expensed as R&D include: equipment, material, labor, overhead, design, testing, engineering, modification, and salaries of research staff. Exceptions to expensing include:

1.1 Alternative Use

Capitalize and then depreciate as R&D expense if alternative use on other future projects is planned (e.g., building will be used for other projects).

1.2 Expense as Operating Expenses (Not R&D)

Routine periodic design changes, market research, executive salaries, quality control testing, post-production costs, and commissions.

Question 1-1   FR-00393

The Holly Company incurred research and development costs in Year 1 as follows:

Equipment acquired for use in various R&D projects	$400,000
Depreciation on the above equipment	60,000
Materials used	100,000
Compensation costs of personnel	200,000
Fees to outside consulting firms	70,000
Indirect costs appropriately allocated	100,000

The total research and development expense in Holly 's Year 1 income statement under U.S. GAAP should be:

1. $930,000
2. $870,000
3. $530,000
4. $470,000

---

2 IFRS

Under IFRS, research costs must be expensed, but development costs may be capitalized if certain criteria are met.

Question 2-1   FR-00770

Hi-Tech Corp. spent $300,000 on research and development to generate new product lines. Only one of the five product lines resulted in a patented item, while the remaining four were considered unsuccessful. The cost of the product that was successfully patented included $30,000 in research costs and $40,000 in development costs. Under IFRS, how much of the $300,000 should be recognized as an expense?

1. $300,000
2. $270,000
3. $260,000
4. $230,000

? Related Questions

For related questions, go to the online question bank:

➤ FR-00769

1 U.S. GAAP

Under U.S. GAAP, costs related to computer software developed to be sold, leased, or licensed, are expensed until technological feasibility has been established and capitalized after that. Capitalized costs are amortized using the greater of the straight-line method or a percentage of revenue basis. For computer software developed for internal use, costs in the preliminary project stage and costs incurred in training and maintenance are expensed. Costs after the preliminary project stage are capitalized. Capitalized costs are amortized on a straight-line basis.

Question 1-1   FR-00408

During Year 1, the James Company incurred costs to develop and produce a routine, low-risk computer software product, as follows:

Detailed program design	$30,000
Coding and testing to establish technological feasibility	40,000
Coding after establishment of technological feasibility	20,000
Other testing after establishment of technological feasibility	30,000
Producing product masters for training materials	50,000
Duplication of software and training materials	15,000
Packaging	10,000

In James' December 31, Year 1 balance sheet, what amount should be reported in inventory under U.S. GAAP?

1. $25,000
2. $185,000
3. $70,000
4. $90,000

? Related Questions

For related questions, go to the online question bank:

➤ FR-00847

2 IFRS

IFRS does not provide specific guidance for computer software development costs. Under IFRS, research costs related to computer software development are expensed and development costs may be capitalized if certain criteria are met.

1 Recognized Subsequent Events

Subsequent events occur after the balance sheet date but before the financial statements are issued.

Subsequent events that provide additional information about conditions that existed at the balance sheet date must be recognized on the financial statements. An example of this type of event is litigation settled after the balance sheet date where the litigation arose before the balance sheet date. The settlement amount is considered in determination of the liability.

2 Nonrecognized Subsequent Events

Subsequent events that provide information about conditions that occurred after the balance sheet date and did not exist at the balance sheet date are not recognized in the financial statements, but may be disclosed if necessary to keep the statements from being misleading.

Question 2-1   FR-00844

Drexler Corp. has a June 30 fiscal year-end and plans to issue its annual (Year 3) financial statements by September 30, Year 3. On August 15, a warehouse fire destroys an estimated $250,000 of inventory. As a result of the fire, in its Year 3 financial statements Drexler should:

   1. Book a journal entry with a disclosure.

   2. Book a journal entry with no associated disclosure.

   3. Disclose the nature of the event with no estimated financial impact.

   4. Disclose the nature of the event along with the estimated financial impact.

? Related Questions

For related questions, go to the online question bank:

➤ FR-00845

Notes

1 Definition

Fair value is the price that would be received to sell an asset or paid to transfer a liability in an orderly transaction between market participants in the principal (or most advantageous) market at the measurement date.

- Fair value is a market-based measure.
- Fair value is an exit price, not an entrance price.
- Fair value does not include transaction costs.

2 Market Determination

- Market participants are buyers and sellers who are independent and willing to enter a transaction.
- If there is a principal market, the price in that market will be used.
- If there is no principal market, the price in the most advantageous market will be the fair value measurement.
- Transaction costs are used to determine the most advantageous market, but are not included in the final fair value measurement.

3 Measuring Fair Value

Entities can use the market approach, the income approach, the cost approach, or a combination of these, as appropriate, when measuring the fair value of an asset or a liability.

Valuation techniques should maximize the use of observable inputs (Level 1 and Level 2) and minimize the use of unobservable inputs (Level 3).

- Level 1 inputs are quoted prices in active markets for identical assets or liabilities.
- Level 2 inputs are other directly or indirectly observable inputs.
- Level 3 inputs are unobservable inputs.

Question 3-1   FR-00858

Which of the following choices correctly matches the type of investment with its most appropriate fair value classification?

Investment Type	Level
1. U.S. Treasury bill	3
2. Mortgage-backed securities	2
3. Limited partnerships	1
4. Large public company common stock	3

? Related Questions

For related questions, go to the online question bank:

➤ FR-00859

IV | State and Local Governments

Notes

1 Fund Structure

A fund is a sum of money or other resource segregated for the purpose of carrying on a specific activity or attaining certain objectives in accordance with specific regulations, restrictions, or limitations and constituting an independent fiscal and accounting entity. Each fund is a self-balancing set of accounts.

The basis of accounting and measurement focus contribute to the accountability objectives of each fund type.

1.1 Fund Categories and Fund Types

Eleven fund types (**GRaSPP SE PAPI**) are classified in the following three generic categories:

1.1.1 Governmental Funds

- **General:** The general fund accounts for the ordinary operations of a governmental unit that are financed from taxes and other general revenues. All transactions not accounted for in some other funds are accounted for in this fund.

- **Special Revenue:** Special revenue funds account for revenues from specific taxes or other earmarked sources that are restricted or committed to finance particular activities of government other than debt service or capital projects.

- **Debt Service:** Debt service funds account for the accumulation of resources and the payment of interest and principal on all "general obligation debt."

- **Capital Projects:** Capital projects funds account for resources used for the acquisition or construction of major capital assets by a governmental unit.

- **Permanent:** Permanent funds are used to report resources that are legally restricted to the extent that income, and not principal, may be used for purposes that support the reporting government's programs.

1.1.2 Proprietary Funds

- **Internal Service:** Internal service funds account for goods and services provided by departments on a cost reimbursement fee basis to other departments.

- **Enterprise:** Enterprise funds account for the acquisition and operation of governmental facilities and services that are intended to be primarily (over 50 percent) self-supported by user charges.

1.1.3 Fiduciary Funds

- **Pension:** Pension trust funds account for resources of defined benefit and defined contribution plans, as well as post retirement benefit plans.

- **Agency:** Agency trust funds account for resources temporarily in the custody of a governmental unit.

- **Private Purpose:** Private purpose trust funds account for all other trust arrangements under which principal and income are for the benefit of specific individuals, private organizations, and other governments.

- **Investment Trust:** Investment trust funds account for external investment pools.

Question 1-1   FR-00488

Payback Parish levied an additional one-cent sales tax intended exclusively for the repayment of Civic Center Bonds. The earnings from this sales tax would most appropriately be recorded in the:

1. General Fund.
2. Special Revenue Fund.
3. Debt Service Fund.
4. Capital Projects Fund.

---

2 Measurement Focus

Measurement focus describes the reporting objective that the application of fund accounting is designed to achieve. There are two measurement focuses:

2.1 Current Financial Resources Measurement Focus

Financial statement readers are focused on the sources, uses and balances of current financial resources. The focus often includes a budgetary element. The governmental fund types use the current financial resources measurement focus.

- Non-current assets and liabilities are not reported on the governmental fund types balance sheets.

- Capital outlay expenditures are reported on the face of the governmental fund types operating statements.

- Proceeds from long-term debt are recorded in the governmental funds as "other financing sources."

- Payment of principal and interest are recorded as "expenditures."

2.2 Economic Resources Measurement Focus

Financial statement readers are focused on the determination of operating income, changes in net assets, financial position and cash flow. The proprietary fund and fiduciary fund types use this focus. Accounting is nearly identical to commercial accounting used in "for profit" entities.

- Non-current assets and non-current liabilities are recorded on the balance sheet.

- Depreciation expense is recorded.

Question 2-1   FR-00405

The Town of Holler has a community development block grant that funds the renewal and revival of economically disadvantaged areas in its jurisdiction. The Town properly accounts for the grant in a special revenue fund. Which one of the following funds would not share the use of the current financial resources measurement focus with the Community Development Block Grant Fund?

1. The Holler Bridge Fund (used to account for the bridge construction financed by general obligation debt).

2. The Holler Bridge Debt Service Fund (used to account for the accumulation of resources for the repayment of general obligation debt issued to finance the construction of the Holler Bridge).

3. The Holler Sound Citizen's Initiative Fund (used to account for collection and disbursement of special assessments that pay debt service obligations which the town is barred by statute from assuming).

4. The Holler Cemetery Perpetual Care Fund (that accounts for resources used for the public cemetery).

---

3 Basis of Accounting

Basis of accounting describes the accounting principles used to accomplish the measurement focus of each fund category. There are two bases:

3.1 Modified Accrual Basis of Accounting

The current financial resources measurement focus is accomplished using the modified accrual basis of accounting. The difference between modified accrual and accrual primarily relates to the timing of revenue recognition.

Revenues are generally accrued when they are *both measurable and available* (due and collected within 60 days of year-end). There are four classifications of non-exchange revenues that serve as the basis for most governmental fund resources. There is no underlying exchange transaction that produces these revenues; the government does not provide a specific service in exchange for the revenue earned:

Modified accrual also creates important expenditure recognition differences, including no interest accrual.

3.1.1 Derived Non-exchange Tax Revenues

A sales tax or an income tax is considered to be "derived" tax revenue; it is a tax that comes as a result of (is derived from) economic activity. Derived non-exchange tax revenues are accrued based on the timing of receipt. Receipts due at year-end and actually received within 60 days of year-end are accrued and recognized as revenue.

3.1.2 Imposed Non-exchange Revenues

Fines and property taxes are imposed non-exchange revenues since the taxpayer's obligation is imposed by an enforceable claim by the government. Imposed non-exchange revenues are typically accrued when billed since collection is not in doubt. Collection of fines is based upon enforcement of a penalty resulting from the violation of law (e.g., driver's licenses can be revoked, cars can be impounded, etc.). Liens on property (allowed by law) are used to enforce property tax collection.

3.1.3 Government Mandated Non-exchange Transactions

Grants are conveyed by one government to another, (a state, or a county) to mandate certain activities.

Revenues are recognized when eligibility requirements are met and the revenues are both measurable and available.

3.1.4 Voluntary Non-exchange Transactions

Resources are willingly conveyed by a government to another for a particular purpose or use without an equal exchange of value. Revenues are recognized when restrictions are met.

3.2 Accrual Basis of Accounting

The economic resources measurement focus is accomplished using the accrual basis of accounting where revenues are recorded when earned and expenses are recorded when incurred.

Question 3-1   FR-00420

The City of Riggsville elected to account for its very small fee-supported trash collection service through its General Fund. Payment for services provided in December, for which payment is not anticipated until March, has not been accrued. The trash collection service shares the same basis of accounting with:

1. The Riggsville Utility Fund, an enterprise fund supported by user charges.

2. The Riggsville Motor Pool, an internal service fund supported by internal user charges.

3. The Riggsville Road and Bridge Fund, used to account for the receipt of gasoline tax funds in a Special Revenue Fund.

4. The Riggsville Employee Retirement Fund, used to account for the pension fund resources that benefit the city's employees.

Question 3-2   FR-00315

Property taxes for the Town of Farrell of $25,000,000 were assessed in October of Year 1 to fund budgeted operations for the fiscal year ended September 30, Year 2. Some $24,000,000 are collected from November Year 1 through March Year 2 with liens of $1,000,000 applied to properties with unpaid property tax bills in May Year 2. Properties subject to delinquent property taxes were auctioned for taxes of $800,000. At September 30, Year 2, government would record property tax revenue of:

1. $25,000,000

2. $24,800,000

3. $24,200,000

4. $24,000,000

? Related Questions

For related questions, go to the online question bank:

➤ FR-00330

➤ FR-00492

A State and Local Government Concepts

Task-Based Simulations

Task-Based Simulation: Basis of Accounting

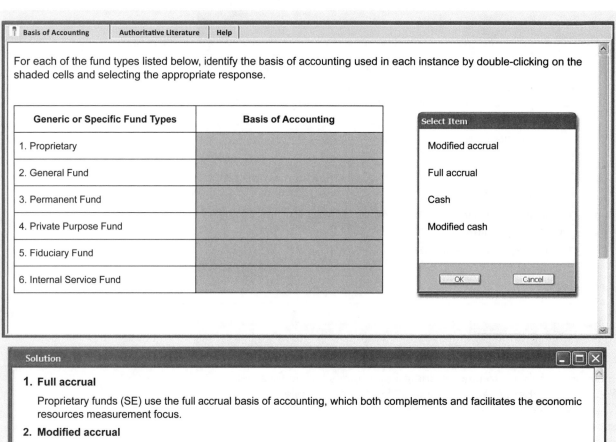

For each of the fund types listed below, identify the basis of accounting used in each instance by double-clicking on the shaded cells and selecting the appropriate response.

Generic or Specific Fund Types	Basis of Accounting
1. Proprietary	
2. General Fund	
3. Permanent Fund	
4. Private Purpose Fund	
5. Fiduciary Fund	
6. Internal Service Fund	

Select Item

Modified accrual

Full accrual

Cash

Modified cash

[OK]   [Cancel]

Solution

1. **Full accrual**

   Proprietary funds (SE) use the full accrual basis of accounting, which both complements and facilitates the economic resources measurement focus.

2. **Modified accrual**

   The General Fund is a Governmental (GRSPP) Fund, which uses the modified accrual basis that both complements and facilitates the financial resources measurement focus.

3. **Modified accrual**

   The Permanent Fund is a Governmental (GRSPP) Fund, which uses the modified accrual basis that both complements and facilitates the financial resources measurement focus.

4. **Full Accrual**

   The Private Purpose Funds are Fiduciary (PAPI) Funds, which use the full accrual basis that both complements and facilitates the economic resources measurement focus.

5. **Full Accrual**

   Fiduciary funds (PAPI) use the full accrual basis of accounting, which both complements and facilitates the economic resources measurement focus.

6. **Full Accrual**

   The Internal Service Funds are Proprietary (SE) Funds, which use the full accrual basis that both complements and facilitates the economic resources measurement focus.

100%

1 Government-wide Reporting

The GASB 34 reporting model (as amended by GASB 63) focuses the reader on both government-wide and fund financial statements using an integrated approach to highlight both the operational and fiscal accountability requirements of the government.

The basic structure includes the presentation of:

- Basic financial statements (comprised of government-wide financial statements, fund financial statements, and notes to the financial statements)
- Required supplementary information

Fund financial statements emphasize fiscal accountability while government-wide financial statements emphasize operational accountability. Financial presentations are integrated by the reconciliation of fund financial statements to government-wide presentations.

Government-wide financial presentations are prepared using the economic resources measurement focus utilizing the accrual basis of accounting. The government-wide financials include presentation of governmental activities and business-type activities such as the enterprise funds. Fiduciary funds are excluded from the government-wide financial statements but are included as part of the fund financial statements.

A matrix to keep in mind for GASB 34 reporting categorizes our fund structure mnemonic as follows for government-wide reporting:

Governmental	Business Type	Excluded
GRaSPP S	E	PAPI

Government-wide financial statements are the:

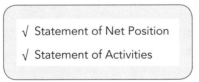

√ Statement of Net Position

√ Statement of Activities

- Required supplementary information (RSI) is presented both before and after the basic financial statements.

  - Preceding the basic financial statements is the management's discussion and analysis, a letter that presents a brief, objective, and easily readable analysis of the government's activities.

  - Following the basic financial statements is RSI that includes multi-year pension data, infrastructure data for governments using the modified approach for infrastructure, and budgetary disclosures.

- Other supplementary information (optional) may be included. Optional information includes budget variances and individual financial statements for nonmajor funds.

- A statement of cash flows is not prepared for government-wide presentations.

Question 1-1   FR-00474

The Municipality of Sykes prepares its financial statements for the year ended December 31, Year 1. The municipality has elected to display all funds in its report including nonmajor funds. The Municipality of Sykes has the option of:

1. Displaying each nonmajor fund in a combining statements of fund balance sheets and statement of revenues, expenditures, and changes in fund balance.

2. Disclosing nonmajor fund activity in the notes to the financial statements.

3. Describing each nonmajor fund in required supplementary information.

4. Displaying a summary of nonmajor funds in the fund financial statements and a combining statement of nonmajor funds in other supplementary information.

---

2 Fund Financial Statements

Fund financial statements are presented for all funds based on their applicable measurement focus and related basis of accounting. Only major funds are reported separately; nonmajor funds are reported in the aggregate. Individual nonmajor funds may be reported as optional supplementary information.

2.1 Governmental Fund Financial Statements

■ **Balance Sheet:** Included in this statement are assets plus deferred outflows of resources, liabilities plus deferred inflows of resources, and fund balance.

■ **Statement of Revenues, Expenditures, and Changes in Fund Balance:** Included in this statement are other financing sources (proceeds from debt and interfund transfers) and other financing uses.

2.2 Proprietary Fund Financial Statements

■ **Statement of Net Position:** Included in this statement are assets plus deferred outflows of resources, liabilities plus deferred inflows of resources, and net position.

■ **Statement of Revenues, Expenses, and Changes in Fund Net Position**

■ **Statement of Cash Flows**

2.3 Fiduciary Fund Financial Statements

■ **Statement of Fiduciary Net Position:** Included in this statement are assets plus deferred outflows of resources, liabilities plus deferred inflows of resources, and net position.)

■ **Statement of Changes in Fiduciary Net Position**

2.4 Determination of Major Funds

GASB 34 as amended by GASB 63 emphasizes reporting by major fund rather than fund type. To qualify as a major fund the two following criteria must be met:

1. An individual fund's total assets plus deferred outflows of resources, or liabilities plus deferred inflows of resources, or revenues, or expenditures/expenses, are at least 10 percent or more of the corresponding total assets plus deferred outflows of resources, or liabilities plus deferred inflows of resources, or revenues, or expenditures/expenses of all governmental funds or enterprise funds (e.g., a special revenue fund's revenues would need to be 10 percent of the revenues for the governmental fund financial statement category; a water and sewer fund's revenues would need to be 10 percent of all enterprise funds' revenues).

2. The same individual fund's total assets plus deferred outflows of resources, or liabilities plus deferred inflows of resources, or revenues, or expenditures/expenses, are at least 5 percent or more of the corresponding total assets plus deferred outflows of resources, or liabilities plus deferred inflows of resources, or revenues, or expenditures/expenses of all governmental funds and enterprise funds combined (e.g., a special revenue fund's revenues would need to be 5 percent of the combined revenues amounts for governmental and enterprise funds; a water and sewer fund's revenues would need to be 5 percent of the combined revenue amounts for governmental and enterprise funds).

2.5   Reconciliation of Fund Statements to Government-wide Statements

Because of the different measurement focus and related basis of accounting used, the governmental fund balance as reported in the balance sheet must be reconciled to net position of government-wide statements as reported in the statement of net position.

■ The difference in measurement focus provides the following reconciling items:

- Add non-current assets.

- Subtract non-current liabilities.

- Add internal service fund net assets.

■ The difference in basis of accounting produces the following reconciling items:

- Adjust for accrual of revenue accounted for on the full accrual basis of accounting rather than the modified accrual basis of accounting.

- Adjust for accrual of expenses accounted for on the full accrual basis of accounting rather than the expenditures accrued on the modified accrual basis of accounting.

- The changes in fund balance displayed in the governmental fund statement of revenues, expenditures, and changes in fund balances must be reconciled to changes in net position of the governmental activities column as reported in the statement of activities of the government-wide statement.

■ The difference in measurement focus produces the following reconciling items:

- Subtract debt proceeds (not accounted for as other financing sources in the government-wide financial statements).

- Add capital outlay (not accounted for as expenses in the government-wide financial statements).

- Add internal service fund changes in net position accounted for in the proprietary funds.

- The difference in basis of accounting produces the following reconciling items:
  - Adjust for accrual of revenue accounted for on the accrual basis of accounting rather than the modified accrual basis of accounting.
  - Adjust for accrual of expenses accounted for on the accrual basis rather than the expenditures accrued on the modified accrual basis.

Balance Sheet	Statement of Revenues, Expenditures, and Changes in Fund Balance
GRaSPP—Fund balance	GRaSPP—Net change in fund balance
Assets (non-current)	Other financing sources
Liabilities (non-current)	Expenditure—capital outlay (net of depreciation)
Service (internal) fund net position	Service (internal) fund net income
Basis of Accounting	Basis of Accounting
Accrued	Additional accrued
Revenues and	Revenues and
Expenses	Expenses

2.6 Statement of Cash Flows

The Statement of Cash Flows is only used for the proprietary funds. The direct method is required and it is prepared in a manner similar to the commercial version, with the following differences:

- There are four categories (instead of the three) and the order of the categories is the following:
  1. Operating activities.
  2. Noncapital financing activities.
  3. Capital and related financing activities.
  4. Investing activities.

- Interest income/cash receipts are reported as "investing activities" (not as operating activities). Interest expense/cash payments are either:
  - capital and related financing; or
  - noncapital financing.

- Capital asset purchases are reported as "financing activities" (not as investing activities).

- Interest expense/cash disbursements are reported as "financing activities" (not as operating activities).

- Many transactions unique to government (e.g., transfers, property tax revenues, and special assessments) are often classified as "non-capital financing activities."

- A reconciliation of operating income (instead of net income) to net cash provided by operations is required.

Question 2-1   FR-00390

The City of Richardson reported a change in fund balances of $2,002,000 in its governmental funds Statement of Revenues, Expenditures, and Changes in Fund Balances for the year ended December 31, Year 1. Additional information:

1. Capital outlay expenditures amounted to $10,000,000 in the modified accrual statement. General government fixed assets amounted to $160,000,000 excluding land and had an average life of 20 years.

2. The modified accrual statement reported proceeds from the sale of land in the amount of $1,000,000. The land had a basis of $800,000.

3. Property taxes had been levied in the amount of $20,000,000. It was estimated that 3% would be uncollected, that $1,000,000 would be collected within 60 days of year-end, and that $400,000 would be collected more than 60 days from year-end. The City had recognized the maximum permitted under modified accrual accounting.

4. $370,000 of property taxes had been deferred at the end of the previous year and was recognized under modified accrual as revenue in the current year.

5. The modified accrual statement reflected debt service expenditures in the amount of $1,000,000 for interest and $1,500,000 for principal. No adjustment was necessary for interest accruals at year-end.

6. Compensated absences charges, on the full accrual basis, amounted to $100,000 more than under the modified accrual basis.

The change in net position in the governmental column in the government-wide Statement of Activities for the year ended December 31, Year 1 is:

1. 4,602,000
2. 5,202,000
3. 3,832,000
4. 4,632,000

? Related Questions

For related questions, go to the online question bank:

➤ FR-00446

➤ FR-00457

➤ FR-00467

➤ FR-00483

➤ FR-00486

3 Infrastructure

Infrastructure can have an impact on both the statement of net assets and statement of activities. Included among the capitalized non-current assets on the government-wide statement of net assets should be eligible infrastructure, such as roads, drainage systems, and bridges. Consequently, depreciation of such assets is required, and should be reported in the statement of activities.

However, if the government is unable to arrive at the cost data for its infrastructure, the use of a modified approach (no capitalization needed) is acceptable, provided that supplementary information describing the infrastructure, its condition, and estimation of expenses needed to maintain condition is included in the RSI. A complete new professional assessment of the infrastructure condition is necessary every three years.

Question 3-1   FR-00480

The Village of James has elected to use the modified approach for reporting infrastructure for the year ended December 31, Year 1. Using the modified approach, the government's asset management system does not need to include:

1. Inventory of assets.

2. Summary of condition assessments.

3. Estimated net realizable value of community infrastructure.

4. Amount necessary to maintain and preserve the condition of the assets.

---

4 Comprehensive Annual Financial Report

Governments often present a Comprehensive Annual Financial Report (CAFR). A CAFR is not required by GASB 34. It is a GFOA designated presentation that adds introductory and statistical sections to the GASB 34 presentation, as follows:

1. Introductory Section (unaudited)

   - Letter of transmittal
   - Organizational chart
   - List of principal officers

2. Basic Financial Statements and Required Supplementary Information (audited)

   - MD&A
   - Government-wide financial statements
   - Fund financial statements
   - Notes to financial statements
   - Required supplementary information

3. Statistical Section (unaudited)

   - Ten years of selected data
   - Ten years of economic data
   - Other data

5 Financial Statements Samples

Progressive Township **Statement of Net Position** December 31, Year 1			
	Primary Government		
	Governmental Activities	Business-type Activities	Total	Component Units
Assets				
Cash	$4,055,000	$2,000,000	$6,055,000	$520,000
Derivative instrument—rate swap	–	40,000	40,000	–
Receivables	1,065,000	670,000	1,735,000	–
Internal balances	450,000	(450,000)	–	–
Inventories	96,000	127,500	223,500	–
Capital assets	2,827,000	2,975,000	5,802,000	–
Total assets	8,493,000	5,362,500	13,855,500	520,000
Deferred Outflows of Resources				
Accumulated decrease in fair value of hedging derivatives	–	35,000	35,000	–
Total deferred outflows of resources	–	35,000	35,000	–
Liabilities				
Accounts payable	1,104,000	400,000	1,504,000	130,000
Forward contract	–	35,000	35,000	–
Other liabilities	95,000	–	95,000	–
Non-current liabilities:				
Due within one year	46,000	337,500	383,500	–
Due in more than one year	3,518,000	2,750,000	6,268,000	–
Total liabilities	4,763,000	3,522,500	8,285,500	130,000
Deferred Inflows of Resources				
Accumulated increase in fair value of hedging derivatives	–	40,000	40,000	–
Total deferred inflows of resources	–	40,000	40,000	–
Net Position				
Net investment in capital assets	1,227,000	450,000	1,677,000	–
Restricted for:				
Capital projects	1,574,000	–	1,574,000	–
Debt service	723,000	1,200,000	1,923,000	–
Unrestricted	206,000	185,000	391,000	390,000
Total net position	$3,730,000	$1,835,000	$5,565,000	$390,000

Progressive Township
Statement of Activities
For the Year Ended December 31, Year 1

| Functions/Programs | Expenses | Indirect Expense Allocation | Program Revenues | | | NET (Expenses) Revenues and Changes in NET Position | | | Component Units |
| | | | Charges for Services | Operating Grants and Contributions | Capital Grants and Contributions | Primary Government | | | |
						Governmental Activities	Business-type Activities	Total	
Primary government:									
Governmental activities:									
General government	$ 555,000	(50,000)	$ 215,000	–	–	(290,000)	–	(290,000)	–
Public safety	1,025,000	$35,000	78,000	–	–	(982,000)	–	(982,000)	–
Culture and recreation	107,500	10,000	–	–	–	(117,500)	–	(117,500)	–
Other functional classifications	1,947,000	5,000	–	$1,260,000	–	(692,000)	–	(692,000)	–
Interest on long-term debt	246,000	–	125,000	–	–	(121,000)	–	(121,000)	–
Total governmental activities	3,880,500	–	418,000	1,260,000	–	(2,202,500)	–	(2,202,500)	–
Business-type activities:									
Water	692,000		700,000	–	–	–	$ 8,000	8,000	–
Sewer	1,038,000		1,050,000	–	$300,000	–	312,000	312,000	–
Parking facilities	465,000		650,000	–	–	–	185,000	185,000	–
Total business-type activities	2,195,000		$2,400,000	–	300,000	–	505,000	505,000	–
Total primary government	6,075,500		2,818,000	$1,260,000	300,000	(2,202,500)	505,000	(1,697,500)	–
Component units:									
Landfill	300,000		500,000	–	–	–	–	–	200,000
Public school system	1,000,000		100,000	–	–	–	–	–	(900,000)
Total component units	$1,300,000		600,000	–	–	–	–	–	(700,000)
	General revenues								
	Taxes:								
	Property taxes—levied for general purposes					$1,620,000	–	$1,620,000	$1,000,000
	Franchise taxes					735,000	–	735,000	–
	Investment earnings					205,000	60,000	265,000	–
	Special item—gain on sale of governmental capital property					425,000	–	425,000	–
	Transfers					12,000	(12,000)	–	–
	Total general revenues, special items, and transfers					2,997,000	48,000	3,045,000	1,000,000
	Change in net position					794,500	553,000	1,347,500	300,000
	Net position—beginning					2,935,500	1,282,000	4,217,500	90,000
	Net position—ending					$3,730,000	$1,835,000	$5,565,000	$ 390,000

Progressive Township
Balance Sheet
Governmental Funds
December 31, Year 1

	General Fund	HUD Programs	Convention Development Tax	Convention Center Bonds	Convention Center Construction	Other Governmental Funds	Total Governmental Funds
Assets							
Cash	$ 800,000	$80,000	$250,000	$505,000	$2,100,000	$270,000	$4,005,000
Receivables	162,000	–	–	125,000	–	–	287,000
Due from other funds	450,000	–	–	60,000	–	–	510,000
Receivables from other governments	620,000	–	50,000	–	–	83,000	753,000
Inventories	55,000	–	–	–	–	6,000	61,000
Total assets	2,087,000	80,000	300,000	690,000	2,100,000	359,000	5,616,000
Liabilities							
Accounts payable	250,000	20,000	56,000	–	600,000	100,000	1,026,000
Due to other funds	50,000	–	60,000	–	–	–	110,000
Payable to other governments	65,000	–	–	–	–	–	65,000
Other liabilities	95,000	–	–	–	–	–	95,000
Total liabilities	460,000	20,000	116,000	–	600,000	100,000	1,296,000
Deferred Inflows of Resources							
Unavailable revenues—special assessments	–	–	–	125,000	–	–	125,000
Total deferred inflows of resources	–	–	–	125,000	–	–	125,000
Fund Balances							
Nonspendable Inventories	55,000	–	–	–	–	6,000	61,000
Restricted for:							
Debt service	–	–	–	565,000	–	158,000	723,000
Capital projects	–	–	–	–	1,500,000	74,000	1,574,000
Committed to:							
Urban renewal	–	60,000	184,000	–	–	–	244,000
Sanitation	45,000	–	–	–	–	–	45,000
Assigned:							
Special revenue funds	–	–	–	–	–	36,000	36,000
Unassigned:							
General fund	1,527,000	–	–	–	–	–	1,527,000
Special revenue funds	–	–	–	–	–	(15,000)	(15,000)
Total fund balances	1,627,000	60,000	184,000	565,000	1,500,000	259,000	4,195,000
Total liabilities, deferred inflows of resources, and fund balances	$2,087,000	$80,000	$300,000	$690,000	$2,100,000	$359,000	$5,616,000

Total governmental fund balances	4,195,000
Capital assets used in governmental activities that are not reported in fund financial statements	2,667,000
Other long-term assets not available to defray the cost of current expenses and are not reported in fund financial statements	125,000
Long-term liabilities including bonds payable not recorded in fund financial statements	(3,420,000)
Internal service fund used for governmental activities	163,000
Net position from governmental activities	$3,730,000

				Progressive Township				

Statement of Revenues, Expenditures, and Changes in Fund Balances
Governmental Funds
For the Year Ended December 31, Year 1

	General Fund	HUD Programs	Convention Development Tax	Convention Center Bonds	Convention Center Construction	Other Governmental Funds	Total Governmental Funds
Revenues							
Property taxes	$1,620,000	–	–	–	–	–	$1,620,000
Fees and fines	120,000	–	–	–	–	–	120,000
Intergovernmental	–	$960,000	$375,000	–	–	$ 660,000	1,995,000
Charges for services	–	–	–	–	–	78,000	78,000
Interest earnings	55,000	–	28,000	$ 36,000	$ 40,000	40,000	199,000
Total Revenues	1,795,000	960,000	403,000	36,000	40,000	778,000	4,012,000
Expenditures							
Current:							
General government	450,000	–	–	–	–	–	450,000
Public safety	1,000,000	–	–	–	–	–	1,000,000
Culture and recreation	80,000	–	17,500	–	–	–	97,500
Other functional classifications	200,000	940,000	–	–	–	757,000	1,897,000
Debt service:							
Principal	–	–	–	250,000	–	110,000	360,000
Interest and other charges	–	–	–	30,000	–	211,000	241,000
Capital outlay	25,000	–	–	–	600,000	162,000	787,000
Total expenditures	1,755,000	940,000	17,500	280,000	600,000	$1,240,000	4,832,500
Excess (deficiency) of revenues over expenditures	40,000	20,000	385,500	(244,000)	(560,000)	(462,000)	(820,500)
Other Financing Sources (Uses)							
Proceeds of long-term capital-related debt	–	–	–	–	2,080,000	–	2,080,000
Transfers in	85,000	–	–	370,000	–	66,000	521,000
Transfers out	(14,000)	–	(250,000)	–	(120,000)	(125,000)	(509,000)
Total other financing sources and uses	71,000	–	(250,000)	370,000	1,960,000	(59,000)	2,092,000
Special Item							
Proceeds from sale of land	500,000	–	–	–	–	–	500,000
Net change in fund balances	611,000	20,000	135,500	126,000	1,400,000	(521,000)	1,771,500
Fund balances—beginning	1,016,000	40,000	48,500	439,000	100,000	780,000	2,423,500
Fund balances—ending	$1,627,000	$ 60,000	$184,000	$565,000	$1,500,000	$ 259,000	$4,195,000

Progressive Township **Reconciliation of the Statement of Revenue, Expenditures, and Changes in Fund Balances of Governmental Funds to the Statement of Activities** For the year ended December 31, Year 1		
Net change in fund balances—total governmental funds		$1,771,500
Bond proceeds	(2,080,000)	
Payments	$360,000	
Excess of bond proceeds over principal payments		(1,720,000)
Proceeds of land sold	(500,000)	
Gain on sale	425,000	
Cost of land sold (excess of proceeds over gain on disposal)		(75,000)
Capital outlay	787,000	
Depreciation expense:		
General government	(35,000)	
Public safety	(25,000)	
Culture and recreation	(10,000)	
Other functional classifications	(50,000)	
Amount by which capital outlay exceeded depreciation in the current period		667,000
Revenues in the statement of activities that do not provide current financial resources are not reported in the funds		125,000
Net revenue (expense) of internal service funds		26,000
Change in net position of governmental activities		$794,500

Notes

1 Reporting Units

Reporting units (the primary government and its component units) are the governmental version of "consolidations." When to consolidate and how to consolidate is important under the GASB 34 model.

1.1 Primary Governments and Component Units

A government is viewed as a stand-alone or primary government if it has a separately elected governing board, it is a legal entity and it is financially independent.

A government that cannot stand by itself is a component unit of another government and should present its financial statements with the primary government.

1.2 Discrete vs. Blended Presentation

Component units are presented either discretely or in a blended format. Generally, component units are presented as discrete (separate columns) on the primary government's financial statements.

Blended presentations are made when the component unit either exclusively serves the primary government or when the component unit's governing body is substantially the same as the primary government's governing body. Blending involves consolidation of activities.

Question 1-1   FR-00434

Geartyville established the Cox Administration Corporation, a nonprofit corporation for the purpose of administering employee welfare benefits for the employees of Geartyville. The city appoints the corporation's Board of Directors. The financial statements of the Cox Administration Corporation should be:

1. Presented discretely as a component unit.
2. Presented as a blended component unit.
3. Only disclosed in the notes to the financial statements.
4. Displayed as a stand alone corporation.

? Related Questions

For related questions, go to the online question bank:

➤ FR-00494

1 Interfund Activity

Interfund activity is subject to specific requirements related to financial statement display and disclosure and can be classified as follows:

- Reciprocal interfund activity
- Nonreciprocal interfund activity

1.1 Reciprocal Interfund Activity

- Includes exchange-type transactions between funds.
- Interfund loans are expected to be repaid and are accounted for as interfund receivables and payables (due from/due to).
- Unrealizable balances are reclassified as transfers.
- Interfund services provided and used represent sales and purchases between funds at external pricing. Transactions of this type are accounted for as revenues and expenses.

1.2 Nonreciprocal Interfund Activity

- Represents non-exchange transactions between funds.
- Interfund transfers of assets between funds without the exchange of equivalent value represent interfund transfers. These are normally reported as other financing sources and uses after nonoperating revenues and expenses.
- Interfund payments of expenses made by one fund on behalf of another fund are accounted for as reimbursements. Interfund reimbursements are not displayed as interfund transactions.

1.3 Government-wide Financial Statement Displays of Interfund Activity

- Interfund activity within a particular column displayed on the governmental activities or business-type activities financial statements (intra-activity transaction between governmental funds and internal service funds) is eliminated prior to the preparation of governmental-wide financial statements.
- Interfund activity between columns displayed on the governmental activities or business-type activities financial statements (inter-activity transaction between governmental funds and enterprise funds) is reported as "internal balances" on the statement of net assets and "transfers" (revenues or expenses) in the statement of activities. They are not eliminated.
- Interfund activity between the primary government and its fiduciary funds should be reported as if between external parties.

2 Fund Accounting Mechanics

Fund accounting mechanics generally focus on the accounting for the governmental funds and require knowledge of the journal entries used to record the budget, actual activities, and encumbrances.

2.1 Budgetary Activity

To record the budget into the accounting records, the following entry is used. Any balancing amounts are posted to budgetary control.

DR	Estimated revenue control	$XXX	
CR	Appropriations control		$XXX
CR	Budgetary control		XXX

Budgetary control can also be a debit. Budgetary accounts are recorded at the beginning of the year and are closed at the end of the year. Budgetary accounts are only impacted when establishing, amending or closing the budget.

2.2 Actual Activity

Actual activities are recorded as they happen throughout the year. Expenditures are typically recorded as they are incurred.

Capital purchases are identified as capital outlay because of their long-term nature but they are accounted for as expenditures and they are not reported in the balance sheet. In addition, no depreciation expense is recorded on governmental fund financial statements. Generally, all spending is recorded currently as "expenditures."

DR	Capital outlay expenditures	$XXX	
CR	Cash or vouchers payable		$XXX

Principal payment on debt is displayed as an expenditure since there is no non-current debt recorded on the governmental fund financial statements.

DR	Debt service—principal expenditure	$XXX	
CR	Cash		$XXX

In addition, new debt proceeds are recorded as other financing sources, a resource inflow:

DR	Cash	$XXX
CR	Other financing sources—debt proceeds	$XXX

The modified accrual basis of accounting records (accrues) revenue when it is measurable and available, generally collected within 60 days of year-end. Only the amount available is recorded as revenue. Note the entry below to record property tax receivable (imposed non-exchange revenue) and the related allowance for uncollectible taxes. Tax receivable is recorded when the tax is levied but only available revenue is recognized. No "bad debt expenditure" is recognized.

DR	Property tax receivable—current	$XXX
CR	Allowance for uncollectible taxes—current	$XXX
CR	Property tax revenue	XXX

2.3 Encumbrance Activity

Encumbrances are recorded when purchase orders are issued. The issuance of a purchase order does not represent a liability, rather, the reserve for encumbrance account acts as a limitation that reduces the available fund balance. Entries to record the encumbrance of funds and the receipt of goods are as follows:

To record the issuance of a purchase order:

DR	Encumbrances	$XXX
CR	Budgetary control	$XXX

Upon receipt of goods the encumbrance of funds associated with the issued order is reversed and the related expenditure is recorded.

DR	Budgetary control	$XXX
CR	Encumbrances	$XXX
DR	Expenditure	$XXX
CR	Vouchers payable	$XXX

2.4 Relationship Between Accounts at Year-End

Governmental funds record budget, actual, and encumbrance activities separately. Both budget and actual activities are recorded during the year and then closed at the end of the year. Encumbrances are recorded and closed throughout the year. At year-end, if encumbrances are still outstanding, they are reported as a component of committed or assigned fund balance and disclosed if appropriations do not lapse.

2.5 Inventory of Supplies

When the government buys supplies, two methods can be used for the transaction: purchase and consumption.

At the time of purchase:

	The Purchase Method				The Consumption Method	
DR	Expenditures	$5,000		DR	Inventory of supply	$5,000
CR	Vouchers payable		5,000	CR	Vouchers payable	5,000

At year-end (assumption: 1,000 of supply is still on hand):

DR	Inventory of supply	$1,000		DR	Expenditures	$4,000
CR	Nonspendable fund balance – inventory		1,000	CR	Inventory of supply	4,000

Under the purchase method the remaining inventory must be placed in the balance sheet (it was all expensed at the beginning) and because it cannot be spent in that year, the fund balance should be reclassified as being nonspendable fund balance—inventory.

Question 2-1 FR-00490

Refund Ridge Township issued General Governmental Refunding Bonds for $1,000,000 at 98 during the year ended June 30, Year 1. The entire amount of the difference between bond proceeds and face amount relates to the original issue discount. The Township would report the following balances in the indicated accounts in its Debt Service Fund financial statements at and for the year ended June 30, Year 1:

	Bonds Payable	Other Financing Sources	Other Financing Uses
1.	1,000,000	0	980,000
2.	0	20,000	1,000,000
3.	0	1,000,000	20,000
4.	0	0	0

Question 2-2   FR-00375

The County of Deutsch appropriated $45,000 in its General Fund for miscellaneous supplies for its fiscal year ended September 30, Year 1. The County found that it had paid $15,000 for miscellaneous supplies in November Year 0 and issued a $30,000 PO to a sole source vendor for miscellaneous supplies in December Year 0. By August Year 1, the County had received $20,000 related to the order but did not pay the vendor until October pending tax receipts. Appropriations do not lapse. What was the County of Deutsch's available appropriation at September 30, Year 1?

1. $0
2. $15,000
3. $10,000
4. $5,000

? Related Questions

For related questions, go to the online question bank:

➤ FR-00345

➤ FR-00360

3 Fund Balance Classifications

Governmental fund balances are classified in any one of five ways (different levels of constraint):

3.1 Nonspendable

Nonspendable fund balances represent resources that are nonspendable because they are not in spendable form (e.g., inventories or prepaid expenditures) or legally or contractually required to be maintained intact (e.g., permanent fund principal).

3.2 Restricted

Restricted fund balances represent resources whose use has been limited by such external sources as creditors (e.g., debt covenants), contributors, other governments, laws, constitutional provisions, or enabling legislation.

3.3 Committed

Committed fund balances represent resources that can only be used for specific purposes pursuant to constraints imposed by formal action of the government's highest level of decision-making authority.

3.4 Assigned

Assigned fund balances are constrained by the government's intent to be used for specific purposes but are neither restricted nor committed.

3.5 Unassigned

Unassigned fund balances is the residual classification for the general fund. This classification represents fund balance that has not been assigned to other funds and that has not been restricted, committed or assigned to specific purposes within the general fund. The general fund should be the only fund that shows a positive unassigned fund balance amount. Over-expenditure of resources in other governmental funds may, however, result in a reported negative unassigned fund balance.

Question 3-1   FR-00496

The least restrictive classification of governmental fund balances is titled:

1. Unreserved
2. Unassigned
3. Unspendable
4. Committed

---

4 Deferred Outflows and Inflows of Resources

GASB 63 requires that certain transactions that do not qualify for treatment as either assets or liabilities be accounted for and reported as deferred outflows of resources or deferred inflows of resources. A deferred outflow of resources is a consumption of net assets that is applicable to a future reporting period. Deferred outflows of resources have a positive effect on net position and are reported following assets but before liabilities. A deferred inflow of resources is an acquisition of net assets that is applicable to a future reporting period. Deferred inflows of resources have a negative effect on net position and are reported following liabilities but before equity.

4.1 Government-wide Statement of Net Position

Governments are encouraged to report net position as the difference between assets plus deferred outflows of resources and liabilities plus deferred inflows of resources.

4.2 Governmental Fund Balance Sheet

Governmental funds should present the statement of financial position in a balance sheet format that displays assets plus deferred outflows of resources equal to liabilities plus deferred inflows of resources plus fund balance.

4.3 Proprietary and Fiduciary Statement of Net Position

Proprietary funds are encouraged and fiduciary funds are required to report net position as the difference between assets plus deferred outflows of resources and liabilities plus deferred inflows of resources (similar to the government-wide statement of net position). Proprietary funds can also use a balance sheet format [(Assets + Deferred outflows of resources) = (Liabilities + Deferred inflows of resources) + Net position].

4.4 Types of Transactions Accounted for as Deferred Outflows and Inflows of Resources

4.4.1 Service Concession Arrangements

Advance payments by vendors that operate infrastructure in exchange for volume based fees are displayed as deferred inflows of resources until earned.

4.4.2 Hedge Accounting

Derivatives used as hedges to mitigate the risk of fluctuations in fair value or cash flows qualify for accounting as deferred outflows of resources and deferred inflows of resources if they are effective. Effectiveness means that changes in the value of a derivative used as a hedge offsets the fluctuations in the fair value or cash flows of the hedged item. A sample entry for the decline in value of a qualifying derivative instrument would be:

DR	Deferred outflows of resources	$XXX
CR	Derivative instrument	$XXX

This is similar to the use of other comprehensive income when recording unrealized gains and losses for a nongovernmental entity.

4.4.3 Other Deferred Outflows/Inflows of Resources

GASB 65, "Items Previously Reported as Assets and Liabilities," revises the treatment of a variety of transactions previously reported as either assets or liabilities on the statement of financial position to classification as either deferred outflows/inflows of resources or recognition as revenue or expense. Transactions addressed in the statement include:

- Refunding of debt
- Imposed non-exchange revenue transactions
- Government-mandated non-exchange transactions and voluntary non-exchange transactions
- Sales of future revenues and intra-entity transfers of future revenues
- Debt issuance costs
- Leases
- Regulated operations
- Assets associated with unavailable revenues
- Certain changes in net pension liability (GASB 68)

Question 4-1   FR-00804

A municipality that appropriately classifies a derivative as a hedge will account for an increase in the value of the derivative, which is reported as an asset, as:

1. An increase in deferred inflows of resources.
2. A decrease in deferred inflows of resources.
3. An increase in deferred outflows of resources.
4. A decrease in deferred outflows of resources.

V | Not-for-Profit Accounting and Reporting

1 Not-for-Profit Entities

Not-for-profit entities possess the following characteristics:

- Contributions of significant amounts of resources received from providers who do not expect commensurate or proportionate return.
- Operating purposes other than to provide goods or services at a profit.
- Absence of ownership interest.

The FASB has the primary responsibility of providing guidance on generally accepted accounting principles for not-for-profit entities.

2 Required Financial Statements

2.1 Basic Financial Statements

All not-for-profit entities are required to prepare three basic financial statements on the full accrual basis:

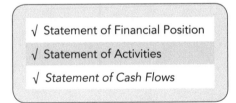

√ Statement of Financial Position

√ Statement of Activities

√ Statement of Cash Flows

2.2 Disclosure of Functional Expenses

Not-for-profit organizations are required to present disclosure of functional expenses, analyzed by object classification.

The objective of the functional expense disclosure is to present the programmatic and support expenses displayed horizontally on the statement of activities in separate columns and to analyze the expenses by object (natural classifications).

The Felix Nursing Home Inc. is a health care provider organized as a not-for-profit organization whose activities are regulated by state licensure rules. The financial information that the Felix Nursing Home Inc. is required to produce are:

	Statement of Financial Position	Statement of Activity	Statement of Cash Flows	Functional Expense Disclosure
1.	Yes	Yes	Yes	Yes
2.	Yes	Yes	Yes	No
3.	Yes	Yes	No	No
4.	Yes	Yes	No	Yes

3 Net Asset Classification

The reporting objectives of not-for-profit organizations include presentation of the net assets at the balance sheet date and the components of the change in net assets on the statement of activities for the year ending on the balance sheet date. There are two net asset classifications:

3.1 Without Donor Restrictions

Net assets free of donor restrictions on usage.

3.2 With Donor Restrictions

Only donors may restrict assets. The management or board can designate or identify assets to be used for a particular purpose. However, a designation is not a restriction. Net assets contributed with donor-imposed restrictions may be either temporary in nature (due to purpose, time, or acquisition of plant) or in perpetuity.

3.2.1 Purpose

The money must be spent as the donor stipulates (e.g., cancer research, youth education).

3.2.2 Time

The donated assets may be donor restricted until a fixed period passes (e.g., a gift of a CD that must be held until maturity and then can be spent as the organization wishes). Time restrictions may also be implied by availability; contributions receivable generally increase net assets with donor restrictions.

3.2.3 Acquisition of Plant

The donated assets are classified as net assets with donor restrictions to purchase or build long-lived assets.

3.2.4 Donor Restrictions in Perpetuity (Endowments)

Net assets contributed with restrictions, such as an endowment fund where the corpus must be retained in perpetuity and interest income can be used by the not-for-profit organization in accordance with the donor's stipulations.

Question 3-1   FR-00404

Andrew contributed $250,000 to an endowment in the name of his late father, Phillip, at Ray Private University on January 2, Year 1. The terms of the bequest require that principal be retained intact and that the earnings from the principal be used to fund the Phil Anthorpist chair for accountancy. If Ray Private University earns $15,000 during Year 1 from the donation, the college would record the following for Year 1:

1. Increases in net assets without donor restrictions of $265,000.
2. Increases in net assets with donor restrictions of $265,000.
3. Increases in net assets without donor restrictions of $250,000 and increases in net assets with donor restrictions of $15,000.
4. Increases in net assets without donor restrictions of $15,000 and increases in net assets with donor restrictions of $250,000.

? Related Questions

For related questions, go to the online question bank:

➤ FR-00344
➤ FR-00473

---

4 Statement of Cash Flows

The statement of cash flows is the same as the statement issued by commercial enterprises with a few unusual features. Either the direct or indirect method can be used. There are three categories of cash flow activities:

4.1 Operating Activities

- Include applicable agency transactions.
- Include receipts of resources without donor restrictions designated by the governing body to be used for long-lived assets.

4.2 Investing Activities

- Include proceeds from the sale of works of art or purchases of works of art.
- Include investment in equipment.
- Include proceeds from the sale of assets that were received in prior periods and whose sale proceeds were donor-restricted to investment in equipment.

4.3   Financing Activities

4.3.1   Proceeds From Donor-Restricted Contributions

■ Include cash received with donor-imposed restrictions limiting its use to purchases of long-term assets or annuity agreements.

- Disbursements of these donor-restricted contributions for either investments or the purpose for which they were intended are classified as investing activities.

4.3.2   Other Types of Financing Activities

Include receipts and disbursements associated with borrowing and receipts of dividends and interest that is donor-restricted to reinvestment.

4.4   Cash and Cash Equivalents

Donor-restricted securities that may otherwise meet the cash equivalent criteria in commercial accounting are excluded.

Question 4-1   FR-00329

Walton Farms Boys Home Inc. is a not-for-profit organization that received marketable securities from a donor with a fair value of $100,000 on July 1, Year 1. The securities were donated with the stipulation that proceeds would be used to build new dormitories. On January 8, Year 2, Walton Farms Boys Home elected to sell the securities for $110,000 and begin construction on the dormitories. On its Statement of Cash Flows for the year ended December 31, Year 2, the Walton Farms Boys Home would display cash flows from the securities transaction as:

	Operating	Investing	Financing
1.	$110,000	$0	$0
2.	$0	$110,000	$0
3.	$10,000	100,000	$0
4.	$0	$0	$110,000

---

1 Revenue and Support Recognition

Not-for-profit accounting focuses on two terms (conditional and restricted) that are often used interchangeably in conversation but have two distinct accounting meanings.

- Classification of net assets relates to presence (with) or absence (without) of donor-imposed restrictions on contributions.

- Recognition of revenue relates to the treatment of gifts or promises to give. Conditional promises are not recorded and conditional gifts received in advance of satisfying conditions are recorded as liabilities.

- Conditional is not the same as restricted.

Resource inflows in not-for-profit organizations are generally displayed in the financial statements as either revenue or other support. Revenues typically represent exchange transactions in which the not-for-profit organization earns resources in exchange for a service performed (e.g., fees). Support often represents unconditional contributions.

1.1 Cash Contributions and Unconditional Promises

Cash contributions and unconditional promises are displayed as support upon receipt or accrual.

1.2 Conditional Promises and Receipts

Cash contributions that can only be used upon meeting a condition and conditional promises to give are not recorded as revenue until the condition is met. A condition is a contingency that must be resolved, rather than a restriction that can be satisfied. Conditional contributions ("good faith deposits") are displayed as a liability titled "refundable advance." Conditional promises to give are not recorded.

1.3 Multi-year Pledges

Unconditional promises receivable over a period of years are recognized as an increase to net assets with donor restrictions since amounts have an implied time restriction. Receivables are recorded at their present value with the difference between face and present value recognized as contribution revenue over time, not interest.

1.4 Other Revenue Transactions and Issues

■ Agency transactions relate to receipts of resources over which the not-for-profit organization has no discretion or "variance power." The absence of variance power over the resources creates a liability rather than revenue.

■ Gifts-in-kind represent noncash contributions recorded as both support and an offsetting expense.

■ Exchange transactions represent the sale of goods or services in exchange for a fee. Exchange transactions are classified as revenues without donor restrictions.

■ Donations with donor restrictions for which restrictions will be satisfied within the year of receipt may be classified as donations without donor restrictions in the event that the not-for-profit organization consistently applies this policy.

Question 1-1	FR-00433

The Darberville Day Care collected $45,000 in day care fees from families during the year ended December 31, Year 1, to provide services. During the same period, the Day Care collected $30,000 from the United Way to provide ongoing funding for the Day Care's early childhood development programming and $10,000 from the Federal School Lunch Program to defray the cost of meals served to children. The Day Care's accounting policies consistently allow for the direct recording of contribution revenue with donor restrictions as contribution revenue without donor restrictions when the terms and conditions of the contributions are met in the year of donation. As a result of the above transactions, the Day Care would record revenues and support without donor restrictions of:

1. $40,000
2. $45,000
3. $75,000
4. $85,000

? Related Questions

For related questions, go to the online question bank:

➤ FR-00419

➤ FR-00479

➤ FR-00482

2 Expense Classification and Display

Expenses are defined as program or support services. Program expenses relate to the mission of the organization while support services relate to the organization's administrative, membership development and fundraising expenses. The total amount of each functional expense (the expenses by individual program or support service) is displayed on the face of the statement of activities or disclosed in the notes to the financial statement.

3 Split-Interest Agreements

Agreements such as charitable remainder trusts represent donor contributions structured to simultaneously donate assets to the not-for-profit organization and share those assets with a beneficiary. Split-interest agreements are displayed separately on the not-for-profit organization's financial statements, measured at their fair value or present value at acquisition, and classified as donor-restricted.

DR	Assets held in trust	$XXX	
CR	Liability to beneficiary		$XXX
CR	Contribution revenue (with donor restrictions)		XXX

Disbursements associated with split-interest agreements are classified as financing activities on the statement of cash flows. All expenses are classified as without donor restrictions in the statement of activities.

Question 3-1   FR-00359

On December 30, Year 1, Albert Altruistic donated $200,000 to the Carton Museum under the terms and conditions of a charitable remainder trust that guarantees Mr. Altruistic a life-time tax free annuity of $20,000 per year and bequeaths the remainder to Carton for use in their operations in furtherance of the mission of the museum. Independent actuaries have estimated that the museum's liability has a present value of $84,250. As a result of his contribution, the Carton Museum would record the following on its December 31, Year 1, financial statements:

1. An increase in net assets without donor restrictions of $200,000.
2. An increase in net assets with donor restrictions of $200,000.
3. An increase in net assets without donor restrictions of $115,750.
4. An increase in net assets with donor restrictions of $115,750.

4 Donated Services and Donated Works of Art

Contributions of services are recorded as revenue some of the time. The services must either enhance a physical asset or meet the following (**SOME**) criteria: they require **s**pecialized skills, are **o**therwise needed, and are **m**easured **e**asily. Services that meet the criteria are recorded as revenues and assets or expenses at their fair value as follows:

DR	Expense or asset	$XXX
CR	Contributions—Nonoperating revenue	$XXX

Donated works of art are not required to be recorded by the recipient if all of the following criteria are met and the capitalization policy is consistently applied:

- The item is held for *public viewing*;
- The work of art is *cared for* by the not-for-profit organization; and
- Proceeds, if the art is sold, must be used to *purchase other works* of art.

Question 4-1   FR-00374

Faith Church decided to replace its electric organ with a multiple rack pipe organ. The church purchased the organ itself for $250,000 and a congregation member stepped forward to assemble the organ and perform the necessary carpentry work for $5,000. The congregation member is a skilled craftsman who normally charges $40,000 for this work. Other congregation members stepped forward to help with general labor assistance valued at $7,000. As a result of the transaction above, Faith Church should record revenues from contributed services of:

1. $35,000
2. $40,000
3. $42,000
4. $47,000

? Related Questions

For related questions, go to the online question bank:

➤ FR-00487

5 Accounting for Marketable Securities

Investments in securities are displayed at their fair values and increases and decreases in the fair value of securities are classified as without donor restrictions in the statement of activities unless there are donor-stipulated restrictions.

Investment income (dividends and interest) are reported in the period earned in the net asset category as either with or without donor restrictions. Investment returns are reported net of any related investment expense.

5.1 Endowments

Not-for-profit organizations account for assets with donor restrictions that are perpetual in nature in endowment funds. Generally, a benefactor will donate an amount and direct that earnings and not principal be used for specific or general purposes of the not-for-profit.

An underwater endowment is a donor-restricted endowment fund for which the fair value at the reporting date is less than either the original gift amount or the amount required to be maintained by the donor or by law.

Underwater endowment funds will report accumulated losses together with the endowment fund in net assets with donor restrictions.

Question 5-1   FR-00493

During the year ended June 30, Year 0, the Aberdeen Care Clinic, a not-for-profit organization, received an endowment for $2,300,000. The endowment is to remain intact with income and appreciation from the investment of the endowment to be used in support of a research program to assist the elderly. By June 30, Year 2, the endowment had accumulated $110,000 in gains. On July 1, Year 2, the company liquidated 65% of the cumulative appreciation of the endowment for use in the research program. During the year ended June 30, Year 3, the endowment earned $30,000, which it spent on the research program but, at year end, suffered market losses that reduced the total value of the investment below its initially recorded value to $2,250,000. The amounts reported as investment losses by net asset category for the year ended June 30, Year 3, would be:

	Without Donor Restrictions	With Donor Restrictions
1.	$0	($88,500)
2.	$0	($50,000)
3.	($88,500)	$0
4.	($50,000)	($38,500)

? Related Questions

For related questions, go to the online question bank:

➤ FR-00445

➤ FR-00491

6 Pass-Through Contributions to Not-for-Profit Beneficiary

FASB ASC 958-605 defines the manner in which separate organizations that either receive or benefit from contributions account for the donations. Principles are largely driven by application of the concept of variance power. The pronouncement considers the common situation of a foundation, the recipient, which raises money for another not-for-profit organization, the beneficiary (e.g., a university). The statement also considers instances where the recipient is a federated or community-wide organization, such as the United Way, and the beneficiary is a smaller not-for-profit organization.

6.1 General Rule: Recipient (e.g., a Foundation)

6.1.1 Without Variance Power

If a recipient organization receives donations on behalf of another not-for-profit and does not have any discretion with regard to the use of the contribution, the donation is recorded as a liability.

DR	Asset	$XXX	
CR	Refundable advance liability		$XXX

6.1.2 With Variance Power

If a recipient organization receives donations on behalf of another not-for-profit and has discretion regarding the use of the contribution, the donation is recorded as revenue.

DR	Asset	$XXX	
CR	Revenue		$XXX

6.2 General Rule: Beneficiary (e.g., a University)

6.2.1 Without Variance Power

If a recipient organization receives donations on behalf of another not-for-profit and does not have any discretion with regard to the use of the contribution, the donation is recorded as revenue on the beneficiary's books.

DR	Receivable	$XXX	
CR	Contribution revenue		$XXX

6.2.2 With Variance Power

If a recipient organization receives donations on behalf of another not-for-profit and has discretion with regard to the use of the contribution, the donation is generally not recorded on the beneficiary's books unless a financial relationship exists.

6.3   Financially Interrelated Recipients and Beneficiaries

Recipients and beneficiaries are deemed to be interrelated if one organization has the ability to influence the decisions of the other and one organization has an ongoing interest in the other. Beneficiaries recognize an interest in the net assets of the recipient when they are financially interrelated with the recipient. The interest is adjusted for the beneficiary's share of the change.

DR	Interest in net assets	$XXX
CR	Change in interest in recipient net assets	$XXX

Beneficiaries recognize a beneficial interest in an unconditional right to receive specified cash flows from pools of assets. Changes in value are recorded on the beneficiary's books as follows:

DR	Beneficial interest	$XXX
CR	Contribution revenue	$XXX

Question 6-1   FR-00456

The Cox Foundation for the Performing Arts was established to support and coordinate the fundraising appeals of the Little Tutu Dance Troupe and the Expressive Community Theater. The bylaws require that the governing body of the foundation include equal representation from the dance troupe and the theater consisting of two thirds of the foundation's board and that the foundation distribute current period collections in the subsequent year. Noted philanthropist L.L. Thayer contributes $250,000 to the foundation on July 1, Year 1, and states in his bequest that the entire amount of the contribution is meant to support the operations of the dance troupe. On its December 31, Year 1, financial statements, the Little Tutu Dance Troupe should:

1. Only disclose the gift to the foundation.

2. Record a $250,000 increase in net assets without donor restrictions and change in interest in the net assets of the foundation.

3. Record a $250,000 increase in net assets with donor restrictions and change in interest in the net assets of the foundation.

4. Record $250,000 in contribution revenue without donor restrictions.

? Related Questions

For related questions, go to the online question bank:

➤ FR-00389

➤ FR-00485

7 Industry Applications

7.1 Health Care Organization Revenue Recognition

Patient service revenue should be accounted for on the accrual basis at usual and customary fees, even if the full amount is not expected to be collected. Although patient service revenue is accounted for on a gross basis, deductions are made from gross revenue for reporting purposes to display revenues net. Charity care, the value of services that a health care organization gives away, is not displayed in the financial statements.

Bad debt expense is recorded when the allowance is established after an evaluation of a patient's ability to pay. Otherwise, bad debts are recorded as a deduction from revenue.

7.2 University and Institutions of Higher Learning Revenue Recognition

Student tuition and fees should be reported at gross amount. Scholarships, tuition waivers, and similar reductions are considered either expenses or a separately displayed allowance reducing revenue.

Question 7-1   FR-00489

Healthy Care Hospital Inc., a private not-for-profit organization, accumulated the following patient service revenue transactions in their records during the June 30, Year 1, fiscal year:

Gross patient fees for all services provided at usual and customary rates	$5,000,000
Contractual allowances for third party payments	800,000
Bad debts written off after an assessment of patient's ability to pay	350,000
Current year bad debt allowance	300,000
Charity care	1,300,000

The amount reported as net patient service revenue for Healthy Care Hospital Inc. for the year ended June 30, Year 1, would be:

1. $5,000,000
2. $4,200,000
3. $2,900,000
4. $2,850,000

Question 7-2
FR-00466

Nadaf University received $4,000,000 in tuition revenue for the year ended December 31, Year 1. In addition to the tuition received, the university offered $500,000 in scholarships but had to refund $200,000 for canceled classes. For the year ended December 31, Year 1, Nadaf would record gross revenue for tuition of:

1. $3,800,000
2. $4,000,000
3. $4,300,000
4. $4,500,000

Financial Final Review

Class Question Explanations

Financial Final Review

Financial I

Topic A

QUESTION 1-1

FR-00365

Choice "4" is correct.

Income from continuing operations should be adjusted for all of the items. The $100,000 in additional depreciation needs to be deducted from income from continuing operations. The $200,000 loss from the strike by the supplier's employees and the $500,000 flood loss should be included in income from continuing operations. The inventory overstatement in the prior year results in a cost of goods sold overstatement in the current year, so $300,000 should be added back to income from continuing operations.

Allison Corporations adjusted income from continuing operations is calculated as follows:

Unadjusted income from continuing operations	$1,000,000
Less: Additional depreciation	(100,000)
Less: Loss from strike	(200,000)
Plus: Adjustment to COGS for inventory misstatement	300,000
Less: Loss from flood	(500,000)
Adjusted income from continuing operations	$ 500,000

QUESTION 2-1

FR-00335

Choice "2" is correct.

Other comprehensive can be remembered by the **PUFER** mnemonic.

Pension adjustments
Unrealized gains and losses on available-for-sale debt securities
Foreign currency items
Effective portion of cash flow hedge
Revaluation surplus (IFRS only)

The only item that fits is the unrealized gain on the available-for-sale debt security. The unrealized gain on the trading debt security is included in income. Dividends are not included in income or other comprehensive income (but as an adjustment to retained earnings). The other items in the list are normal income statement items and thus are not part of other comprehensive income.

QUESTION 3-1

FR-00850

Choice "1" is correct.

Disclosure of current vulnerabilities to certain concentrations is a requirement in the notes to the financial statements. Receiving over half of its grant funding from one agency represents a significant concentration of business from a single source, and users of the financial statements will need this information in order to properly evaluate the university. If the funding source went away, the university would have a significant shortfall to overcome and may have difficulty fulfilling its financial obligations (paying faculty and staff, paying interest to bondholders, etc.) in the absence of this funding.

Choice "2" is incorrect. This disclosure does not necessarily indicate the need for other funding sources; it merely discloses the most significant funding source.

Choice "3" is incorrect. Although the disclosure would seem to indicate that there is a strong relationship between the government and the university, that is not specifically the intent of the disclosure.

Choice "4" is incorrect. The disclosure is not likely to quantify the impact on future revenue if this funding source went away.

Financial I

Topic B

QUESTION 2-1 FR-00323

Choice "3" is correct.

Depreciation is a part of operating activities and is added back since it was subtracted to produce net income in the first place. This question is a question on the SCF although it does not look like the question is phrased in exactly that manner.

Looking at the facts, an accumulated depreciation account analysis format can be used. The beginning and ending balances are available. The format is as follows:

Beginning balance	$600,000
Add: depreciation charged to operations	?
Subtract: A/D on equipment sold	?
Ending balance	$800,000

To obtain the accumulated depreciation of the property sold, subtract the $40,000 carrying amount from the $50,000 original cost, and the difference is the accumulated depreciation that was eliminated when the equipment was sold.

Beginning balance	$600,000
Add: depreciation charged to operations	?
Subtract: A/D on equipment sold	(10,000)
Ending balance	$800,000

In this account analysis format, the depreciation charged to operations is $210,000.

Or another way to look at it:

Accumulated Depreciation

$600,000	given
10,000	asset sold
590,000	*subtotal*
210,000	to balance account
$800,000	given

They said depreciation charged to operations in this question to differentiate it from any depreciation that might have been charged to work-in-progress and might have become a part of inventory cost.

QUESTION 3-1

Choice "2" is correct.

In order to compute the cash paid to suppliers, the Black Knights Company must determine how much inventory was purchased and the change in accounts payable. AP increases with purchases and decreases with payments. Thus:

Purchases	=	COGS + Change in inventory
	=	$450,000 + ($160,000) = $290,000

However, since AP decreased, The Black Knights Company paid more cash to suppliers than just the amount for purchases:

Cash paid	=	Purchases − Change in AP
	=	$290,000 − ($40,000) = $330,000

Choice "1" is incorrect. The decrease in AP is added to purchases (subtraction of a negative number). Recall that the decrease in AP means The Black Knights Company paid more cash to suppliers than just the amount for purchases.

Choice "3" is incorrect. The decrease in inventory is subtracted from COGS to determine purchases. (Remember, COGS = beginning inventory + purchases − ending inventory; beginning inventory − ending inventory = net change in inventory.)

Choice "4" is incorrect. The decrease in AP is added to purchases (subtraction of a negative number). Recall that the decrease in AP means The Black Knights Company paid more cash to suppliers than just the amount for purchases. In addition, the decrease in inventory is subtracted from COGS to determine purchases. (Remember, COGS = beginning inventory + purchases − ending inventory; beginning inventory − ending inventory = net change in inventory.)

QUESTION 4-1

Choice "4" is correct.

Net cash used in investing activities is calculated as follows:

Cash paid to purchase fixed assets	$(50,000)
Cash proceeds from the sale of fixed assets	10,000
Net cash used in investing activities	$(40,000)

The depreciation adjustment to the operating section of Cool Tool's statement of cash flows is calculated as follows:

Accumulated depreciation, Year 10	$41,000	
− Sale of fixed assets	(12,000)	= $18,000 cost − $6,000 BV
+ Depreciation expense	24,000	
Accumulated depreciation, Year 11	$53,000	

Choice "1" is incorrect. This answer incorrectly uses the cost of the fixed assets sold rather than the cash received from the sale to determine the net cash used in investing activities. This answer also incorrectly uses the amount of accumulated depreciation related to the asset sold as the depreciation expense for the period.

Choice "2" is incorrect. This answer incorrectly uses the cost of the fixed assets sold rather than the cash received from the sale to determine the net cash used in investing activities.

Choice "3" is incorrect. This answer incorrectly uses the amount of accumulated depreciation related to the asset sold as the depreciation expense for the period.

Financial I

QUESTION 5-1   FR-00308

Choice "1" is correct.

In this question, they want to know the net cash used in financing activities. Normally when they ask this kind of question, they provide a list of amounts, some of which are financing activities and some of which are not.

The first amount on the list is a payment for retirement of the company's long-term bonds. The payment certainly is cash used in financing, so that is $750,000 to start with. Dropping down to the last transaction, the proceeds from the sale of the treasury stock of $95,000 is financing, a source of cash and thus a positive use. That gives a total of $655,000 ($750,000 − $95,000) cash used. Moving up to the third transaction, conversion of stock of whatever kind into common stock is a non-cash item that only has to be disclosed.

$655,000 cannot be the answer since it is not one of the selections. In the second transaction, cash dividends of $62,000 were paid. That payment is certainly cash used in financing; once that amount is added to the $655,000, the total cash used is $717,000 ($655,000 + $62,000), which is a selection.

QUESTION 7-1   FR-00383

Choice "4" is correct.

The U.S. Treasury bill is considered to be a cash equivalent item so purchasing the T-bill merely changes the form of cash held, it does not change the cash position of the entity. Thus, the purchase is not reported on the statement of cash flows.

QUESTION 9-1   FR-00463

Choice "2" is correct.

A supplemental disclosure of the reconciliation of net income to net cash provided by operating activities is only required when the *direct* method is used under U.S. GAAP. It is not required when the indirect method is used as the operating activities section of the statement of cash flows prepared under the indirect method shows this reconciliation.

Choice "1" is incorrect. A supplemental disclosure of income taxes paid is required when the indirect method is used.

Choice "3" is incorrect. A supplemental disclosure of interest paid is required when the indirect method is used.

Choice "4" is incorrect. A supplemental disclosure of non-cash investing and financing activities is required under both the direct and indirect methods.

Topic C

QUESTION 3-1   FR-00846

Choice "1" is correct.

The market value of the outstanding common shares for Brevard is equal to $240 million ($40 x 6 million shares), which makes it an accelerated filer. Accelerated filers have 75 days after the fiscal year-end to file their annual report (10-K) and 40 days after the fiscal quarter ends to file their quarterly report (10-Q).

Choice "2" is incorrect. 75 days for the annual report is correct, but 45 days only applies to non-accelerated filers (any company with a market capitalization less than $75 million).

Choice "3" is incorrect. 60 days is the deadline for large accelerated filers (market capitalization of $700 million or more) for the 10-K report.

Choice "4" is incorrect. Both filing deadlines (60 days for the 10-K and 45 days for the 10-Q) are incorrect.

Financial I

QUESTION 6-1

Choice "4" is correct.

Under Regulation S-X, an entity's audited financial statements filed with the SEC should include balance sheets for the *two* most recent fiscal years and the statements of income, changes in owners' equity, and cash flows for the three fiscal years preceding the date of the most recent audited balance sheet.

Topic D

QUESTION 2-1

Choice "2" is correct.

$1.78 and $1.75 EPS Year 11 and Year 10.

	Year 11	Year 10
Net income	$ 410,000	$ 350,000
Weighted Avg. Shares	÷ 230,000	÷ 200,000
EPS	$ 1.78	$ 1.75

	Shares O/S		Mo's O/S		Stock Split	Total
Jan. 1 to April 1	100,000	×	3	×	2	600,000
April 1 to July 1	120,000	×	3	×	2	720,000
July 1 to Dec. 31	240,000	×	6	×	1	1,440,000
			12			2,760,000

Weighted shares O/S (2,760,000 ÷ 12) = 230,000

It is important to note that stock splits (and stock dividends) are applied retroactively to all prior periods presented.

QUESTION 3-1

Choice "2" is correct.

With the same data as in the previous question, the convertible preferred stock and convertible bonds now have to be taken into account. For both types of securities, the if-converted method will be used.

For the convertible preferred stock, the dividends that were paid are assumed not to have been paid (since the convertible preferred stock was assumed to have been converted). They are not "added back" but they are not subtracted like they were in the basic EPS computation. For the convertible bonds, the interest that really was paid on the bonds is assumed not to have been paid (since the convertible bonds were assumed to have been converted). After-tax interest on the bonds of $140,000 ($2,000,000 × 0.10 × 0.70) is "added back" to the numerator. The numerator is thus $1,140,000 ($1,000,000 + $140,000).

The denominator is the 200,000 weighted average number of shares plus the 40,000 shares from the assumed conversion of the convertible preferred stock plus 100,000 shares from the assumed conversion of the convertible bonds ($2,000,000 / $1,000 × 50), for a total of 340,000 shares. $1,140,000 / 340,000 = $3.35

Financial I

Topic E

QUESTION 2-1

FR-00318

Choice "4" is correct.

The first thing that should come to mind for a segment question is the 10% rule. But the question is 10% of what? 10% of revenue for one thing, but 10% of what revenue? The rule is combined revenue from both sales to outsiders and intersegment sales, which in this question is a total of $88,000. 10% of that amount is $8,800. The overall corporate headquarters is ignored.

QUESTION 2-2

FR-00437

Choice "4" is correct.

An operating segment is considered to be a reportable segment if it accounts for at least 10 percent of total revenues (external and intercompany) or total profits/losses or total assets. In this problem, 10 percent of total revenues is $132,500, so Ice and Steam qualify as reportable segments based on total revenues; 10 percent of total profits is $63,500, so Rain, Ice, and Steam qualify based on total profits; and 10 percent of total assets is $209,000, so Rain, Snow, Ice, and Steam qualify based on total assets. Hail is the only operating segment that does not qualify as a reportable segment based on the 10 percent size tests. Note that Rain, Snow, Ice, and Steam together account for $1,230,000 or 93 percent of total outside sales, which means that Water Works is reporting sufficient segment information based on the rule that reportable combined outside sales must be at least 75 percent of total outside sales.

Choices "1", "2", and "3" are incorrect, based on the above explanation.

Financial II

Topic A

QUESTION 1-1 FR-00362

Choice "3" is correct.

The general format of an account analysis is beginning, add, subtract, ending.

They provided the beginning and ending balances. They also provided sales; when something is sold on account, accounts receivable is increased so sales is an add in the account analysis format.

They also provided the amount of the bad debt write-off for the year; when an account is written off, accounts receivable is decreased so the write-off is a subtract. Cash collections is another subtract, and that is what they are asking for.

Beginning balance	$150,000	
Plus: Sales	600,000	
Less: Collections	(535,000)	(originally a plug)
Less: Write-off of accounts	(40,000)	
Ending balance	$175,000	

QUESTION 1-2 FR-00448

Choice "1" is correct.

Using the percentage of ending AR method, Red Rock's December 31, Year 3, allowance for doubtful accounts should be $46,100 ($922,000 x 5%). Bad debt expense can be determined using the company's beginning and ending allowance balances and the write-off and collection activity for the year:

	Beginning Allowance	$45,000
-	Write-offs	(35,000)
+	Recoveries	18,000
+	**Bad debt expense**	**18,100**
	Ending Allowance	$46,100

Choice "2" is incorrect. This is the amount of write-offs in Year 2. Under the allowance method, write-offs are not charged to bad debt expense, but are written-off against the allowance for doubtful accounts.

Choice "3" is incorrect. This is the allowance for doubtful accounts on 12/31/Y3. As is shown in the calculation above, the ending allowance balance is not equal to Red Rock's bad debt expense in Year 3.

Choice "4" is incorrect. This would be the Year 3 bad debt expense if Red Rock calculated bad debt expense using the percentage of credit sales approach, assuming the 5% of credit sales are expected to be uncollectible ($3,000,000 x 5% = $150,000).

QUESTION 3-1 FR-00377

Choice "2" is correct.

The receivables were sold without recourse, with no control being retained by Stanberry. The transfer thus meets the requirements of an asset sale, and a gain or a loss should be recognized. The loss is realized, and the difference is not a receivable from Cork Company.

Financial II

Topic B

QUESTION 1-1   FR-00328

Choice "4" is correct.

The first transaction is $28,000 of tools included in the physical inventory count and still sitting on the loading dock at 5:00 PM on December 31. Because the tools have not yet left the loading dock, the sale has not yet occurred and the tools should have been counted in the physical inventory count. They were counted so there is no adjustment for the first transaction.

The second transaction is $50,000 of inventory coming the other way. The goods were in transit from a vendor and were shipped FOB shipping point from that vendor. Because they were shipped by December 31, they should have been included in Mixon's inventory but were not since they were not there to be counted. The inventory of $1,750,000 should be increased to $1,800,000 ($1,750,000 + $50,000).

The accounts payable and sales information is irrelevant.

QUESTION 2-1   FR-00373

Choice "1" is correct.

Under the lower of cost or market, market starts at the $20 replacement cost. It is then limited to a ceiling and a floor. The ceiling is the selling price less cost of completion and/or selling. In this case, the selling price is $30, and the costs of completion are $2; the ceiling is thus $28 ($30 − $2). No problem exists here because the $20 replacement cost is already under the ceiling.

The floor is the ceiling less the normal profit margin. The ceiling is $28, and the normal profit margin is $7; the floor is thus $21 ($28 − $7). Because the market cannot be lower than the floor, it is $21.

The lower of the cost ($26) and the market ($21) is $21.

Financial II

QUESTION 3-1

FR-00432

Choice "4" is correct.

Under the FIFO method, the first units purchased are the first units sold. In this problem, there are 750 units available for sale (150 + 100 + 200 + 300) and 500 units sold, leaving 250 units of ending inventory. This ending inventory must come from the last purchase of 300 units at $500/unit, so the cost of ending inventory is 250 units x $500/unit = $125,000.

Choice "1" is incorrect. This answer incorrectly calculates the cost of ending inventory using the $400/unit cost from the items in beginning inventory.

Choice "2" is incorrect. This is the cost of ending inventory using the LIFO method. Under the LIFO method, the last units purchased are the first units sold. In this problem, there are 750 units available for sale (150 + 100 + 200 + 300) and 500 units sold, leaving 250 units of ending inventory. This ending inventory must come from the 150 units on hand at $400/unit plus first purchase of 100 units at $440/unit, so the cost of ending inventory is (150 units x $400/unit) + (100 units x $440/unit) = $104,000.

Choice "3" is incorrect. This is the cost of ending inventory using the weighted average method. Under the weighted average method, both the cost of goods sold and the cost of ending inventory are determined using the weighted average cost per unit, calculated as follows:

> Cost of goods available for sale / Number of units available for sale = [(150 x $400) + (100 x $440) + (200 x $460) + (300 x $500)] / (150 + 100 + 200 + 300) = $346,000 / 750 = $461.33

In this problem, there are 750 units available for sale (150 + 100 + 200 + 300) and 500 units sold, leaving 250 units of ending inventory. Therefore, the cost of ending inventory under the weighted-average method is $115,333 ($461.33 x 250), which is closest to $115,000.

QUESTION 3-2

FR-00358

Choice "2" is correct.

The first thing to account for is the physical units. There were 150 units in beginning inventory, 600 units purchased (100 + 200 + 300), and 500 units sold. Ending inventory was thus 250 units.

Using the LIFO method, the 250 units in the ending inventory would be assumed to be the earliest units, in this case the 150 units in the beginning inventory and 100 units from the first purchase. Ending inventory cost would thus be $104,000 (150 × $400 + 100 × $440).

Financial II

QUESTION 3-3

FR-00444

Choice "3" is correct.

Under the weighted average method, both the cost of goods sold and the cost of ending inventory are determined using the weighted average cost per unit, calculated as follows:

Cost of goods available for sale / Number of units available for sale = [(150 x $400) + (100 x $440) + (200 x $460) + (300 x $500)] / (150 + 100 + 200 + 300) = $346,000 / 750 = $461.33

In this problem, there are 750 units available for sale (150 + 100 + 200 + 300) and 500 units sold, leaving 250 units of ending inventory. Therefore, the cost of ending inventory is $115,333 ($461.33 x 250), which is closest to $115,000.

Choice "1" is incorrect. This answer incorrectly calculates the cost of ending inventory using the $400/unit cost from the items in beginning inventory.

Choice "2" is incorrect. This is the cost of ending inventory using the LIFO method. Under the LIFO method, the last units purchased are the first units sold. In this problem, there are 750 units available for sale (150 + 100 + 200 + 300) and 500 units sold, leaving 250 units of ending inventory. This ending inventory must come from the 150 units on hand at $400/unit plus first purchase of 100 units at $440/unit, so the cost of ending inventory is (150 units x $400/unit) + (100 units x $440/unit) = $104,000.

Choice "4" is incorrect. This is the cost of ending inventory using the FIFO method. Under the FIFO method, the first units purchased are the first units sold. In this problem, there are 750 units available for sale (150 + 100 + 200 + 300) and 500 units sold, leaving 250 units of ending inventory. This ending inventory must come from the last purchase of 300 units at $500/unit, so the cost of ending inventory is 250 units x $500/unit = $125,000.

Topic C

QUESTION 2-1

FR-00406

Choice "2" is correct.

The cost of the land includes all purchase related costs plus any costs incurred to get the land ready for use:

	Purchase price	$750,000
+	Legal fees	32,000
+	Title insurance	15,000
+	Timber clearing costs	18,000
−	Lumber sale proceeds	(7,000)
	Cost of land	$808,000

The cost of land does not include the excavation costs for the office building, which will be included in the total cost of the building.

Choice "1" is incorrect. This answer incorrectly excludes the timber clearing costs and the lumber sale proceeds from the calculation of the cost of the land.

Choice "3" is incorrect. This answer incorrectly excludes the lumber sale proceeds from the calculation of the cost of the land.

Choice "4" is incorrect. This answer incorrectly includes the excavation costs for the office building. These costs should be included in the total cost of the building.

Financial II

QUESTION 3-1 FR-00421

Choice "3" is correct.

In Year 1, Bluebird's interest payments on the construction borrowing total $900,000 ($10 million × 9%). Of the interest paid, Bluebird would capitalize interest related to the construction of the office building as follows:

Capitalized interest = Weighted average accumulated construction expenditures × Interest rate on construction debt = $3,750,000 × 9% = $337,500

Therefore, interest expense of $562,500 would be reported on the Year 1 income statement, calculated as the difference between the total interest payments and the capitalized interest ($900,000 − 337,500 = $562,500).

Choice "1" is incorrect. This is the interest that would be capitalized and added to the total cost of the office building. See the calculation in the explanation above.

Choice "2" is incorrect. This answer is not supported by the facts in this question.

Choice "4" is incorrect. This is the total interest paid in Year 1 on Bluebird Inc.'s construction debt. Only a portion of this amount is reported as interest expense on the income statement, as calculated above.

QUESTION 4-1 FR-00376

Choice "3" is correct.

Note that the question could have just as easily asked for depreciation expense or for carrying amount (book value).

In this question, they are asking about depreciation after a change in accounting estimate. The change in accounting estimate is a change in the depreciation life of a machine and a change in the salvage value.

The machine was originally purchased on January 1, Year 1 for $250,000. With a salvage value of $50,000 and a useful life of 10 years, depreciation for Year 1 was $20,000. The carrying amount at 12/31/Y1 was thus $230,000.

Depreciation for Year 2 was another $20,000, and the carrying amount at 12/31/Y2 was $210,000. Accumulated depreciation at that date was $40,000.

During Year 3, the change in accounting estimate occurred. The useful life was reduced from 10 years to 5 years (3 more years at 12/31/Y2) and the salvage value was reduced from $50,000 to $0. The net result was that the full $210,000 remaining would be depreciated over the remaining 3 years at $70,000 per year. Accumulated depreciation at December 31, Year 3 would thus be $110,000 ($40,000 + $70,000).

Financial Final Review

Financial II

Topic D

QUESTION 1-1   FR-00391

Choice "4" is correct.

On this transaction, since the exchange has commercial substance, Bizzell will recognize a gain on the exchange. Gains and losses in exchanges having commercial substance are computed as the difference between the fair value and the book value of the asset given up. The fair value of the asset given up (the new land) was $500,000. The book value of the asset given up (the old land) was $350,000. The gain was thus $150,000.

The Journal Entry is as follows:

DR	New land	$450,000*	
DR	Cash	50,000	
CR	Old land		$350,000
CR	Gain on exchange		150,000**

* Pate gave and Bizzell received
** $150,000 = $500,000 − $350,000

The asset will be recorded on Bizzell's books at $450,000, its fair value.

For Pate, the fair value of the asset given up (the new land) was $450,000. The book value of the asset given up was $320,000 (the old land). The gain was thus $130,000. The Journal Entry is as follows:

DR	New land	$500,000*	
CR	Cash		$ 50,000
CR	Old land		320,000
CR	Gain on exchange		130,000**

* Bizzell gave and Pate received
** $130,000 = $450,000 − $320,000

If the exchange had lacked commercial substance, the Journal Entry for Bizzell would have been as follows:

DR	New land	$315,000	
DR	Cash	50,000	
CR	Old land		$350,000
CR	Gain on exchange		15,000

Because Bizzell received cash (boot), Bizzell would record a gain in proportion to the cash received:

$$(500,000 - 350,000) \times \frac{50}{500} = \$15,000$$

Financial II

The Journal Entry for Pate would have been as follows:

DR	New land	$370,000*	
CR	Cash		$50,000
CR	Old land		320,000

* Bizzell gave and Pate got

The basis of the new land would have been $320,000 for an exchange that lacked commercial substance. However, it was increased to take the cash paid into account. Note that because boot was paid by Pate, Pate does not recognize a gain on the transaction.

QUESTION 2-1   FR-00458

Choice "3" is correct.

Statements II and III are both correct. Statement I is incorrect because a fair value approach is used to record an exchange that has commercial substance. If an exchange lacks commercial substance, then a book value approach is used. Statement IV is incorrect because the gain or loss is calculated by comparing the book value and the fair value of the asset given.

Topic E

QUESTION 1-1   FR-00339

Choice "1" is correct.

$55,000 unrealized holding gain on trading debt securities reported in Year 2 income statement:

Trading Portfolio	Fair Value
12/31/Y2	$155,000
12/31/Y1	(100,000)
Unrealized gain, reflected in income	$ 55,000

Rule: Unrealized gains and losses are reported as follows: trading debt securities-reported at fair value with unrealized gains and losses included in earnings (along with "realized" gains and losses, if any).

Available-for-sale debt securities-reported at fair value with unrealized gains and losses reported as a separate component of other comprehensive income until realized.

Financial II

Choice "1" is correct.

The unrealized gain to be recorded on MNE's Year 2 statement of comprehensive income is calculated as follows:

Sale of Alpha Corp. debt	(3,000)	Write-off unrealized gain (see JE)
Unrealized gain—Beta Corp.	8,000	($38,000 – 30,000)
Unrealized loss—Omega Corp.	(3,000)	($24,000 – 27,000)
Net change in AFS securities	2,000	

JE to record sale of investment in Alpha Corp.:

DR	Cash	$57,000	
DR	Unrealized gain—OCI	3,000	
CR	Investment in Alpha Corp. debt		$53,000
CR	Realized gain		7,000

Choice "2" is incorrect. This is the unrealized gain on the Alpha Corp. debt, which is written off in Year 2 when the security is sold.

Choice "3" is incorrect. This is total accumulated other comprehensive income to be reported on the balance sheet related to the available-for-sale debt securities, not the current period unrealized gain on available-for-sale debt securities to be reported on the statement of comprehensive income.

Choice "4" is incorrect. This is the unrealized gain to be reported in Year 2 on the Beta Corp. debt, not the total unrealized gain on all available-for-sale debt securities in Year 2.

Choice "3" is correct.

The accumulated other comprehensive income to be reported on MNE's Year 2 balance sheet can be calculated as follows:

	Accumulated OCI 12/31/Y1	Year 2 Unrealized Gain/Loss	Adjustment for Sale	Accumulated OCI 12/31/Y2
Alpha Corp.	$3,000	$ --	$(3,000)	$ --
Beta Corp.	(5,000)	8,000		3,000
Omega Corp.	6,000	(3,000)		3,000
	$4,000			$6,000

Choice "1" is incorrect. This is the current period unrealized gain on available-for-sale debt securities to be reported on the statement of comprehensive income.

Choice "2" is incorrect. This is the unrealized gain on the Alpha Corp. debt, which is written off in Year 2 when the security is sold.

Choice "4" is incorrect. This is the unrealized gain to be reported in Year 2 on the Beta Corp. debt, not the total accumulated OCI related to these securities.

QUESTION 3-1

FR-00438

Choice "2" is correct.

Red Crown will account for its investment in Red Hand using the equity method, as ownership of at least 20 percent of the voting common stock of a company generally implies that the investor can exercise significant influence over the investee. Under the equity method, Red Crown will report its share of the earnings of Red Hand on its Year 1 income statement:

Red Hand net income x Ownership % = $300,000 x 25% = $75,000

Red Crown will account for its investment in Red Leaf using the fair value method, as ownership of any percentage of nonvoting stock generally does not allow the investor to exercise significant influence or control over the investee. Under the fair value method, Red Crown will report its share of Red Leaf's Year 1 dividends on its Year 1 income statement:

Red Leaf preferred dividends x Ownership % = $200,000 x 40% = $80,000

Therefore, the total income from these two investments on Red Crown's Year 1 income statement will be $155,000 ($75,000 + 80,000).

Choice "1" is incorrect. This answer incorrectly accounts for both the Red Hand and Red Leaf investments using the fair value method. As described above, the Red Hand investment should be accounted for using the equity method.

Choice "3" is incorrect. This answer incorrectly accounts for the Red Hand investment using the fair value method and the Red Leaf investment using the equity method. As described above, the Red Hand investment should be accounted for using the equity method and the Red Leaf investment should be accounted for using the fair value method.

Choice "4" is incorrect. This answer incorrectly accounts for both the Red Hand and Red Leaf investments using the equity method. As described above, the Red Leaf investment should be accounted for using the fair value method.

Financial II

Topic F

QUESTION 1-1   FR-00436

Choice "4" is correct.

Under U.S. GAAP, the $900,000 spent to develop the product is considered research and development and must be expensed when incurred. However, the legal and other patent registration fees can be capitalized. Therefore, when the patent is granted on June 30, Year 1, the company will record an intangible asset in the amount of $20,000 which will be amortized over 10 years (the lesser of the patent's legal and economic lives). In Year 1, patent amortization will total $1,000 ($20,000/10 × 6/12), resulting in a 12/31/Y1 net book value of $19,000 ($20,000 cost – $1,000 amortization).

When the legal fees related to the successful defense of the patent are recorded on January 1, Year 2, they will be capitalized and added to the book value of the patent:

Beginning book value	$19,000
Legal fees related to successful defense	76,000
	$95,000

This amount will then be amortized over the remaining 9.5 year life of the patent on a straight line basis:

$95,000 / 9.5 years = $10,000

Choice "1" is incorrect. This is the amount of amortization recorded in Year 1.

Choice "2" is incorrect. This is the amount of amortization that would have been recorded in Year 1 if the patent had been granted on January 1.

Choice "3" is incorrect. This is the amount of amortization that would be recorded in Year 2 if the patent were amortized over 10 years, rather than 9.5 years. Ten years cannot be used as the amortization period because only 9.5 years of the patent's economic life is remaining on 1/1/Y2.

QUESTION 1-2   FR-00347

Choice "2" is correct.

Two intangible assets were acquired at the beginning of the year. The first has a finite life and thus should be amortized; the second has an indefinite life and cannot be amortized. The second asset looks like it might be impaired, but they did not ask for the impairment loss.

The acquisition cost of the first intangible asset was $5,000,000. That cost is amortized over the life of 50 years, for an annual amortization of $100,000.

Topic G

QUESTION 2-1

FR-00766

Choice "4" is correct.

Under U.S. GAAP, impairment analysis begins with a test for recoverability in which the net carrying value of the asset is compared to the undiscounted cash flows expected from the asset. If the net carrying value exceeds the undiscounted cash flows, then an impairment loss is recorded equal to the difference between the carrying value and fair value of the asset. In this problem, the carrying value of $750,000 exceeds the undiscounted future cash flows of $740,000, so an impairment loss of $50,000 ($700,000 fair value – $750,000 net carrying value) will be reported on the income statement.

Choice "1" is incorrect. The asset's carrying value of $750,000 exceeds the undiscounted future cash flows of $740,000, so an impairment loss of $50,000 ($700,000 fair value – $750,000 net carrying value) must be recognized on the income statement.

Choice "2" is incorrect. The impairment loss is equal to the difference between the fair value and carrying value of the asset, not the difference between the carrying value of the asset and the undiscounted future cash flows expected from the asset.

Choice "3" is incorrect. The impairment loss is not equal to the difference between the fair value of the asset and the undiscounted future cash flows expected from the asset.

QUESTION 2-2

FR-00767

Choice "3" is correct.

Under IFRS, an impairment loss is recorded for the excess of the carrying value of an intangible asset over its recoverable amount. The recoverable amount is the greater of the asset's fair value less costs to sell and the asset's value in use (present value of future cash flows). In this problem, the value in use of $710,000 exceeds the fair value less costs to sell of $700,000 and an impairment loss of $40,000 must be reported on the income statement:

Impairment loss = $710,000 recoverable amount – $750,000 carrying value = $(40,000)

Choice "1" is incorrect. An impairment loss must be recorded under IFRS because the carrying value of the trademark exceeds the trademark's recoverable amount.

Choice "2" is incorrect. The impairment loss is not equal to the difference between the fair value less costs to sell and the present value of the future cash flows expected from the trademark.

Choice "4" is incorrect. The trademark's $710,000 value in use exceeds the $700,000 fair value less costs to sell, so the value in use is the trademark's recoverable amount and is used to calculate an impairment loss of $40,000.

Financial II

QUESTION 3-1

Choice "3" is correct.

Under U.S. GAAP, goodwill impairment exists because the $890,000 fair value of the reporting unit is less than its $950,000 carrying value of the reporting unit. After allocating $840,000 of the fair value of the reporting unit to its assets and liabilities other than goodwill, the $50,000 unallocated fair value is the implied fair value of the goodwill and the goodwill impairment loss is:

Impairment loss = Goodwill implied fair value – Goodwill book value

Impairment loss = $50,000 – $130,000 = -$80,000

Choice "1" is incorrect. This is the implied fair value of the goodwill, not the goodwill impairment loss.

Choice "2" is incorrect. This is the difference between the book value and fair value of the reporting unit, not the goodwill impairment loss. The goodwill impairment loss is calculated using the implied fair value of the goodwill determined after allocating the fair value of the reporting unit to all assets and liabilities of the unit.

Choice "4" is incorrect. The goodwill impairment loss is not equal to the difference between the book value of the reporting unit less the fair market value assigned to the assets and liabilities of the reporting unit.

QUESTION 4-1

Choice "4" is correct.

Impairment is a two-step process, the first of which is to determine if impairment exists, and the second of which is to measure the loss.

To determine if an impairment loss exits, we compare the undiscounted cash flows from the machine to the carrying amount of the machine. The undiscounted cash flows are $900,000 ($45,000 × 20 years remaining life), and the carrying amount is $1,000,000 (in this case, they provided the carrying amount; in a longer problem, it might have to be calculated). Since the undiscounted cash flows are less than the carrying amount, there is an impairment loss.

The amount of the impairment loss is the difference between the fair value of the machine and its carrying amount ($800,000 – $1,000,000) or $200,000.

Topic H

QUESTION 1-1

Choice "2" is correct.

Accretion is the increase in the ARO over time. At the end of the four years, the cumulative accretion and accumulated depreciation should combine to equal the asset retirement obligation (ARO) of $200,000. The present value of a four-year obligation at a 7 percent rate and a future value of $200,000 is equal to $152,579. This asset must be fully depreciated over four years, while the liability must accrue from $152,579 to $200,000, a difference of $47,421. (The present value can be calculated this way: $200,000 / 1.07^4. This is equal to $200,000 / 1.3108. Or, if you were given a present value table, you would look up the factor for the present value of $1, 4 periods, 7 percent to obtain 0.7629. Multiply this factor by $200,000 to obtain $152,579.)

Choice "1" is incorrect. The accretion is correct, but the asset will be booked at a present value of $152,579 and this becomes the amount that will ultimately be depreciated over four years.

Choice "3" is incorrect. The combined total is correct, but the amounts in each column are reversed.

Choice "4" is incorrect. The combined total must equal the ultimate liability of $200,000.

Financial II

Choice "3" is correct.

The employee portion represents both the income tax withholding ($5,000 x 15% = $750) and the Social Security/Medicare withholding ($5,000 x 7.65% = $382.50). Therefore, the payable on behalf of the employee is equal to $750 + $382.50, or $1,132.50. The employer will book an expense for just the amount "owed" by the employer, which is $5,000 x 7.65 percent, or $382.50.

Choice "1" is incorrect. The payable must also include the amount the employee owes for income taxes ($750).

Choice "2" is incorrect. The expense represents the employer (rather than employee) portion.

Choice "4" is incorrect. The employer will only book an expense for the amount it is responsible for, which is just $5,000 x 7.65 percent, or $382.50.

Topic I

Choice "4" is correct.

The selling price of a bond is equal to the present value of the principal and interest payments calculated using the effective rate (or market yield), as follows:

PV of principal:	$1,000,000 × 0.4632	$ 463,200
PV of interest:	$90,000* × 6.7101	603,909
		$1,067,109

* Interest payments = $1,000,000 × 9% = $90,000

Choice "1" is incorrect. This is the face amount of the bond times 92% (100% − 8%).

Choice "2" is incorrect. This is the issue price of the bonds (and the approximate present value using the stated rate).

PV of principal:	$1,000,000 × 0.4224	$422,400
PV of interest:	$90,000 × 6.4177	577,593
		$999,993

Choice "3" is incorrect. This is approximately the amount if the effective rate of 8% were used to calculate the present value of the principal, but the stated rate of 9% were used to calculate the present value of the interest.

Financial II

QUESTION 1-2 FR-00307

Choice "1" is correct.

Watch the dates in bonds questions because the dates can make a big difference.

In this question, they are asking for the unamortized discount two years after issuance. The bonds pay interest annually, and the effective interest method is used, as follows.

Unamortized bond discount, 7/1/Year 1		$61,000
Bond discount amortization, 7/1/Year 1 to 6/30/Year 3:		
Amortization for 7/1/Year 1 to 6/30/Year 2:		
Bonds payable carrying amount, 7/1/Year 1	$939,000	
Effective interest rate 10%	× 0.10	
Interest expense, 7/1/Year 1 to 6/30/Year 2	93,900	
Interest payment ($1,000,000 × 9%)	90,000	(3,900)
Amortization for 7/1/Year 2 to 6/30/Year 3:		
Bonds payable carrying amount, 7/1/Year 2 ($939,000 + $3,900)	$942,900	
Effective interest rate 10%	× 0.10	
Interest expense, 7/1/Year 2 to 6/30/Year 3	94,290	
Interest payment ($1,000,000 × 9%)	90,000	(4,290)
Unamortized bond discount, 6/30/Year 3		$52,810

Note that, for each year, the interest (expense) component is equal to the carrying amount of the bond at the beginning of the year times the effective interest rate. The difference between the interest component and the interest payment is the amortization of the discount, and the amortization adjusts (increases) the carrying amount of the bond by decreasing the unamortized discount.

The interest expense will change each year, but the interest payment will remain constant.

The schedule above is a small part of a bond amortization table. Know these calculations.

QUESTION 3-1 FR-00842

Choice "3" is correct.

A debt modification that lowers future cash flows below the carrying value of the debt will result in a gain as well as a reduction in the carrying value of the liability, with the gain recorded in current operations.

Choice "1" is incorrect. Debt modifications are normally handled prospectively, but not when the future cash outflows are less than the carrying value of the debt.

Choice "2" is incorrect. Debt modifications are normally handled prospectively, but not when the future cash outflows are less than the carrying value of the debt.

Choice "4" is incorrect. The modification results in a gain, not a reduction, of interest expense.

Financial II

Topic J

QUESTION 1-1

Choice "1" is correct.

Common stock (5,000 shares × $1 stated value)	**$ 5,000**
Preferred stock (1,500 shares × $10 par value)	**$15,000**

Additional paid-in capital from:		
Common stock ($15 – $1) × 5,000 shares =	$70,000	
Preferred stock ($25 – $10) × 1,500 shares =	22,500	
	$92,500	

$5,000, common stock; $15,000 preferred stock; $92,500 APIC.

QUESTION 2-1

Choice "3" is correct.

Under the cost method, Black Dog would record the following journal entries for its Year 1 stock transactions:

Jan. 1, Year 1—Issue 30,000 shares of $5 par common stock for $9/share:

DR	Cash	$270,000	
CR	Common stock		$150,000
CR	APIC—CS		120,000

June 30, Year 1—Repurchase 10,000 shares for $8/share:

DR	Treasury stock	$80,000	
CR	Cash		$80,000

Sept. 15, Year 1—Resell 5,000 shares for $12/share:

DR	Cash	$60,000	
CR	Treasury stock		$40,000
CR	APIC—TS		20,000

Therefore, total APIC on Black Dog's balance sheet at December 31, Year 1 would be $140,000 ($120,000 from original sale + $20,000 from sale of treasury stock).

Choice "1" is incorrect. This is the amount of APIC—Treasury Stock recorded as a result of the resale of treasury stock on Sept. 15, Year 1 (see the explanation above). The question asks for total APIC.

Choice "2" is incorrect. This is the amount of APIC—Common Stock recorded as a result of the original issuance of common stock on Jan. 1, Year 1.

Choice "4" is incorrect. This is the amount of total APIC that would be reported on the Dec. 31, Year 1 balance sheet under the par value method.

Financial II

QUESTION 3-1

FR-00311

Choice "3" is correct.

There are both common and preferred shareholders. The dividends are $100,000, and some of it has to go to the preferred shareholders since none of the answers is $100,000.

The preferred goes first (since it is preferred) at 5% of par value or $15,000 (5% × 30,000 × $10). Since the preferred is "fully participating," the common shares are initially treated the same way as the preferred. The common thus gets its 5% or $10,000 (5% × $200,000 × $1). Then everybody shares in relation to their relative par values.

Total par value common	$200,000	(200,000 shares × $1)
Total par value preferred	300,000	(30,000 shares × $10)
Total par value	$500,000	

The preferred gets 3/5 of what is left, and the common gets 2/5. The amount left over is $75,000; the preferred gets $45,000 of that and the common gets $30,000. Putting this all together, the common gets a total of $40,000 and the preferred gets a total of $60,000.

Topic K

QUESTION 3-1

FR-00407

Choice "2" is correct.

Year 1 gross profit (loss) is calculated as follows:

	Project 1	Project 2
Contact price	$690,000	$425,000
Estimated total cost	(600,000)	(450,000)
Gross profit	$ 90,000	$ (25,000)

Under the completed contract method, only the Project 2 estimated total loss of $25,000 will be recognized in Year 1. The Project 1 gain will not be recognized until the project is complete.

Under the percentage of completion method, the Year 1 gain is calculated as follows:

Year 1 Percent complete	= Cost to date / Total estimated cost:
Project 1	= $200,000 / 600,000 = 33.3%
Project 2	= Irrelevant—losses are recognized in total when incurred

Gross profit earned to date = (Gross profit × % complete) – Gross profit recognized in prior periods:

Project 1 =	($90,000 × 33.3%) – $0 =	$ 30,000
Project 2 =	[$(25,000) ×100%] – $0 =	$(25,000)
		$ 5,000

Choice "1" is incorrect. The gross loss under the completed contract method is incorrectly calculated based on the fact that Project 2 is only 50% complete. Under both the completed contract and percentage of completion methods, losses are recognized in full, whether or not the project is complete.

Financial II

Choice "3" is incorrect. The gross profit (loss) under both the percentage of completion and completed contract methods are incorrectly calculated based on the fact that Project 2 is only 50% complete. Under both the completed contract and percentage of completion methods, losses are recognized in full, whether or not the project is complete.

Choice "4" is incorrect. The gross profit (loss) under the percentage of completion method is incorrectly calculated based on the fact that Project 2 is only 50% complete. Under both the completed contract and percentage of completion methods, losses are recognized in full, whether or not the project is complete.

Topic L

QUESTION 1-1   FR-00325

Choice "3" is correct.

U.S. GAAP requires that the funded status (Fair value of plan assets − PBO) of a company's defined benefit pension plan(s) be reported on the balance sheet as a non-current asset (if overfunded) or a current/non-current liability (if underfunded). Do It Right will report a non-current asset of $650,000 ($5,580,000 − 4,930,000) on its December 31, Year 7, balance sheet because the company's pension plan is overfunded (FV of plan assets > PBO).

Choice "1" is incorrect. Although the difference between the fair value of 329the plan assets and the PBO is $650,000, this is an overfunded pension plan which must be reported as a non-current asset. The funded status of a pension plan is only reported as a current liability to the extent that the expected benefits payable in the next 12 months exceed the fair value of the plan's asset, which is not the case in this situation.

Choice "2" is incorrect. $2,180,000 is the difference between the fair value of the plan assets and the ABO. The ABO is not used to calculate the funded status of defined benefit pension plans. Additionally, the funded status of Do It Right's pension plan would not be reported as a non-current liability because Do It Right's pension plan is overfunded.

Choice "4" is incorrect. $2,180,000 is the difference between the fair value of the plan assets and the ABO. The ABO is not used to calculate the funded status of defined benefit pension plans. Additionally, GAAP does not allow the funded status of a pension plan to be recorded as a current asset.

QUESTION 1-2   FR-00310

Choice "4" is correct.

What should come to mind immediately are those items that make up the formula for net periodic pension cost. A number of those very items are listed in the facts of the question, and the major difficulty is remembering which of those items should be added and which should be subtracted.

Start with the service cost of $160,000. Add the $50,000 of annual interest on the pension obligation, and that gives $210,000, a possible answer. The actual and expected gain of $35,000 would reduce the $210,000 to $175,000, and the $5,000 amortization of unrecognized prior service cost would add to it to produce $180,000.

The $40,000 loss on plan assets related to the disposal of a subsidiary in Year 1 looks like it might be a factor, but that loss would have been included in the loss on the disposal of the subsidiary (probably in discontinued operations) and not the net periodic pension cost (if it had been added, the total would have $220,000).

Financial II

QUESTION 2-1 FR-00854

Choice "1" is correct.

The APBO (accumulated postretirement benefit obligation) represents the present value of the liability associated with vested future benefits. The EPBO (expected postretirement benefit obligation) is equal to the APBO, plus the present value of the liability associated with nonvested future benefits. If there are no nonvested benefits, the APBO and EPBO will be equal; if there are nonvested benefits, the EPBO will be greater than the APBO.

Choice "2" is incorrect. Churchill is a public company under U.S. GAAP, which means the health care trend rate assumed by the company must be included as a disclosure.

Choice "3" is incorrect. If Churchill uses the expected rate of return in order to calculate net postretirement benefit expense/cost, then any differences between the expected return and actual return will result in a gain or loss that can either be booked as an expense in the current period (on the income statement) or booked in other comprehensive income (OCI) and amortized over time.

Choice "4" is incorrect. In order to accrue for these costs, they must represent benefits earned as a result of services already rendered.

QUESTION 3-1 FR-00341

Choice "4" is correct.

Compensatory stock options should be valued at the fair value of the option on the grant date. On the grant date (January 1, Year 1), the option had a fair value of $61 per option, so the total compensation cost is $6,100 ($61 x 100 options).

Topic M

QUESTION 1-1 FR-00425

Choice "2" is correct.

	Situation 1	Situation 2
Income tax payable	$16,000	$32,000
Change in deferred tax asset	(1,000)	–
Change in deferred tax liability	–	1,000
Income tax expense	$15,000	$33,000

When taxable income is larger than book income, a deferred tax asset is recognized.

To summarize, deferred tax assets are created by transactions that defer the tax benefits of expenses or which recognize tax income before book income.

Remember that the situations are independent. The question asks for the Income tax expense (which is the total of the current and deferred income tax expense).

Current tax expense is the product of taxable income times the tax rate.

Deferred tax expense either increases or decreases tax expense depending on whether it is an increase in a deferred tax asset (decrease) or an increase in a deferred tax liability (increase).

Financial II

The computations related to situation #1 are as follows:

Current tax expense ($40,000 in income × 40% tax rate) = $16,000 in current income tax payable

Deferred tax assets (future deductible amounts) are $2,000 in the current year ($5,000 × 40% tax rate) representing a $1,000 change from the $1,000 beginning deferred tax asset balance.

Current tax expense would be reduced by the $1,000 increase in the tax asset to arrive at income tax expense of $15,000.

The computations related to situation #2 are as follows:

Current tax expense ($80,000 in income × 40% tax rate) = $32,000 in current income tax payable

Deferred tax assets (future deductible amounts) are $4,000 in the current year ($10,000 × 40% tax rate) representing no change from the $4,000 beginning deferred tax asset balance.

Deferred tax liabilities (future taxable amounts) are $2,000 in the current year ($5,000 × 40% tax rate) representing a $1,000 change from the $1,000 beginning deferred tax asset balance.

Current tax expense would be increased by the $1,000 increase in the deferred tax liability to arrive at income tax expense of $33,000.

QUESTION 4-1   FR-00410

Choice "4" is correct.

	Situation	
	1	*2*
Future deductible amount	$5,000	$10,000
Tax Rate	40%	40%
Deferred tax asset ending balance	$2,000	$ 4,000

QUESTION 6-1   FR-00461

Choice "1" is correct.

Under U.S. GAAP and IFRS, all deferred tax assets/liabilities are reported as non-current on the balance sheet. Deferred tax assets and deferred tax liabilities may be netted if the entity has a legally enforceable right to offset current tax assets against current tax liabilities and the deferred tax assets and deferred tax liabilities relate to income taxes levied by the same tax authorities.

Choices "2", "3", and "4" are incorrect, per the explanation above.

Financial II

QUESTION 7-1

Choice "3" is correct.

Zeus will utilize $35,000 of the Year 6 NOL to receive a refund of taxes paid in Year 4 and Year 5. The amount of the refund is calculated as follows:

Year 4: $20,000 × 30% =	$6,000
Year 5: $15,000 × 25% =	3,750
Total Refund	$9,750

The remaining $65,000 ($100,000 − $35,000) of the Year 6 NOL will be carried forward to offset the Year 7 taxable income of $70,000. Therefore, a fully realizable deferred tax asset can be calculated using the Year 7 tax rate:

$65,000 × 40% = $26,000

Zeus's Year 6 income tax journal entry will be:

DR	Income tax refund receivable	$ 9,750	
DR	Deferred tax asset—current	26,000	
CR	Income tax benefit		$35,750

Choice "1" is incorrect. This is the $100,000 NOL multiplied by the Year 6 tax rate. This is not the method used to calculate the income tax benefit from an NOL.

Choice "2" is incorrect. This is the deferred tax asset related to the NOL carryforward, not the amount of the tax benefit.

Choice "4" is incorrect. This answer incorrectly uses the Year 7 income of $70,000, rather than the carryforward of $65,000 to calculate the income tax benefit.

Financial III

Topic A

QUESTION 1-1   FR-00327

Choice "3" is correct.

The accounting change is a change in accounting estimate, which is handled prospectively.

Before the change, depreciation was calculated on the straight-line basis using a life of 6 years. The depreciable base was $600,000, so the accumulated depreciation for the 3 years before the change was $300,000 ($600,000/6 × 3). Thus, the carrying amount at the date of the change was also $300,000.

A change in accounting estimate is handled prospectively. In this case, the remaining carrying amount of $300,000 is depreciated over the new remaining life of 5 years (8 − 3). The new depreciation expense each year is $60,000.

Note that the question is asking about depreciation expense. It just as easily could have been accumulated depreciation or it could have been the net book value of the asset.

QUESTION 2-1   FR-00342

Choice "4" is correct.

This particular change is from weighted average to FIFO. It is a change in accounting principle. Accounting changes are reported on the statement of retained earnings net of tax. In this question, the cumulative effect before taxes is $800,000. Net of tax, it is $560,000 ($800,000 × 0.70).

QUESTION 2-2   FR-00312

Choice "3" is correct.

A change in accounting principle is normally recorded using retrospective adjustment where the cumulative effect of the adjustment on prior years is reported in beginning retained earnings of the earliest year presented, net of the related tax effect. There are exceptions, and this particular change in accounting principle is one of the exceptions. Therefore, there is no cumulative effort reporting because such a change in depreciation method is treated as a change in estimate and accounted for prospectively.

QUESTION 4-1   FR-00372

Choice "1" is correct.

The cash basis for financial reporting is not a generally accepted basis of accounting (GAAP); therefore, it is an error. Correction of an error from a prior period is reported as a prior period adjustment to retained earnings.

Choice "2" is incorrect. Cash basis reporting is not acceptable under accrual basis accounting principles. Thus, the change from cash basis is not reported as a change in accounting principle.

Choice "3" is incorrect. Correction of prior period errors has no effect on the current year's income statement.

Choice "4" is incorrect. An error correction is recorded by restating retained earnings. Error corrections are not reported on the income statement.

Financial Final Review

Financial III

Topic B

QUESTION 2-1   FR-00394

Choice "4" is correct.

The conveniently named Philadelphia Corporation (P as in parent) has acquired the Saxon Corporation (S as in subsidiary) in a business combination transaction treated as a purchase. Philadelphia issued 200,000 shares of $10 par value stock valued at $18 for all of Saxon's common stock. That was $3,600,000 (200,000 × $18) in total. If 200,000 shares were issued for $8 over par, then $1,600,000 went to additional paid-in capital from that transaction. But there was already $1,300,000 there. The total of the two is $2,900,000 ($1,300,000 + $1,600,000). Saxon's additional paid-in capital is eliminated when the financial statements are consolidated.

QUESTION 2-2   FR-00778

Choice "3" is correct.

Under the IFRS partial goodwill method, noncontrolling interest on the balance sheet is calculated as follows:

NCI = fair value of subsidiary net assets × NCI %

Therefore, the NCI is:

NCI = $11,500,000 × 20% = $2,300,000

QUESTION 2-3   FR-00460

Choice "2" is correct.

At the time of the sale, Pico and Sepulveda would have recorded the following journal entries:

Pico—record sale to Sepulveda:

DR	Accounts receivable	$400,000	
CR	Sales revenue		$400,000
DR	Cost of goods sold	320,000*	
CR	Inventory		320,000

* $320,000 = $400,000/1.25

Sepulveda—record purchase from Pico:

DR	Inventory	$400,000	
CR	Accounts Payable		$400,000

Because this is an intercompany transaction, the intercompany sales revenue, cost of goods sold and profit on inventory must be eliminated. In this problem, the intercompany profit on inventory is $80,000 ($400,000 cost of inventory on Sepulveda's books – $320,000 original cost of inventory on Pico's books). Because Sepulveda has sold half of the inventory purchased from Pico, half of the intercompany profit must be eliminated from cost of goods sold and half of the intercompany profit must be eliminated from ending inventory. The journal entry to record this elimination is as follows:

DR	Sales revenue	$400,000	
CR	Cost of goods sold		$360,000
CR	Inventory		40,000

Therefore, at year-end, consolidated inventory is equal to Pico's inventory + Sepulveda's inventory – Eliminated intercompany profit = $390,000 + 480,000 – 40,000 = $830,000.

Choice "1" is incorrect. This answer option incorrectly calculates ending inventory as follows:

Sepulveda	[$480,000 – (50% × $400,000)]	$280,000
Pico		390,000
		$670,000

Choice "3" is incorrect. This is the sum of the inventory amounts on each of the balance sheets without the elimination entry for the intercompany profit of $40,000 [$390,000 + $480,000 = $870,000].

Choice "4" is incorrect. This answer option incorrectly adds (rather than subtracts) the intercompany profit on the inventory of $40,000 to the ending balance sheet amounts of inventory for each [$390,000 + $480,000 + $40,000].

QUESTION 3-1   FR-00856

Choice "4" is correct.

Once an entity is deemed to meet the qualifications of a variable interest entity, the question is raised as to whether the entity must be consolidated. Two factors used to make this determination include whether the investor has the power to direct significant economic activities for the VIE and whether the investor is the "primary beneficiary" of the VIE. As a primary beneficiary, the investor would absorb at least 50 percent of the VIE's expected losses or gains. So if it is a case that the VIE incurs losses, and the investor does not absorb at least 50 percent of them, then they are not the primary beneficiary and the VIE would not be consolidated.

Choice "1" is incorrect. This condition would imply that the investor is the primary beneficiary and as such, it would lend itself to consolidation.

Choice "2" is incorrect. A VIE that requires significant financial support to exist would not present an argument against consolidation.

Choice "3" is incorrect. Current equity holders lacking substantive voting rights would not present an argument against consolidation.

Financial III

Topic C

QUESTION 2-1   FR-00475

Choice "2" is correct.

Only the probable loss from the first product liability lawsuit would be recorded on the balance sheet. Because a range of losses is given, the lowest amount in the range is recorded on the balance sheet as a contingent liability and the range is disclosed in the footnotes along with the details of the case. The possible loss from the second product liability lawsuit and the probable contingent gain are not recorded on the balance sheet, but instead are disclosed in the footnotes.

Choice "1" is incorrect. This answer incorrectly offsets the probable gain of $500,000 against the probable loss of $800,000. Probable gains cannot be accrued on the balance sheet, but can only be disclosed in the footnotes.

Choice "3" is incorrect. This answer incorrectly accrues the $1,000,000 possible loss on the second product liability lawsuit. A possible loss should not be accrued on the balance sheet, but should instead be disclosed in the footnotes.

Choice "4" is incorrect. This answer incorrectly accrues the $1,000,000 possible loss on the second product liability lawsuit. A possible loss should not be accrued on the balance sheet, but should instead be disclosed in the footnotes. Additionally, this answer accrues the $2,000,000 high end of the range of probable losses on the first product liability lawsuit. Generally, the low end of the range is accrued.

Topic D

QUESTION 1-1   FR-00382

Choice "4" is correct.

Both carrying value (amount) and fair value must be disclosed for most financial instruments (when it is practicable to estimate fair value).

QUESTION 2-1   FR-00471

Choice "1" is correct.

Statement III is the only correct statement. Statement I is incorrect because a derivative must have one or more underlyings *and* one or more notional amounts. Statement II is incorrect because derivatives can be reported as assets or liabilities. Statement IV is incorrect because changes in the fair value of a fair value hedge are reported on the income statement.

Choices "2", "3", and "4" are incorrect, based on the above explanation.

Financial III

Topic E

QUESTION 1-1

FR-00449

Choice "2" is correct.

Statements II and III are correct. Statement I is incorrect because a company's financial statement must be in conformity with GAAP before translation/remeasurement. Statement IV is incorrect because translation gains are reported in other comprehensive income, while gains and losses from remeasurement are reported on the income statement.

Choices "1", "3", and "4" are incorrect, based on the above explanation.

QUESTION 2-1

FR-00459

Choice "4" is correct.

On November 1, Year 1, Western would record the transaction as follows:

DR	Accounts receivable (25,000 euros × $1.19)	$29,750	
CR	Revenue		$29,750

On December 31, Year 1, Western would record a foreign exchange transaction loss of $750 [25,000 euros x ($1.19 − 1.16)] due to the decrease in the exchange rate:

DR	Foreign exchange transaction loss	$750	
CR	Accounts receivable		$750

On February 15, Year 1, when Western receives the payment from its customer, the company would record a foreign exchange transaction gain of $1,750 [25,000 euros x ($1.23 − 1.16)]:

DR	Cash (25,000 euros × $1.23)	$30,750	
CR	Accounts receivable ($29,750 − 750)		$29,000
CR	Foreign exchange transaction gain		1,750

Choice "1" is incorrect. This answer incorrectly identifies the Year 1 loss as a gain. Additionally, it incorrectly identifies the Year 2 gain as a loss and incorrectly calculates the Year 2 amount by multiplying the $0.04 difference between the 11/1/Y1 exchange rate and the 2/15/Y2 exchange rate ($1.23 − $1.19 = $0.04) by 25,000 euros ($0.04/euro x 25,000 euros = $1,000).

Choice "2" is incorrect. This answer incorrectly identifies the Year 1 loss as a gain. Additionally, it incorrectly identifies the Year 2 gain as a loss.

Choice "3" is incorrect. This answer incorrectly calculates the Year 2 gain by multiplying the $0.04 difference between the 11/1/Y1 exchange rate and the 2/15/Y2 exchange rate ($1.23 − $1.19 = $0.04) by 25,000 euros ($0.04/euro x 25,000 euros = $1,000).

Financial III

Topic F

QUESTION 1-1

FR-00336

Choice "4" is correct.

In this question, they want to know the amount charged to expense for what looks like an operating lease. An amount of $1,200,000 was paid on December 1, Year 1.

$200,000 of the $1,200,000 was for actual rent. However, the lease agreement indicated that the rent would double halfway through the lease. The total rent that will be paid for the entire 10 years is thus $36,000,000, for an equivalent monthly rent of $300,000 ($36,000,000 / 120).

The other amount that would be charged to expense (the question does not say rent expense, just expense) would be the amortization of the leasehold improvement. The leasehold is the office space, the improvement is the new carpet for the executives, and the amortization would be on the straight-line basis over 120 months, for $5,000 per month.

The total expense would thus be $305,000.

QUESTION 2-1

FR-00306

Choice "2" is correct.

In this question, they want to know the capital (finance) lease liability. They are paying $50,000 every year for the next 10 years, and they provide the present value of the minimum lease payments of the lease as of December 31, Year 1. Watch the dates; they are there for a reason.

The first payment is made on signing the lease, i.e., at the beginning of the period. The liability after that payment is $288,000 ($338,000 − $50,000). The question asks what the long-term liability is one year later.

$288,000 × 10% is $28,800. That amount is the interest component of the second payment. The difference between the $50,000 payment and the $28,800 is $21,200, and the $21,200 is the reduction of the long-term liability of the second payment; therefore the liability after the second payment is $266,800 ($288,000 − $21,200).

It all started with the first payment. All the other answers have a wrong turn.

QUESTION 2-2

FR-00396

Choice "3" is correct.

The excess of the present value of the lease payments over the cost of the equipment is recorded as profit on the sale.

Present value of lease payments	$ 3,150,000
Cost of equipment	(2,950,000)
Profit on sale	$ 200,000

Choice "1" is incorrect. Because this is a sales-type lease, profit will be recorded at the inception of the lease.

Choice "2" is incorrect. This is the difference between the $3,300,000 list price of the equipment and the actual sales price of the equipment, which is equal to the $3,150,000 present value of the lease payments.

Choice "4" is incorrect. This is the difference between the list price of the equipment and the carrying value of the equipment. In this problem, the equipment was sold for less than the list price. The actual selling price, not the list price, should not be used to calculate the profit on the sale.

Financial III

QUESTION 3-1

Choice "4" is correct.

Under U.S. GAAP, Smalltime retains "substantially all" rights to Plane #1 because the $469,440 ($80,000 × 5.868) present value of the annual lease payments is greater than 90% of the fair value of the plane (90% × $500,000 = $450,000). Therefore, the entire $300,000 ($500,000 sales price – $200,000 carrying amount) gain on the sale of the plane will be deferred.

Smalltime retains less than "substantially all" but greater than "minor" rights to Plane #2 because the $547,200 ($200,000 × 2.736) present value of the annual lease payments is between 10% – 90% of the fair value of the plane. Therefore, of the $600,000 ($900,000 sales price – $300,000 carrying amount) gain on the sale, an amount equal to the present value of the annual lease payments of $547,200 will be the deferred gain, and $52,800 will be recognized as gain immediately.

Therefore, the total deferred gain on these transactions is $300,000 + $547,200 = $847,200.

Choice "1" is incorrect. This is the portion of the gain on the sale of Plane #2 which will be recognized immediately.

Choice "2" is incorrect. This is the deferred gain from Plane #1. A portion of the gain on the sale of Plane #2 should also be deferred, as described above.

Choice "3" is incorrect. This is the portion of the gain on the sale of Plane #2 that should be deferred. The entire gain on Plane #1 should also be deferred, as described above.

Topic G

QUESTION 1-1

Choice "3" is correct.

In this question, all of the costs except the cost of the equipment acquired for the various R&D projects are considered R&D costs. Since the equipment has alternative future uses (on various research projects), the depreciation on the equipment is an R&D expense.

QUESTION 2-1

Choice "3" is correct.

All of the research and development costs related to the unsuccessful product lines must be expensed. The $30,000 in research costs related to the product that was successfully patented must also be expensed because all research costs are expensed under IFRS. The $40,000 in development costs will most likely be capitalized because they related to a successfully patented product and development costs can be capitalized under IFRS. Therefore, the entity should expense $260,000 ($300,000 – $40,000).

Financial III

Topic H

QUESTION 1-1

FR-00408

Choice "1" is correct.

Until technological feasibility has been established for a product, costs incurred in creating a computer software product should be charged to research and development expense when incurred. Technological feasibility is established upon completion of a detailed program design or a working model. In this question, $70,000 would be recorded as research and development expense ($30,000 for detailed program design and $40,000 for coding and testing to establish technological feasibility).

Costs incurred from the point of technological feasibility until the time when product costs are incurred are capitalized as software costs. In this question, $100,000 ($20,000 + $30,000 + $50,000) is capitalized as software cost.

Product costs that can be easily associated with the items to be inventoried are reported as a part of the inventory cost (in this question, $15,000 for duplication of software and training materials and $10,000 for packaging, for a total of $25,000).

Topic I

QUESTION 2-1

FR-00844

Choice "4" is correct.

Although the fire occurred after the balance sheet date of June 30, the nature of the event and estimated financial impact were known before the financial statements were due to be issued on September 30. Therefore, the correct approach for Drexler is to disclose the nature of the event along with the estimated financial impact.

Choice "1" is incorrect. The entirety of the event occurred after June 30, so there is no need to book a journal entry to reflect it in the Year 3 balance sheet/income statement. The entry will be booked in the Year 4 statements.

Choice "2" is incorrect. The entirety of the event occurred after June 30, so there is no need to book a journal entry to reflect it in the Year 3 balance sheet/income statement. The entry will be booked in the Year 4 statements. In addition, a disclosure should also be included to help users of the financial statements understand the nature and impact of the event.

Choice "3" is incorrect. Because an estimated financial impact is known, the nature of the event should be disclosed along with the estimated financial impact.

Financial III

Topic J

Choice "2" is correct.

An asset-backed security is an investment whose value and income payments are driven by a pool of underlying assets. A mortgage-backed security is a type of asset-backed security that is secured by a mortgage or mortgages. Level 2 investments may trade in active markets, but tend to be based on dealer quotations or alternative sources supported by observable investments or inputs that trade in inactive markets. A mortgage-backed security will most likely fall under a Level 2 classification.

Choice "1" is incorrect. A U.S. Treasury bill represents a short-term fixed obligation of the United States government, which means it has a very active market and quoted market prices are readily available. As a result, this type of investment will be categorized under Level 1.

Choice "3" is incorrect. Limited partnerships allow investors to take advantage of opportunities without incurring the risks and liabilities of a general partnership. These types of investments trade infrequently (if at all), and as a result have significant unobservable inputs that therefore requires that they fall under Level 3.

Choice "4" is incorrect. A large company's common stock will have a very active market and therefore have quoted market prices. As a result, the most appropriate categorization is Level 1.

Financial Final Review **CQ-37**

Notes

Topic A

QUESTION 1-1   FR-00488

Choice "3" is correct.

Earnings from a tax to be used exclusively to repay specific debt would most likely be accounted for in the debt service fund associated with that debt. Fund financial reporting, particularly for the governmental funds, demonstrates compliance with laws rules and regulations. The display of revenues restricted for debt repayment in the debt service fund would demonstrate compliance with the law that levied the tax.

Choice "1" is incorrect. The General Fund would not serve to demonstrate the use of the sales tax for repayment of debt as clearly as the debt service fund.

Choice "2" is incorrect. The Special Revenue Fund would not serve to demonstrate the use of the sales tax for repayment of debt as clearly as the debt service fund.

Choice "4" is incorrect. The Capital Projects Fund accounts for construction monies, not funds anticipated for the repayment of debt. The Capital Projects Fund would not be appropriate.

QUESTION 2-1   FR-00405

Choice "3" is correct.

The Holler Sound Citizen's Initiative Fund is an agency fund that would account for the debt service associated with a special assessment for which the municipality had no obligation. An agency fund is accounted for using the economic resources measurement focus and would not share the same basis of accounting with the Community Development Block Grant Fund.

Choice "1" is incorrect. The Holler Bridge Fund is a capital projects fund that would use the current financial resources measurement focus in the same manner as the special revenue fund used to account for the community development block grant.

Choice "2" is incorrect. The Holler Bridge Debt Service Fund is a debt service fund that would use the current financial resources measurement focus in the same manner as the special revenue fund used to account for the community development block grant.

Choice "4" is incorrect. The Holler Cemetery Perpetual Care Fund is a permanent fund established to benefit the general public and would use the current financial resources measurement focus in the same manner as the special revenue fund used to account for the community development block grant.

QUESTION 3-1   FR-00420

Choice "3" is correct.

The trash collection service is accounted for in the General Fund, a governmental fund that uses the modified accrual basis of accounting, the basis of accounting that will not recognize revenues until measurable (amount is defined) and available (amount is collected within 60 days of year-end). The Road and Bridge Fund uses the same basis of accounting as the trash collection service.

Choice "1" is incorrect. The utility fund is an enterprise fund that uses the full accrual basis of accounting that recognizes revenue when earned.

Choice "2" is incorrect. The motor pool is an internal service fund that uses the full accrual basis of accounting that recognizes revenue when earned.

Choice "4" is incorrect. The retirement fund is a pension fund that uses the full accrual basis of accounting that recognizes revenue when earned.

Financial IV

QUESTION 3-2

FR-00315

Choice "2" is correct.

Property tax revenue is an imposed non exchange revenue that would be recorded when levied to the extent that it is both measurable and available. The fact pattern indicates that the following revenues were recognized:

Tax revenue collected	$24,000,000
Delinquent taxes collected	800,000
Total tax revenue available	24,800,000
Uncollected revenue	200,000
Total tax levy	$25,000,000

General Rule: Property taxes generally meet the definition of non-exchange revenues and are recognized in the period in which an enforceable legal claim to the taxes arises and the revenues are available. Availability is defined as collection within the period levied or soon enough to pay liabilities of the current period (60 days after year-end). Governments may refer to the date the enforceable legal claim arises as either the lien date or the assessment date. Property taxes received in advance are displayed as deferred inflows of resources.

Topic B

QUESTION 1-1

FR-00474

Choice "4" is correct.

Combining statements of nonmajor funds may be displayed in "Other Supplementary Information" at the option of the issuer.

Choice "1" is incorrect. Presentation of nonmajor funds in the fund financial statements is inappropriate except in summary.

Choice "2" is incorrect. Nonmajor fund detail should not be exclusively displayed in the notes to the financial statements.

Choice "3" is incorrect. Display of nonmajor grant activity is not required.

Financial IV

QUESTION 2-1

Choice "4" is correct.

City of Richardson
Reconciliation of the Statement of Revenues, Expenditures, and Changes
in Fund Balances of Governmental Funds to the Statement of Activities
December 31, Year 1

Net change in fund balances-total governmental funds:	$ 2,002,000
Governmental funds report capital outlays as expenditures. However, in the Statement of Activities, the cost of those assets is allocated over their estimated useful lives as depreciation expense. This is the amount by which capital outlays exceeded depreciation in the current period. 160,000,000 / 20 (10,000,000 − 8,000,000).	2,000,000
In the Statement of Activities, only the gain on the sale of land is reported, whereas in the governmental funds, the proceeds from the sale increase financial resources. Thus, the change in net position differs from the change in the fund balance by the cost of the land sold.	(800,000)
Revenues in the Statement of Activities that result from changes in accrual balances (property taxes).	
– Current Year Accrual	400,000
– Prior Year Accrual	(370,000)
Repayment of bond principal is an expenditure in the governmental funds, but the repayment reduces long-term liabilities in the Statement of Net Position.	1,500,000
Some expenses in the Statement of Activities do not require the use of current financial resources and therefore are not reported as expenditures in the governmental funds.	(100,000)
Change in net position of governmental activities:	**$4,632,000**

QUESTION 3-1

Choice "3" is correct.

The net realizable value of infrastructure is not a required element of a government's asset management system when the government uses the modified approach.

The asset system must include:

- An inventory of assets.
- Summary of asset condition.
- Amount required to preserve the asset condition.

Financial IV

Topic C

QUESTION 1-1

FR-00434

Choice "2" is correct.

Rule: Component units include legally separate organizations (governmental, not-for-profit, or for profit) for which elected officials of the primary government are financially accountable. A primary government is financially accountable if it appoints a voting majority of the organization's governing body. A component unit should be included in the reporting entity financial statements using the blending method when the component unit provides services entirely or almost entirely to the primary government or otherwise exclusively or almost exclusively benefits the primary government even though it does not provide services directly to it.

The Cox Administration Corporation is a component unit since its governing body is appointed by the City. The corporation would be presented as a blended component unit since it was established by the primary government to administer its employee benefit programs in a manner that exclusively benefits the primary government even though it provides services to the employees rather than directly to the primary government itself.

Choice "1" is incorrect. The Cox Administration Corporation primarily serves the primary government and would be presented as a blended not discrete component unit.

Choice "3" is incorrect. The Cox Administration Corporation's financial statements are presented as a blended component unit, not simply disclosed.

Choice "4" is incorrect. The Board of Directors of the Cox Administration Corporation is appointed by the primary government; the corporation is a component unit, not a stand alone corporation.

Topic D

QUESTION 2-1

FR-00490

Choice "3" is correct.

Proceeds from refunding debt would be displayed at face value as "Other Financing Sources" in the debt service fund associated with the refunded debt with any original issue discount displayed as "Other Financing Uses." Underwriter's fees (as distinct from original issue discount) netted against bond proceeds would have been charged to expenditures. The transaction associated with the issuance of the debt would appear on the Statement of Revenues, Expenditures and Changes in Fund Balance.

Choice "1" is incorrect. The non-current debt, bonds payable, would not be recorded in the governmental fund financial statements, it would only be recorded in the government-wide financial statements under the governmental activities column. "Other Financing Sources" would be displayed at the face amount of the bond and any difference between the face amount and proceeds associated with the original issue discount would be displayed as "Other Financing Uses."

Choice "2" is incorrect. Refund bonds would be recorded in the debt service fund associated with the refunded debt. The face amount of the bonds would be displayed as proceeds under the "Other Financing Sources" classification while any discount associated with an original issue discount would be displayed beneath the "Other Financing Uses" classification. Charges associated with underwriter's fees that are netted against bond proceeds would be displayed as an expenditure.

Choice "4" is incorrect. The issuance of refunding bonds would be recorded in the debt service fund financial statements as bond proceeds under the category "Other Financing Sources" at face value with any original issue discount reported as "Other Financing Uses." It would not be either recorded exclusively on the government-wide financial statements or recorded in another fund.

QUESTION 2-2

Choice "1" is correct.

The County's available appropriation is computed as the difference between the original appropriation and the funds either expended or encumbered.

Appropriation		$45,000
Less:		
Expended by November, Year 0		(15,000)
Accrued by August, Year 1		(20,000)
Budgetary control (purchase order)	$30,000	
Order received	(20,000)	
Budgetary control		(10,000)
Available appropriation		$ 0

The County would record activity as follows:

To record initial expenditures related to miscellaneous supplies:

DR	Expenditures	$15,000	
CR	Cash		$15,000

To record encumbrances for issued purchase order:

DR	Encumbrances	$30,000	
CR	Budgetary control		$30,000

To reverse encumbrances associated with liabilities incurred related to items received:

DR	Budgetary control	$20,000	
CR	Encumbrances		$20,000
DR	Expenditures	20,000	
CR	Accounts payable		20,000

Financial IV

QUESTION 3-1

FR-00496

Choice "2" is correct.

Unassigned fund balances represent spendable resources that are the least limited as to use.

Choice "1" is incorrect. "Unreserved" is older terminology. Although unreserved and undesignated fund balance classifications approximated the meaning of the "unassigned" fund balance prior to implementation of GASB 54, the terminology is now obsolete and a distracter.

Choice "3" is incorrect. There is no such classification as "unspendable." This is a distracter. There is a classification titled "nonspendable." These residual amounts may indeed be unassigned, but they are not available and would not be less limited as to use than resources classified as unassigned.

Choice "4" is incorrect. Committed funds are internally limited by formal action of the government's highest level of decision-making authority and would not be less limited as to use than resources classified as unassigned.

QUESTION 4-1

FR-00804

Choice "1" is correct.

Increases in derivatives classified as assets are accounted for as increases in deferred inflows of resources, a classification of transactions below liabilities and above fund equity.

Choice "2" is incorrect. Increases in derivatives classified as assets are accounted for as increases, not decreases in deferred inflows of resources.

Choices "3" and "4" are incorrect. Changes in the value of derivatives classified as assets result in increases in deferred inflows of resources, a classification of transactions displayed between liabilities and fund equity, not deferred outflows of resources, a classification of transactions appearing between assets and liabilities.

Topic A

QUESTION 2-1

Choice "1" is correct.

All not-for-profit organizations are required to produce a statement of financial position (balance sheet), statement of activity (income statement), and statement of cash flows along with disclosures of functional expenses as displayed on the statement of activities analyzed by object classification.

Choice "2" is incorrect. Functional expense disclosure is required, not optional.

Choice "3" is incorrect. The statement of cash flows and functional expense disclosures are required.

Choice "4" is incorrect. The statement of cash flows is required.

QUESTION 3-1

Choice "2" is correct.

The initial contribution in which the donor stipulates that the principal must remain intact would be classified as an increase in net assets with donor restrictions along with the earnings, whose use is restricted but which the university can satisfy by implementing programming (the chair for accountancy). No distinction is made for purposes of financial statement display between the items restricted by the donor in perpetuity and the items for which restrictions are temporary in nature.

Choice "1" is incorrect. Contributions for an endowment with earnings restricted for use to fund a chair in accountancy would be reported as an increase to net assets with donor restrictions.

Choice "3" is incorrect. Both the contribution to fund the endowment and related earnings restricted as to use would be accounted for as an increase in net assets with donor restrictions.

Choice "4" is incorrect. Both the contribution to fund the endowment and related earnings restricted as to use would be accounted for as an increase in net assets with donor restrictions.

QUESTION 4-1

Choice "2" is correct.

Proceeds from the sale of assets that were received in prior periods and whose sale proceeds were donor-restricted to investment in long-lived assets are displayed on the Statement of Cash Flows as cash flows from investing activity.

Choice "1" is incorrect. Proceeds from the sale of assets that were received in prior periods and whose sale proceeds were donor-restricted to investment in long-lived assets are displayed on the Statement of Cash Flows as cash flows from investing activity, not an operating activity.

Choice "3" is incorrect. Proceeds from the sale of assets that were received in prior periods and whose sale proceeds were donor-restricted to investment in long-lived assets are displayed on the Statement of Cash Flows as cash flows from investing activity, gains are not segregated as an operating activity.

Choice "4" is incorrect. Proceeds from the sale of assets that were received in prior periods and whose sale proceeds were donor-restricted to investment in long-lived assets are displayed on the Statement of Cash Flows as cash flows from investing activity, not a financing activity.

Financial V

Topic B

QUESTION 1-1   FR-00433

Choice "4" is correct.

Revenues and support without donor restrictions would consist of:

Revenues	
Fees (exchange transactions)	$ 45,000
Support	
United Way support	30,000
Federal grant earned as a result of satisfying restrictions in the same year the grant was awarded	10,000
Total revenue and support without donor restrictions	$ 85,000

Choice "1" is incorrect. Revenues and support without donor restrictions include fees per above.

Choice "2" is incorrect. Revenues and support without donor restrictions include both the United Way support and grant monies whose restrictions are satisfied in the same year as the award.

Choice "3" is incorrect. Revenue and support without donor restrictions include grants with donor restrictions whose restrictions are satisfied in the same period in which the revenues are awarded.

QUESTION 3-1   FR-00359

Choice "4" is correct.

Assets of a charitable remainder trust are measured at fair value when received and the liability is measured at the present value of expected future cash flows to be paid to the beneficiary. Contributions are not available until a future period (when the liability is fully satisfied) and is therefore an increase in net assets with donor restrictions. Carton would use the following entry.

To record acquisition of assets subject to a charitable remainder trust:

DR	Assets held in charitable remainder trust	$200,000	
CR	Liability under trust agreements		$ 84,250
CR	Contribution revenue, with donor restrictions		115,750

Choice "1" is incorrect. The net assets of this transaction relate to the contribution less the value of the liability, not the value of the asset itself.

Choice "2" is incorrect. The net assets of this transaction relate to the contribution less the value of the liability, not the value of the asset itself.

Choice "3" is incorrect. The net assets of this transaction relate to the contribution less the value of the liability, and is subject to donor restrictions associated with time requirements, not classified as an increase in net assets without donor restrictions.

Financial V

QUESTION 4-1

Choice "3" is correct.

Rule: Not-for-profit organizations record donated services **SOME** of the time, when services meet the following criteria:

Specialized skill
Otherwise needed
Measured
Easily

Services are also recognized when a long-lived asset is enhanced.

The services for the construction of the pipe organ meet all criteria. The construction requires a specialized skill, the musical instrument is necessary equipment and there is a market price for the service. In addition, unskilled labor was used to enhance a long-lived asset.

The church would record $35,000 in revenues from contributed specialized services per the rule above (40,000 fair value minus $5,000 paid) and would record $7,000 in revenue for the general labor used to enhance the long-lived asset.

Value for specialized service	$40,000
Amount paid	(5,000)
Net specialized service donated	35,000
General labor used to enhance long-lived asset	7,000
Total donated service revenue	$42,000

Choices "1", "2", and "4" are incorrect per the explanation above.

Financial V

QUESTION 5-1   FR-00493

Choice "1" is correct.

The value of investments at the beginning of the year was $2,410,000. Investments experienced a $160,000 reduction in value accounted for in part by the sale of assets ($110,000 × 65% = $71,500) and a loss of $88,500 ($160,000 – $71,500). All activity is accounted for as with donor restrictions. Underwater endowments will absorb their own losses.

	Without Donor Restrictions	With Donor Restrictions	Total
Beginning of Year	$ –	$ 2,300,000	$ 2,300,000
Accumulated gains	–	110,000	110,000
Liquidation	–	(71,500)	(71,500)
Gains	–	–	–
Losses	–	(88,500)	(88,500)
End of Year	**$ –**	**$2,250,000**	**$2,250,000**

Choice "2" is incorrect. Although the net decline is appropriately accounted for as net assets with donor restrictions, the amount does not appropriately account for all activity (a liquidation of a portion of the value that inflates the loss).

Choice "3" is incorrect. Losses on endowment funds (even to the extent that they reduce the original value of the endowment, thereby creating an underwater endowment) are accounted for as changes in net assets with donor restrictions.

Choice "4" is incorrect. Losses on endowment funds (even to the extent that they reduce the original value of the endowment, thereby creating an underwater endowment) are accounted for as changes in net assets with donor restrictions.

QUESTION 6-1   FR-00456

Choice "3" is correct.

Little Tutu Dance Troupe is a financially interrelated beneficiary of collections made by the foundation, the recipient. Little Tutu Dance Troupe board members serve on the foundation's board and can influence its operations. Beneficiaries recognize an interest in the net assets of the recipient when the organizations are financially interrelated, as follows:

DR	Interest in net assets of Cox Foundation	$250,000	
CR	Change in interest in net assets of Cox Foundation		$250,000

Because the donation has an implied time restriction because it will only be received in the subsequent period, the net asset classification by Little Tutu is with donor restrictions.

Choice "1" is incorrect. Donations to affiliated recipients involving implied time restrictions are recorded as net assets with donor restrictions on the beneficiaries' financial statements, not simply disclosed.

Choice "2" is incorrect. Donations to affiliated recipients involving implied time restrictions are recorded as net assets with donor restrictions on the beneficiaries' financial statements, not without donor restrictions.

Choice "4" is incorrect. Donations to affiliated recipients involving implied time restrictions are recorded as with donor restrictions net assets on the beneficiaries' financial statements, not without donor restrictions.

QUESTION 7-1

Choice "3" is correct.

Net patient service revenues reported on a hospital statement of activities are comprised of gross earnings net of contractual allowances and exclude charity care. Net patient service revenues are computed as follows:

Gross patient fees	$ 5,000,000
Contractual allowances	(800,000)
Charity care	(1,300,000)
Net patient service revenue	**$2,900,000**

Choice "1" is incorrect. Net patient service revenues reported on a hospital statement of activities are comprised of gross earnings net of contractual allowances and exclude charity care. This choice does not reduce patient service revenue by any of the appropriate deductions.

Choice "2" is incorrect. Net patient service revenues reported on a hospital statement of activities are comprised of gross earnings net of contractual allowances and exclude charity care. This choice only reduces patient service revenue by contractual allowances.

Choice "4" is incorrect. Net patient service revenues reported on a hospital statement of activities are comprised of gross earnings net of contractual allowances and exclude charity care. This choice not only reduces patient service revenue by appropriate deductions but also improperly reduces revenue by the net change in the allowance account. Bad debt expense is matched against revenue as an expense when the allowance was established after an evaluation of the patient's ability to pay. Revenue associated with doubtful accounts is recognized and would be included as a component of net patient service revenue. The change in the allowance is not relevant.

QUESTION 7-2

Choice "3" is correct.

Read the requirements first. Notice the dates.

Gross revenues for tuition would be computed as follows:

Tuition revenue	$4,000,000
Scholarship	500,000
Refunds	(200,000)
Total	$4,300,000

Choice "1" is incorrect. Gross revenues includes scholarships.

Choice "2" is incorrect. Gross revenues include scholarships net of refunds.

Choice "4" is incorrect. Gross revenues are net of refunds.